THE OTTOMAN STATE AND SOCIETIES IN CHANGE

When the Ottoman Empire undertook reforms to re-centralise and westernise in the first half of the 19th century, the first task was to introduce a new taxation system. Such a system necessitated the inspection of the population -- For this reason, just after the declaration of Tanzimat, taxpayers in the empire and their income were investigated. This volume examines *temettuat defterleri* belonging to five cities from Balkan to Anatolia and examines various socio-economic aspects of the period of change.

ISLAMIC AREA STUDIES

SERIES EDITOR
Sato Tsugitaka

Published
Volume 1
SLAVE ELITES IN THE MIDDLE EAST AND AFRICA: A COMPARATIVE STUDY
Edited by Miura Toru and John Edward Philips

Volume 2
THE CONCEPT OF TERRITORY IN ISLAMIC LAW AND THOUGHT
Edited by Yanagihashi Hiroyuki

Volume 3
ISLAM IN POLITICS IN RUSSIA AND CENTRAL ASIA
Edited by Stéphane Dudoignon and Komatsu Hisao

Volume 4
THE INFLUENCE OF HUMAN MOBILITY IN MUSLIM SOCIETIES
Edited by Kuroki Hidemitsu

Volume 5
THE OTTOMAN STATE AND SOCIETIES IN CHANGE
Edited by Hayashi Kayoko and Mahir Aydin

Islamic Area Studies

The Islamic Area Studies Project plans to do multidisciplinary research on Muslim societies in both the Islamic and non-Islamic worlds, by reflecting the fact that areas with close ties to Islam now encompass the world. The series presents the important new knowledge and debate achieved through international joint research about Islam as a religion and civilization, particularly emphasizing comparative and historical analysis. The series will hopefully provide multifaceted, useful information to deepen the reader's understanding of the Islamic world.

Project Leader: Sato Tsugitaka
The University of Tokyo

THE OTTOMAN STATE AND SOCIETIES IN CHANGE

A Study of the Nineteenth Century Temettuat Registers

Edited by

HAYASHI Kayoko and Mahir AYDIN

Routledge
Taylor & Francis Group
LONDON AND NEW YORK

First published in 2004 by
Kegan Paul International

This edition first published in 2010 by
Routledge
2 Park Square, Milton Park, Abingdon, Oxfordshire OX14 4RN

Simultaneously published in the USA and Canada
by Routledge
711 Third Avenue, New York, NY 10017
First issued in paperback 2014

Routledge is an imprint of the Taylor & Francis Group, an informa business

© Kegan Paul, 2004

All rights reserved. No part of this book may be reprinted or reproduced or utilised in any form or by any electronic, mechanical, or other means, now known or hereafter invented, including photocopying and recording, or in any information storage or retrieval system, without permission in writing from the publishers.

British Library Cataloguing in Publication Data
A catalogue record for this book is available from the British Library

ISBN 978-0-710-30801-6 (hbk)
ISBN 978-1-138-01076-5 (pbk)

Publisher's Note
The publisher has gone to great lengths to ensure the quality of this reprint but points out that some imperfections in the original copies may be apparent. The publisher has made every effort to contact original copyright holders and would welcome correspondence from those they have been unable to trace.

CONTENTS

LIST OF CONTRIBUTORS

Japanese names are given using the surname first.

Tevfik GÜRAN	Istanbul University, Istanbul
TAKAMATSU Yoichi	Tokyo University of Foreign Studies, Tokyo
Svetla IANEVA	Institute of History in Bulgarian Academy of Sciences, Sofia
Mahir AYDIN	Istanbul University, Istanbul
EGAWA Hikari	Ritsumeikan University, Kyoto
Arzu TERZİ	Istanbul University, Istanbul
Haydar ÇORUH	Trakya University, Edirne
HAYASHI Kayoko	Tokyo University of Foreign Studies, Tokyo

PREFACE

The present volume is the result of joint research, enabled within the Islamic Area Studies Project (IASP) and sponsored by the Japanese Ministry of Education, Culture, Sports, Science and Technology by means of a five-year grant-in-aid for scientific research.

In July 1999, as an activity of Unit 6 of IASP, I organized a small round-table conference entitled "Source materials of Islamic area studies," inviting Prof. Mahir Aydın from Istanbul to an uncomfortably hot and humid Tokyo. I set up the Ottoman Temettuat registers as the conference topic, knowing that in 1988 the Prime Ministry Ottoman Archives of Turkey, in Istanbul, had made available to researchers for the first time approximately 17,500 volumes of the Temettuat registers. Joint research seemed inevitable because these registers had comprehensive and complicated contents. At the round-table in Tokyo, three contributors to the present volume, Takamatsu Yoichi, Egawa Hikari, and Mahir Aydın, presented papers based on their research at the Prime Ministry Ottoman Archives. Since the language of the conference was Turkish, the participants were few, but we enjoyed a lively discussion. Thereafter we continued working on Temettuat registers, and some colleagues kindly accepted our invitation to join the project and bring more examples of Temettuat register analysis.

Because the contents of these Temettuat registers are so comprehensive and complicated, drawing a coherent picture of them would not be possible within such short-term research as ours. Our aim is rather to present examples of how to use the newly available registers for research into Ottoman socio-economic history. We have looked at five cities of the Ottoman Empire, Samokov, Tatarpazarcığı, Balıkesir, Güzelhisar-ı Aydın and Erzurum, and have also examined the process of conducting surveys for compilation of the registers. Our analyses can hopefully give new images of Ottoman cities and provinces in the period of change, thereby introducing the possibility of investigation based on new historical materials.

During the preparation of this volume, we received various types of assistance. First we would like to express our gratitude to the director and staff of the Prime Ministry Ottoman Archives of Turkey in Istanbul (Başbakanlık Osmanlı Arşivi) for giving us full facilities for research. We would also like to thank Prof. Sato Tsugitaka, Prof. Komatsu Hisao, and Prof. Miura Toru, the director, vice-director, and publication section chief of IASP respectively, for their support to our joint research and publication. Finally, we give special thanks to Janet O. Philips, Ph.D., for her prompt and helpful editing as this volume took shape.

July 2004
HAYASHI Kayoko

Map: The Ottoman Empire in 1840's and the Location of the Five Cities

THE OTTOMAN STATE AND SOCIETIES IN CHANGE

A Study of the Nineteenth Century Temettuat Registers

Introduction

Temettuat Registers as a Resource about Ottoman Social and Economic Life

Tevfik GÜRAN

In the twentieth century, the interest of historians shifted from the analysis of leading historical individuals and political and military events to the analysis of society and social groups. This shift of interest and widening of the content of study has produced new areas of research but also some new problems.

New questions emerged, making it crucial to discover and analyze new sources hitherto untouched. In most cases, this analysis has required new research techniques and critical approaches to given data, rather than traditional methods. In this context, contemporary historians have used not only qualitative knowledge of the past but, especially, quantitative knowledge and methods as a means.

The effects of this shift of interest can be traced in the research on Ottoman history. The increasing speed and expansion of recent research on Ottoman social and economic history, especially research using the *tapu tahrir* registers of the sixteenth century, directly reflect the expansion of content, sources, and methods mentioned above. These registers have become a fundamental qualitative source in comprehensive studies about the population, forms of population and administration, agricultural production, and taxation systems of various parts of the Ottoman Empire.

On the other hand, even though the *tapu tahrir* registers were opened to researcher quite a while ago, research based on the information in them has taken place only at a regional level. No serious criticism has appeared on the importance of these registers as far as Ottoman social and economic history is concerned. Nor have their potential — and inadequacy — for further research been considered and criticized as yet. Besides, and more important, we own not only the *tapu tahrir* registers but also the richest archives in the world, and the discovery and analysis of new sources is not yet complete.

In the present volume, we will introduce another kind of Ottoman register, also important for Ottoman historical research. The registers were called, "*emlak, arazî, hayvanat ve temettüat tahrir defterleri,*" which means "survey registers of real estate, land, animals and income": in short, Temettuat registers, compiled in the first half of the nineteenth century.

1. The Objective

Historical data does not reflect a true reality but, instead, how the organizers of that data saw it. Temettuat registers were the official registers for which the central Ottoman bureaucracy determined and put into practice purpose and content, with the participation of provincial bureaucracy. To evaluate precisely the quality and research possibilities these registers provide, we need to know the Ottoman bureaucracy's purpose in keeping them. Clearly, Temettuat registers were kept not merely to collect statistical data but for functional reasons, as were most other document collections in the Ottoman archives. In fact, these survey registers were just one product of a wide and comprehensive reform movement called Tanzimat.[1]

In the Tanzimat period, administrators believed that social unity and administrative integrity were fundamental for continuation of the state. They therefore believed the success of all administrative reforms depended on establishment of a strong financial basis. The solution of financial problems was possible only if the state had sufficient and reliable revenue; the most important aspect of fiscal reform in Tanzimat administration, therefore, was regulation of taxation.

The fiscal reforms in nineteenth century Ottoman administration started before the Tanzimat period. In this context, the basic change made was the

1 The implementation of the survey and compilation of the registers will be introduced in detail by Takamatsu Yoichi in the Chapter 1 of this volume.

total abolition of a number of *örf* taxes (i.e., conventional tax), the imposition and collection of which had become exceedingly complicated. Instead, a single type of tax was put into practice, based on ability to pay, that is, "according to proportion of each individual's real estate (*emlak*), agricultural land (*arazi*) and income (*temettü*), and according to calculation of per thousand (*binde hesabı*)."

In 1839, the Tanzimat Decree stated that a reasonable tax should be imposed, depending on individual circumstances such as property and ability to pay. Soon, in order to implement these fiscal reforms on the regional level, a *muhassıl* (tax collector) system was established in the provinces. One of the main responsibilities of *muhassıl*s was to find out the number of people who lived in the provinces and their economic strength, so that an appropriate tax could be collected.

In 1840, the *muhassıl*s and their scribes started to record all taxpayers and their real estate, land, and animals, as well as the approximate annual income of all tradesmen and craftsmen. As a result of the surveys, *muhassıl*s were expected to determine the distribution of tax, which would be the base for the fair taxation according the economic power of each person. But, as can be seen from the limited number of registers in the archives from this survey, it could be conducted in only a few regions. The objectives had not yet been realized, the attempt to survey property and income ended in failure, and the *muhassıl* system was given up in 1842.

In the period between the declaration of the Tanzimat Decree and 1845, the reform attempt did not get any important results. For the success of the reform, the members of the Supreme Council of Judicial Ordinances (*Meclis-i Vala*) of the Ottoman government had to begin to understand that a better knowledge of regional problems was urgent. Local problems were to be identified in detail first, and only then could the necessary regulations be introduced.

To obtain more data about local problems, then, two notables from each province were summoned as representatives. In the reports these representatives produced, the most frequent problems mentioned were discontent about the higher amounts of tax and the uneven distribution. They demanded a lower and more fairly distributed tax. To solve this fundamental problem, the Tanzimat government reached a conclusion that allowed all taxpayers throughout the empire, by means of a wide-ranging survey, to pay according to their economic ability.

Table 1: Number of Temettuat Registers Classified as ML.VRD.TMT. in the Prime Ministry Ottoman Archives of Turkey

Province	Number of *kaza*	Number of Registers
Ankara	42	1,401
Aydın	96	1,411
Bolu	96	2,299
Cezayir-i Bahr-ı Sefid	8	26
Edirne	31	1,623
Erzurum	5	316
Hüdavendigar	59	2,491
Konya	67	1,025
Niş	12	817
Rumeli	21	45
Selanik	3	370
Silistre	23	987
Sivas	61	2,297
Üsküb	9	365
Vidin	10	316
Miscellaneous		1,751
Total	543	17,540

It was urgent that these surveys be done quickly. In 1845, a special instruction was given to all provinces of the Empire. In addition, instructions and some sample copies, demonstrating a model form of writing, were issued to carry out the surveys according to an established procedure and avoid problems that might arise (see Appendix III).

As a result, in an extensive part of the Empire known as *dâhil-i dâire-i Tanzîmât* (provinces included in the Tanzimat reform), the application of the surveys and sending of the register to the center was realized. Eventually, the elaborate collection of registers, thousands of registers kept in the Prime Ministry Ottoman Archives of Turkey, emerged. All of these registers are classified as "Maliye Nezareti-Varidat Muhasebesi, Temettuat Defterleri (ML. VRD. TMT)" in the Prime Ministry Ottoman Archives, with a few exceptions that are classified into the fonds of Kamil Kepeci and "Maliyeden Müdevver Defterleri." Most of these registers are from the survey that started in 1845, while some of them contain the results of the 1840 survey.

Most of the registers are the originals sent from the provinces, comprising a single settlement unit such as a quarter of the city, or a village of the countryside. At the end of each register is the sealed assent of the officials who performed the survey. Several comprehensive registers, each comprising more than one village or quarter, were reproduced as fair copies of the originals made by the clerks of the Ministry of Finance in Istanbul. The total number of registers included in ML. RDV. TMT is 17,540, and distribution of these documents with respect to region is as shown in Table 1.

Unlike the previous financial surveys of 1840, the surveys started in 1845 were not made by officials appointed from the administrative center; instead, they were processed by the local headmen and religious leaders (*muhtar* and *imam* in Muslim communities, *kocabaşı* and priest in non-Muslim communities) under the supervision of the agriculture director (*ziraat müdürü*) and agents sent from Istanbul.

The fundamental aim of the surveys was to determine individual incomes, that is, the actual tax-paying ability of the population living in the Empire, so that the tax burden would be distributed fairly among persons and among regions. The method of the survey was determined with respect to this aim.

2. Contents

In the survey, which was based on households, information determined per household was classified into four groups as follows:

1. Information related to the person
    - The name and status of the head of the household
    - The profession of the head of the household

2. Tax payments
    - The amount of tax (*vergi-i mahsusa*) paid by the head of the household, in *kuruş* in previous year (1844)
    - If the household is made up of non-Muslims, the category of the *cizye* that the members of the family are to pay
    - The amount and financial return of the tithes (*âşar*) paid in kind with respect to the products
    - The amount of the tithes and other taxes paid in cash

3. Movable and Immovable Properties (In the survey, three kinds of property possessed by the household were distinguished.)

- The amount of garden, vineyard or pasture cultivated or fallowed, and belonging to the household, stated in *dönüm*; the amount of land rented or let out for rent by the household, in *dönüm*; the identity of the leaseholder or tenant
- The kind and number of livestock possessed by the household
- If the household possessed immovable property such as mill, shop, or winter quarters, the number and size of the property in question

4. Income

- Profit or rental income annually derived from the movable or immovable property held or possessed by the household
- Income received from artisanship, trade and labor by the head of the household and family members

In order to estimate the yield from farms, gardens, vineyards and pastures, in some regions ninefold of tithe, paid in the previous year, 1844, was recorded with respect to the income derived from the land. In registers kept like this, the income derived from the land indicates the value of the product the head of the household had after the tithe was deducted. In other regions, tenfold of tithe, paid in the previous year, was recorded as the income from the land. In this case, the amount of the money shown as income included the tithe tax.

On the other hand, the annual income from the land indicates the gross profit because throughout the surveys the cost of seeds and other production expenses were not deducted. Income for the year 1845 was shown in estimated figures because production had not yet been realized.

Half the gross profit obtained from the land managed by sharecropping was designated as belonging to the owner of the land, and the other half as belonging to the person who tilled the land. The wages paid on the land belonging to farms operated by labor based on wages were deducted from the total gross profit. On the other hand, for rented land the rental income was assigned to the owner of the land, the gross product to the tenant.

In the calculation of profit derived from animals, profit rates with respect to location were used. Annual rent was recorded as income derived from immovables let out for rent. Income derived from professions other than farming, such as trade, artisanship and workmanship, was shown as an estimate. The above indicates the general method of the survey, despite the fact that it varied from one region to another.

Considering that these surveys were made with respect to the tax regulations, we might expect the reliability of the data in the surveys to be low and the information given not accurate because of incomplete or incorrect statements. The emergence of historical data as a by-product of the functional efforts of bureaucracy does not mean, however, that this information is always less reliable than data produced with the direct purpose of obtaining statistical data.

An independent evaluation of the reliability of information supplied in the Temettuat registers would be prudent. In the surveys, the most reliable information was probably given with respect to elements of property, such as land and animals. Data related to taxes and income from agricultural production will also have a higher rate of reliability. Because these data were estimated according to the tithe, we have no reason to expect that the statements would show great deviations from actual production values.

The greatest problem with respect to data on agricultural production arises from the issue of whether the year 1844 was a normal year of production or not. If the year 1844 had been a productive year, agricultural production figures would be higher than usual; if an unfruitful year, they would be lower. The variations by region for the same kinds of products could also be cited. This problem arising from the fluctuations in the products would not be mentioned, however, with respect to the agricultural income.

On the other hand, since the income derived by the farmer households from other than agriculture, and the income derived by the artisans and the tradesmen from their industrial and commercial activities, were arrived at solely by estimation, the most noticeable deviations were expected in this field, in the form of incomplete statements. However, the relative information available with respect to the economic condition of those who lived in a limited social environment such as a quarter or village would reduce the rate of coincidence in these estimations considerably.

As a result, we can evaluate the data supplied in the surveys as data determined by experts, with a rather high rate of reliability. We cannot, however, assert that the information supplied here indicates absolute truth or exact figures. The average values calculated with respect to data supplied in these surveys are therefore open to argument; moreover, this degree of accuracy would show some differences depending on the regions in which the surveys were made. On the other hand, these data can be used with confidence in the comparison of relative conditions of households and social groups, and of settlement areas in the same region.

3. The Possibilities with Respect to Research

Temettuat registers were essentially the results of the surveys for tax, property and income in the mid-nineteenth century, as applied over an extensive part of the Empire on a certain date and according to the same method, with 1.1 million households included. Since the surveys were based on households, the information they supplied becomes more elaborate and turns the surveys into a giant statistical inquiry.

The Temettuat registers supply a comprehensive field of research. They provide information on the settling order of the population, agricultural production, property and income of the households, and taxation. No matter how much in research resources the surveys supplied, however, criticism by researchers about the shortcomings and insufficiencies of the surveys is nonetheless necessary.

These shortcomings and deficiencies can be classified into two groups. First are shortcomings with respect to the survey data, which were usually far from sufficient for the requirements of present-day researchers due to differences in concepts of property and income between the time of the surveys and today. Second are insufficiencies with respect to the application of surveys in some regions. In using the Temettuat registers, the researchers should have a critical approach towards the degree of accuracy and deviations pertaining to the data included in the survey with respect to a certain research area, apart from considering the general insufficiencies.

The main difficulty in evaluation of the shortcomings and insufficiencies is the impossibility of testing data accuracy by using alternative sources. Sources that reach the same kinds of data are scarce, or do not exist.

Another insufficiency of the Temettuat registers with respect to research on nineteenth century Ottoman economic and social history is that they enable us to make only a static analysis because they were applied as of a certain date. Neither at the beginning nor at the end of the nineteenth century was any similar survey made. This deficiency is the basic reason for both their superiority and their insufficiency. In their range and resources, the registers are a unique source for research, yet they are not suitable for the analysis that would enable us to understand the changes that took place in that century.

Even though the surveys are insufficient to make a dynamic analysis with respect to the dimension of time, they provide research possibilities for the comparative studies of regions and social groups because they were applied everywhere at the same time and with the same method.

Temettuat registers are suitable both for general evaluations (after choosing enough samples to represent an extensive part of the empire) and for multi-faceted comparative studies aimed at the observation of differences between social and ethnic groups in the cities or rural areas of a certain region or regions.

In addition, the arrangement of data by households, which were the fundamental elements of social life and were at that time also assuming a greater role with respect to economic and social functions, supplies an elaborate data net for the research to be done on the economic activities, properties, and social status of those who lived in the cities or rural areas.

Historical research based on individuals is typical of present-day historians. Despite all the shortcomings and insufficiencies of the Temettuat registers, the Ottoman archives are undoubtedly a comprehensive and resource-filled reference for this kind of research, for which historical data are often difficult to obtain. The farm household is the most common and interesting example of the social unit expressed as a household. It produced mostly to meet the necessities of the family, with a labor force of members of the family plus a couple of oxen on a small piece of land, and was the fundamental producer type of the classical period of Ottoman agriculture. The Temettuat registers were resourceful enough for extensive field research at the household level to conceive and expound the forms of the configuration based on this small-scale production in the nineteenth century, and the regional variations that emerged.

Another important example of activity to be carried out with respect to the households, based on the Temettuat registers, is the issue of social differentiation. Pre-industrial societies were substantially egalitarian and unified communities as to social configuration. Nevertheless, even among the individuals who constitute these communities, considerable differentiation in social status might occur. Social status was a complex variant that had different parameters for different communities. Identifying the elements that determine social status and the social status groups is difficult. The Temettuat registers could provide a vast field of examples for sociological models that would enable us to observe the social differentiation that emerged in Ottoman society in the nineteenth century,

We can cite many material and cultural parameters with respect to social modification among individuals. The most important material element of social status is undoubtedly differences in property. Preferences of people as to acquisition of property are determined by their culture. Their possessions influence social status in the community considerably. Even though the Temettuat registers of the nineteenth century have some insufficiencies as to amount and composition of property belonging to individuals within Ottoman society, these registers still enable us to obtain accurate and comprehensive information. Having prepared the cross-categories base on this data, we could present tables as to the amount of property and preferences in acquisition of them for people who live in various regions, or who live in cities and villages, or who belong to different ethnic groups.

An important insufficiency of the Temettuat surveys as a source of information about property variations is that these registers do not comprise all the elements that constitute wealth. We are able to determine only the tangible wealth that supplies income to the owner directly. From this perspective, the properties bringing agricultural income, such as arable fields, vineyards, gardens and pastures, as well as the immovable properties supplying rental income, such as inns, baths, shops, mills, and animals, were included in this survey, in general. On the other hand, the houses in which the owners live, the shops in which the artisans and tradesmen perform their professions, the money possessed, the household items, and the instruments of industrial and commercial management were not included in this survey. Besides, with the exception of the physical elements of property, the survey excludes the main constituents of financial property such as assets and liabilities.

Owing to these shortcomings, the Temettuat registers do not have the qualifications that would enable us to put forward a table for comparison as to the amount of property belonging to the families. However, the risk created by research into accumulation of wealth, especially in rural areas, and investigations about the differentiation of wealth among social layers, is substantially reduced because much of the property belonging to individuals consisted of land and animals in the pre-industrial societies.

Income level is another material parameter of social differentiation, for both individuals and social groups. Income derived as a consequence of the economic activities of the households constitutes the most comprehensive field of the surveys. Using these registers, it is possible to obtain resource-filled quantitative information about economic activities of regions and individuals in the Empire in the mid-nineteenth century, and the income derived from these activities, even though the reliability of this kind of data is somewhat problematic. By evaluating the data carefully, however, we learn about the distribution of income obtained from economic activities by sector, the amount and formation of the agricultural production that makes up the bulk of this income, the size of agricultural managements, the forms of land possession, the relationship between the leaseholder and the tenants, and the kinds of income derived from industrial and commercial activities.

By making use of the data supplied in the Temettuat registers, we can account for the functional distribution of the income and also determine distribution of income to individuals. The amount of income received by the poor and those of a medium income level, their composition, tax burdens, and the effect of taxes with respect to the sharing of income in the region in question—all these can be evaluated using the tables. It is also possible to make some analysis to indicate the effects of miscellaneous variants such as profession, amount of property, and ethnic group in determining the income level.

At this point, having supplied the basic characteristics of the Temettuat registers, some sample subjects of research to be derived from this data are emphasized. It is clear that all the researchers, by the questions they could ask within the perspective of their relative fields of interest and by the hypotheses they propose, would get information from the Temettuat registers, in a variety of fields.

Temettuat surveys emerged as a by-product of tax regulation activities of the Tanzimat reform, which was the summit of efforts to enhance the centralization and effectiveness of Ottoman administration in the nineteenth century. Temettuat surveys, which were applied to taxes, property and income on the basis of household in an extensive part of the Empire, on the same date and within the same method, are resource-filled documents that would enable us to perform comprehensive research, with a predominantly quantitative aspect, on Ottoman economic and social history — even though they have some shortcomings and insufficiencies, and provided we use them only after some serious criticism.

Paying attention to these points, in the present volume, we will try to show the possibility of the research using volumes of the remaining Temettuat registers. First of all, we will deal with the process in which the Temettuat survey was put into practice, describing the planning of the survey and the confusion caused by it, and pointing out the reason why the attempt for the financial reform had ended in failure. The following five chapters will provide analyses of Temettuat registers of five cities and their surroundings, to compare the contents of the registers one by one. Sample cities are Tatarpazarcığı and Samakov in present-day Bulgaria, Balıkesir and Aydın in Western Anatolia, and Erzurum in Eastern Anatolia. The characteristics in common and differences of these five cities in the middle of the nineteenth century will be brought to light. If this volume has helped to make a index for comparison of contents of Temettuat registers, it will have fulfilled its purpose.

Chapter 1

Ottoman Income Survey (1840-1846)

TAKAMATSU Yoichi

Introduction

The Ottoman Empire conducted two comprehensive surveys on individual income and property during the Tanzimat era, one in 1840 (1255H) and another from 1845 till the following year (1261-62H). The resulting registers, currently called "*temettuât defterleri*" (Temettuat registers), most of which are classified as "Maliye Nezareti-Vâridât Muhasebesi, Temettuât Defterleri (ML.VRD.TMT)" at the Prime Ministry Ottoman Archives of Turkey in Istanbul, are unique sources that provide abundant and detailed data about the economic status of individuals. Also unique is that, after those simultaneous surveys in a large number of domains in the 1840s, this type of register was never compiled again in Ottoman history. Thanks to the recent opening of these registers to researchers, a series of studies based on them has been conducted, and undoubtedly they are bringing more and more light to many studies of the nineteenth century Ottoman Empire and its society and economy.

Until very recently, however, the main focus of studies on the Temettuat registers has been on the data per se, rather than on how those registers were compiled and used.[1] The author believes that to properly appreciate those

1 On the general characteristics of the Temettuat registers and the method of survey, see M. S. Kütükoğlu, "Osmanlı Sosyal ve İktisâdî Tarihi Kaynak-

sources, and also to shed light on the reason for their unique position in Ottoman history, it is necessary not only to analyze the data of the registers but also to clarify the methods and the results of compiling them by seeking out and interpreting peripheral documents.

The recent accomplishment by Said Öztürk successfully clarified the Porte's decisions on the twice-conducted income surveys. Thanks to his

---

larından Temettü Defterleri," *Belleten*, no. 59/225, 1995, pp. 395-412; Tevfik Güran, "19. Yüzyıl Temettüat Tahrirleri," in Halil İnalcık and Şevket Pamuk (eds.), *Osmanlı Devleti'nde Bilgi ve İstastik*, Ankara, T. C. Başbakanlık Devlet İstastik Enstitüsü, 2000, pp. 73-94; Nuri Adıyeke, "Temettuat Sayımları ve Bu Sayımları Düzenleyen Nizamname Örnekleri," *Ankara Üniversitesi Osmanlı Tarihi Atarştırma ve Uygulama Merkezi Dergisi*, no. 11, 2000, pp. 769-823. See also, "Introduction" by Tevfik Güran in the present volume. The Temettuat registers which have been published are: İsmail Demir (ed.), *Kayseri Temettuât Defteri (H. 1250/M.1834 Tarihli)*, 3 vols., Kayseri, 1998-99; Ahmed Akgündüz and Said Öztürk (eds.), *Yozgat Temettuat Defterleri*, n.p., 2000; Ahmet Yılmaz, *19.yy. İlk Yarısında Yabanâbâd Kazası Sosyal İktisadi Durumu*, Ankara, n.d.; Ahmed Akgündüz and Said Öztürk (eds.), *Darende Temettuat Defterleri*, 3 vols., Istanbul, 2002.

Temettuat registers classified into the fonds of Kamil Kepeci and "Maliyeden Müdevver Defterleri" of the Prime Ministry Ottoman Archives were first introduced by Tevfik Güran, before the series of ML.VRD.TMT became available to researchers. See Tevfik Güran, *Structure économique et sociale d'une région de compagne dans l'Empire Ottoman vers le milieu du XIXe s., étude comparée de neuf villages de la nahiye de Koyuntepe, sandjak de Filibe*, Sofia, 1980 and its Turkish version : "19.Yüzyıl Ortasında Bir Kırsal Bölgede Ekonomik ve Sosyal Yapı: Filibe Sancağının Koyuntepe Nahiyesine Bağlı Dokuz Köy Üzerinde Yapılmış Bir Karşılaştırma Çalışması," *19. Yüzyıl Osmanlı Tarımı Üzerine Araştırmalar*, İstanbul, 1998, pp. 179-228). Another important publication of the same author is: "Osmanlı Tarım Ekonomisi," *Türk İktisat Tarihi Yıllığı (1987)*, 1987, pp. 225-303. After the opening of ML.VRD.TMT, studies based on the Temettuat registers are increasing more and more. The latest example is İlbeyi Özer, *Darende, Tanzimat Döneminde Bir Anadolu Şehri (1844): 19. Yüzyıl Ortalarında Şehrin Sosyal, Ekonomik ve Demografik Yapısı*, İstanbul, 2000. See also the notes of the above-mentioned studies, in particular Akgündüz and Öztürk (eds.), *Yozgat Temettuat Defterleri*. The earliest reference by a non-Turkish scholar to the Ottoman income survey is Stanford Shaw, "The Nineteenth Century Ottoman Tax Reforms and Revenue System," *International Journal of Middle East Studies*, no. 6, 1975, pp. 421-59; unfortunately, this information is completely inaccurate.

work, we now have dramatically accurate knowledge about the background in which the Temettuat registers were compiled.[2] It is not yet clear, however, how the surveys had been conducted and how local societies had reacted to this unprecedented attempt in Ottoman history to simultaneously survey individual properties and incomes on a huge scale.

The purpose of this chapter is to explain chronologically how these income surveys were accepted and then conducted in the provinces, and what policies the Porte adopted. We made extensive use of the documents found in "Bâb-ı Âlî, Sadâret Mektûbî Kalemi Belgeleri (A.MKT)" of the Prime Ministry Ottoman Archives, which had not previously drawn much attention from researchers in terms of these surveys. For the second survey, because of the large amount of available correspondence between the Porte and local administrators, it is possible to delve into the details of the policies, even more so than the study by Öztürk. This can help explain why the Temettuat registers ended up as a unique presence in the empire's history. We must say, however, that materials from the 1840 survey (1255H) are rather limited.[3] Thus, descriptions in this paper come mainly from the second survey, conducted from 1845 to the following year (1261-62H).

1. The 1840 Survey

As is generally known, the Tanzimat reform was launched by issuing an imperial decree commonly called the *Gülhane Hatt-ı Hümayunu* (Rescript of the Rose Chamber) in November 1839. One key fact was that an item of this decree was to "introduce a fair taxation system according to the individual's property and ability."[4] The goal of this comprehensive survey of income and property was to realize precisely this. The 1840 survey, however, may not have been the first one ever. At least, we now know that in 1834-35 during the reign of Mahmud II a survey was conducted in Kayseri.[5] Because the

2 Said Öztürk, "Temettuat Tahrirleri," *Akademik Araştımalar Dergisi,* no. 4-5, 2000, pp. 537-91. Much the same text as this paper is found in *Yozgat Temettuat Defterleri,* pp. 15-54, with some facsimiles of documents.

3 This could be explained by the fact that in the Ottoman Empire the modern archives (*Hazine-i Evrak*) were not established until in 1846.

4 On the text of this imperial decree, see *Takvîm-i Vekâyî,* no. 187 (15 N 1255, 22/11/1839).

5 Demir (ed.), *Kayseri Temettuât Defteri (H.1250/M.1834 Tarihli).*

register compiled as the result of that survey is very similar to the one in the 1840 survey, possibly it was a survey preliminary to the later one. We have, however, no data sufficient to determine clearly whether a similar survey was conducted in areas other than Kayseri, or whether any other survey had been conducted earlier. In any case, it is worth noting that, like any other reform program during the Tanzimat era, the survey for individual's property and income originated in the reign of Mahmud II. Clearly, however, no large-scale survey was conducted until 1840, as an integral part of the Tanzimat reform.

Not surprisingly, the Ottoman government needed massive funding to implement a series of reform programs. To attain that, an efficient tax system was also needed. Thus, in 1840 the Porte abolished the long-established tax farming system and, in its place, founded the *muhassıl* (tax collector) system, in which salaried *muhassıl* from Istanbul would collect the taxes in the provinces. This was a landmark endeavor and clearly one of the kernels of early Tanzimat reform. In this period, only the places where the *muhassıl* system had been introduced were considered part of the area where the Tanzimat came into force. In other words, the *muhassıl* system represented the Tanzimat reform. Or, to be more specific, the register compiled after the 1840 survey was integral to the introducing of the *muhassıl* system, and thus was the centerpiece of the Tanzimat reform.

The tax system prior to the Tanzimat reform was excessively complex. The numerous tax items and tax exemption privileges were tangled and convoluted. The purpose of the *muhassıl* system, therefore, was to make the system simpler, fairer and more efficient.[6] The unfair tax system had long been a major financial problem. The tax rate was inconsistent depending on the place: the tithe was always 1/8 of the produce in the European region of

---

6 On the *muhassıl* system and the financial reforms of the Tanzimat era in general, see Abdurrahman Vefik, *Tekâlif Kavâ'idi*, 2nd. Part, Istanbul, 1330, pp.3-38; Süleyman Sûdî, *Defter-i Muktesid*, Vol.1, Istanbul, 1307, pp.78-92; Reşat Kaynar, *Mustafa Reşit Paşa ve Tanzimat*, Ankara, 1954, pp. 115-20; Abdüllatif Şener, *Tanzimat Dönemi Osmanlı Vergi Sistemi*, Istanbul, 1990, pp. 36-44; Musa Çadırcı, *Tanzimat Döneminde Anadolu Kentleri'nin Sosyal ve Ekonomik Yapıları*, Ankara, 1991, pp. 208-18; Thomas Scheben, *Verwaltungsreformen der frühen Tanzimatzeit: Gesetze, Maßnahmen, Auswirkungen; von der Verkündigung des Ediktes von Gülhane 1839 bis zum Ausbruch des Krimkrieges 1853*, Peter Lang: Frankfurt am Main, 1991, pp. 76-83.

the Empire, yet it could be 1/10, 1/8, 1/7 or 1/5 in the Asian region.[7]

Muhassıls appointed to individual areas under the new tax system were assigned to conduct the survey; under those *muhassıls*, *emlâk kâtibis* (scribes for immovable property), also from Istanbul, were in charge of the actual survey. From the job-description manual given to the *muhassıls*, we can see they were ordered to record how much immovable property, land, and livestock were owned, and a rough calculation of annual income if the survey subject was a commercial or industrial worker.[8] Interestingly, the job of the *muhassıls* also included conducting a population census. The fact that the 1840 register featured physical characteristics such as color of eyes and beard reflects similarities to the census register. In addition to the job-description manual, an example showing how to register was also sent for the *muhassıls*.[9]

Although only a few documents convey information about execution of the 1840 survey in the provinces, we know that in Edirne four *nahiye* (sub-divisions of *kaza*) were divided into eight, and each area was surveyed by a group of five people: an official appointed by the *muhassıl*, another official selected by the residents, a scribe, a Greek Orthodox *kocabaşı* (non-Muslim administrative leader), and an Orthodox *yazıcı* (secretary). But, since 750 *kuruş* was the salary of each of them every month, the total monthly salary of 40 people jumped to 30,000 *kuruş*. Ultimately, the number of staff had to be reduced.[10]

As is commonly known, those radical reform programs of abolishing

---

7 İrade Mesâil-i Mühimme 9 lef 1. The members of the Tanzimat government argued as to whether the tithe had to be evened up to 1/10 or not, and a vote on this matter was taken among them. İrade Mesâil-i Mühimme 9 lef 2, lef 3.

8 Kamil Kepeci 60/7, p. 2-8. For the transcription of this document, see Öztürk, "Temettuat Tahrirleri," pp. 551-52; *Yozgat Temettuat Defterleri,* pp. 28-29. This manual was printed out and delivered to the *muhassıls*. The printed text was as followed: "*Bi-tevfikihi te'âlâ te'sîs ve icrâsı der-dest olan tanzîmât-ı hayriyyeden tahrîr-i emlâk ü nüfûs ile ta'yîn vergü mâddesi ve memleket umûru rü'yet ve hüsn-i idâresi zımnında iktizâ eden mahallere me'mûr buyurulacak muhassıl-ı evmâl yedlerine verilecek ta'lîmât-ı seniyyedir.*" *Mecmû'a-i Kānûnnâme-i Cezâ ve Ta'lîmâtnâme*, Süleymaniye Ktp. Es'ad Efendi, no. 1877. Thanks to Dr. Jun Akiba for this information. See also Abdurrahman Vefik, *op. cit.*,2nd. Part, pp.7-38.

9 ML.VRD.TMT. no. 17534. For the transcription of the document, see Adıyeke, *op. cit.*, pp. 787-94.

10 İrade Dahiliye 567.

tax farming and introducing the *muhassıl* system resulted in a drastic reduction in tax revenue. As a result, the *muhassıl* system was soon abolished and the once-defunct tax farming system was brought back. For this reason, the 1840 survey did not contribute to actual taxation and ended in failure.

The population census, which had been one of the *muhassıl* tasks, continued even after the abolishment of the *muhassıl* system. Even though some may have avoided the population census to evade military service, surveying individual property and income must generally be more difficult than conducting a census. Furthermore, the first population census had already been conducted in the 1830s. Thus, surveying the increase-decrease ratio of the population sufficed. On the other hand, the survey for property and income had to be started without any foundation.[11]

Not many registers remain from the 1840 survey, as compared to registers compiled later on, and we can also assume the area they covered was extremely narrow. Also, although standardized examples were sent for *muhassıl*s, these earlier registers were not precisely unified as to the listed items and formats,[12] a conspicuous difference from the 1845-46 registers. The same can be said of the reliability of data. When the Porte issued another imperial decree for survey in 1845, they admitted that the 1840 survey result had lacked credibility and ended in failure.

Almost all registers resulting from the 1840 survey are classified under the name "*temettuât defterleri*" at the Prime Ministry Ottoman Archives. We cannot claim with certainty, however, that the 1840 registers were initially called the "*temettuât*" (income) registers. The reason is that, whereas the 1845 survey clearly called its surveyed subjects "*temettuât*" and the resulting register "*temettuât defterleri,*" the documents concerning the 1840 survey call its surveyed subjects "*emvâl ve emlâk*" (movable and immovable property) without mentioning the word "*temettuât*" and also do not mention register books as "*temettuât defterleri.*"[13] Furthermore, as mentioned, several listed contents such as physical characteristics of persons are also

---

11 On the population census, see Mahir Aydın, "Sultan II. Mahmud Döneminde Yapılan Nufûs Tahrirleri," *Sultan II. Mahmud ve Reformları Semineri 28-30 Haziran 1989 Bildiriler*, İstanbul Üniversitesi Edebiyat Fakültesi Tarih Araştırma Merkezi: Istanbul, 1998, pp. 81-106.

12 Öztürk, "Temettuat Tahrirleri," pp. 559-61; *Yozgat Temettuat Defterleri,* pp. 42-45.

13 In the volume of *Yozgat Temettuat Defterleri*, the editors called the 1840 registers "*emlak defterleri*" (immovable property registers).

different between the two surveys. Considering these differences, then, registers from the two surveys should be categorized separately. It is also true, however, that the ultimate objective of both surveys was to establish a taxation system worthy of a series of Tanzimat reform programs.

2. The 1845-46 Survey

The Decision and Commencement of the Survey

As mentioned in the previous section, the 1840 survey was a failure in terms of both scale and accuracy of data. Nonetheless, the Ottoman Empire still faced an urgent need to reform its finances by introducing a fair tax system. The next large-scale survey of taxpayer income was therefore inevitable. As early as March 1843, a plan for re-surveying was made, but the Porte was too afraid of opposition from the people to carry it out.[14]

A change in climate took place in 1845. The Tanzimat reform had begun six years earlier but had made little progress, as demonstrated by the failed attempt of the *muhassıl* system. This time the authorities decided to heed more voices in the provinces. As a result, in February 1845, they invited delegates from among the provincial notables — one Muslim and one Non-Muslim for each location — to Istanbul to discuss various regional issues at the Supreme Council of Judicial Ordinances (*Meclis-i Vala*). This was utterly unprecedented in Ottoman history. The selected local delegates were said to be so at a loss they could not fully express their opinions. Yet, they managed to present several issues and plead for improvement. According to the memorial (*lâyiha*) submitted by the delegates, the most important local issues were road construction, and the unfair taxation system.[15]

---

14 Öztürk, "Temettuat Tahrirleri," p. 555; *Yozgat Temettuat Defterleri*, p. 38.

15 On the summons of provincial notables and the results of this event, see *Takvîm-i Vekâyi*, no. 282 (20 S 1261, 28/2/1845), *varaka-i mahsûsa* (7 Ra 1261, 15/4/1845), no. 286 (23 R 1261, 1/5/1845), no. 287 (17 Ca 1261, 24/5/1845); Ahmed Lûtfi Efendi, *Târîh-i Lûtfî*, Vol. 8, Istanbul, pp. 9-10, 15-17; Kaynar, *op.cit.*, pp. 633-37; Çadırcı, *op.cit.*, pp. 199-202; Ed. Engelhardt, *la Turquie et le Tanzimat*, Vol.1, Paris, 1882, p. 76; Bernard Lewis, *The Emergence of Modern Turkey*, second edition, Oxford University Press: London, 1968, pp. 112-13.

In light of this, the Supreme Council divided the areas where the Tanzimat reform was underway into ten divisions, and established *Mecâlis-i Muvakkate-i İmâriyye* or *İmar Meclisi* (the temporary Committee of Public Works) in each division and conduct a new survey for the reform of the existing tax system.[16]

Between late April and early May of 1845, establishment of the Committee of Public Works was announced to the local administrators (i. e., governors, *defterdar*s and *kaymakam*s) in the Tanzimat reform regions (*dâhil-i dâire-i Tanzîmât*) and also 21 copies were sent of an imperial decree regarding the income survey to be conducted for all residents. Included in those regions were the provinces of Erzurum and Diyarbakır in Anadolu and the *sancak*s of Elviye-i Selâse (Yanya, Avlonya and Delvine) in Rumeli, where the Tanzimat reform was launched only in March of the same year.[17] The imperial decree began by mentioning the invitation of provincial delegates to Istanbul and then announced the decision by the Supreme Council. The decree also touched on the failed survey to record individual property, land and income in the early Tanzimat era (1840). Finally, it stated that no new officials were to be appointed for the new survey, and the survey result would be reflected in the collection of tax in 1262 of the financial solar calendar. Implementation of the survey would be entrusted to the local

---

16 Mühimme Defteri 259, p. 19, no. 90; A.MKT. 24/36 (An order from Grand Vezir Rauf Paşa to Mehmed Tayyar Paşa, *kaymakam* of Tırhala, dated in 11 Ca 1261, 8/5/1845). There is no reference in *Takvîm-i Vekâyî* concerning the commencement of the survey, however. On the *İmar Meclisi*, see Çadırcı, *op. cit.*, pp. 199-202 and Scheben, *op. cit.*, pp. 91-94. The bounds of each of ten Committees of Public Works are Konya and Aydın; Hüdâvendigâr, Bolu and Biga; Sivas and Ankara; Diyarbakır and Ma'âdin-i Hümâyûn; Erzurum; Vidin and Niş; Çirmen and Silistre; Üsküp and Rumeli; Selânik and Tırhala; Elviye-i Selâse. Three officials were dispatched from Istanbul to each. The members of the Committee of Public Works were to counsel about reform issues with the local administrators, visiting *sancak* by *sancak*. For the detailed information, see *Takvîm-i Vekâyî*, *varaka-i mahsûsa* (7 Ra 1261, 15/4/1845), no. 286 (23/R1261, 1/5/1845).

17 Mühimme Defteri 259, pp. 19-21, nos. 90 through 110. As for the expansion of provinces included in the Tanzimat reform, see *Takvîm-i Vekâyî*, no. 281 (29 M 1261, 7/2/1845). The survey was therefore never implemented in the provinces where the Tanzimat reform was not enforced, such as Bosna, Adana, Van, Trabzon and all Arab provinces.

administrators in each area under supervising of the newly established Committee of Public Works.

This decree also shows that both printed examples from the Department of Imperial Finance (*Hazîne-i Celîle-i Mâliyye*), demonstrating how to fill out the survey, and a handwritten manual (*yazma ta'lîm-nâme*) were sent to each area.[18] The Grand Vezir also sent each area a letter with the same purpose as the imperial decree.[19] This decree for commencement of the survey was expressed in abstract terms, and therefore the actual survey would be conducted based on the example and the manual.

We could not find the original copy of the printed example. Yet, it is highly probable that the form was a single sheet of paper, since the expression "*matbû' nümûne evrâk*" (sheets of printed example) was used to describe survey examples. We can also easily imagine that a large number of printed copies were sent to the local administrators. For instance, initially 3,000 copies were sent to Hüdavedigâr Province, then later an additional 1,000 copies.[20] To Erdek and Ayvalık, independent *kaymakamlıks* (sub-governorships) though bordering on Hüdavedigâr Province, at first no copies of examples had arrived even in July, but later, 50 copies for every *kaza*, 350 copies in all, were sent.[21] Assuming at least 50 copies for each *kaza*, one can see that a huge number of copies were sent to the greater part of the Ottoman Empire, where the Tanzimat reform was enforced. Lack of appointment of new officials for the survey meant that local officials would conduct the survey without any benefits, so that any burden on the imperial treasury could be avoided. At the same time, this explains the large number of examples distributed to local officials, who were not used to compiling the register.

The text of the manual is found at the Prime Ministry Ottoman Archives.[22] According to this, the survey was targeted at revenues from

---

[18] Mühimme Defteri 259, no. 90. On the *Hazîne-i Celîle-i Mâliyye*, see Yavuz Cezar, *Osmanlı Maliyesinde Bunalım ve Değişim Dönemi (XVIII. yy dan Tanzimat'a Mali Tarih)*, n.p., 1986, pp. 290-301.

[19] For the draft of the letter see A.MKT. 32/55.

[20] A.MKT. 26/8; A.MKT. 26/19/2 (25 C 1261, 1/7/1845).

[21] A.MKT. 26/19 (19 C 1261, 25/6/1845); A.MKT. 26/19/2 (25 C 1261, 1/7/1845); A.MKT. 26/19/3 (23 C 1261, 29/6/1845); A.MKT. 26/19/4 (19 C 1261, 25/6/1845); A.MKT. 26/19/5.

[22] İrade Mesâil-i Mühimme no. 58, lef 5. Öztürk, "Temettuat Tahrirleri," p. 556; *Yozgat Temettuat Defterleri*, p. 38.

immovable property such as farmland, vineyards, fruit orchards, water mills, caravansaries, shops, and rented houses; at the annual income of commercial and industrial workers; and at the amount of tax paid by peasants. Instead of officials from Istanbul, *imams* and *muhtars* (or priests and *kocabaşıs* in non-Muslim villages) conducted the survey; a *ziraat müdürü vekili* (agent of the agricultural director) oversaw it. The *imam* and *muhtar* then approved the resulting register by signing and sealing it before submitting it to the *kaza* chief (*kaza müdürü*). Next, the *kaza* council inspected the register to be submitted to the *kaymakam* or governor, and *defterdar*. The submitted register was put in a sack by *kaza* without making a fair copy of it, and then presented to the Department of Imperial Finance.[23] If a suspicion was raised or inappropriate behavior was detected in the process of compiling the register, governor, *defterdar* and *kaymakam* could make a visit for supervision.[24]

Local administrators, on receiving the imperial decree, example and manual from the Porte, began to prepare for the survey immediately. For example, in Selânik Province, the governor summoned *kaymakams* and consulted on the matter with *defterdar* and members of the Committee of Public Works.[25] The manuals were handed over to the *kaza* chiefs and the members of the *kaza* council, who had been convened to the centers of the *sancaks*.[26]

To announce implementation of the new survey to the local officials in *kazas*, copies were made of the imperial decree received in individual provinces; these were signed and sealed by the governor and sent to *kazas*. In each *kaza*, the copy was recited at the *kaza* council or court. The receipt of the imperial decree was reported to the Porte in a document called *mazbata* (report) under joint seals by the *kaza* chief, members of *kaza* council, *imams*, *muhtars*, and non-Muslim representatives. *İlam*, a report written by *kadı*, was

---

23 Öztürk, "Temettuat Tahrirleri," pp. 556-7; *Yozgat Temettuat Defterleri,* p. 39. A.MKT. 24/19 (gurre-i CA 1261, 8/5/1845, a report by Mehmed Tayyar Paşa, *kaymakam* of Tırhala); A.MKT. 25/72 (9 B 1261, 14/7/1845); A.MKT. 25/90 (12 B 1261, 17/7/1845, a report by Mehmed Lebib, *defterdar* of Rumeli). For the local administration of the Tanzimat period, see Çadırcı, *op.cit.* and Scheben, *op. cit.*

24 A.MKT. 25/90.

25 A.MKT. 24/19.

26 A.MKT. 25/55 (Ankara, 5 B 1261, 10/7/1845); A.MKT. 25/90 (Manastır, 12 B 1261, 17/7/1845).

also attached.[27] Of them, we know that the *mazbata* from the *kaza* council of Bursa[28] and *mazbata* and *ilam* from eleven *kaza*s of the *sancak* of Vize,[29] which had been collectively submitted through the governor of Edirne, were examined at the Supreme Council and then submitted to the Sultan.[30]

Those reports express appreciation to the Sultan for the implementation of the survey. But of course that is just a formality, the rhetoric of the documents. Once an imperial decree is received, the receipt must be sent. Interestingly, there is a dispersion of the dates of reports. Although coming

---

27 *Mazbata* from Güzelhisar-ı Aydın: A.MKT. 25/9 (18 C 1261, 24/6/1845). *İlam* from each *kaza* of the *sancak* of Biga (Çan, Kumkal'e, Lapseki, Ezine-i Kazdağı, Kızılca Tuzla, Bayramiç, Biga, Kal'e-i Sultâniyye, Dimetoka): A.MKT. 25/4 (17 C 1261, 23/6/1845); A.MKT. 25/15 (21 C 1261, 27/6/1845); A.MKT. 25/16/1 (21 C 1261, 27/6/1845); A.MKT. 25/17 (22 C 1261, 28/6/1845); A.MKT. 25/20 (23 C 1261, 29/6/1845); A.MKT. 25/27 (25 C 1261, 1/7/1845); A.MKT. 25/30/1 (27 C 1261, 3/7/1845); A.MKT. 25/32 (27 C 1261, 3/7/1845); A.MKT. 25 /48 (2 B 1261, 7/7/1845). *Mazbata* from each *kaza* of Biga (Çan, Kumkal'e, Lapseki, Ezine-i Kazdağı, Biga, Kal'e-i Sultâniyye, Dimetoka): A.MKT. 25/4/2; A.MKT. 25/36 (21 C 1261, 27/6/1845); A.MKT. 25/16/2; A.MKT. 25/18/1 (22 C 1261, 28/6/1845); A.MKT. 25/36/2 (27 C 1261, 3/7/1845); A.MKT. 25/32/3; A.MKT. 25/46/1.

28 *Mazbata* from Bursa: İrade Dahiliye 5220/1 (19 CA 1261, 26/5/1845).

29 *İlam* from each *kaza* of the *sancak* of Vize (Bürgos, Sarayvize, Silivri, Pınarhisarı, Vize, Ereğli, Ahyolu, Midye, Çorlu, Kırkkilise): A.MKT. 25/63 (9 B 1261, 14/7/1845); A.MKT. 25/68 (9 B 1261, 14/7/1845); A.MKT. 25/72 (9 B 1261, 14/7/1845); A.MKT. 25/75 (10 B 1261, 15/7/1845); A.MKT. 25/77 (10 B 1261, 15/7/1845); A.MKT. 25/64 (19 B 1261, 24/7/1845); A.MKT. 25/79 (21 B 1261, 26/7/1845); A.MKT. 26/20 (21 B 1261, 26/7/1845); A.MKT. 26/32 (23 B 1261, 28/7/1845); A.MKT. 26/48 (27 B 1261, 1/8/1845). *Mazbata* from each *kaza* of Vize (Sarayvize, Pınarhisarı, Ereğli, Misivri, Midye, Ahyolu): A.MKT. 25/68/1 (9 B 1261, 14/7/1845); A.MKT. 25/75/1 (21 B 1261, 26/7/1845); A.MKT. 25/95 (13 B 1261, 18/7/1845); A.MKT. 25/99 (15 B 1261, 20/7/1845); A.MKT. 25/77/1 (19 B 1261, 24/7/1845); A.MKT.25/79/1. In all eleven *ilam*s and eleven *mazbata*s should have been sent to the Porte from the *sancak* of Vize (İrade Mesâil-i Mühimme 72 lef 2), but we could have found only ten *ilam*s and six *mazbata*s. In some cases, these *mazbata* were called *mazhar* or *arzuhal* by the senders themselves, but the Porte, recipient of the documents, called them *mazbata*. İrade Mesâil-i Mühimme 72 lef 3 (10 Ş 1261,14/8/1845, letter from the governor of Edirne and *irade*).

30 On the Bursa case: İrade Dahiliye 5220. The Vize case: İrade Mesâil-i Mühimme 72 lef 1 (20 Ş 1261, 24/8/1845), lef 2, lef 3.

from a location close to the Imperial Capital, the latest one from the *kaza* of Kırkkilise of the *sancak* of Vize is dated August 1 (27 B 1261), approximately three months after the proclamation of the imperial decree. The imperial decree seems as if it had arrived late; however, since the first register from Kırkkilise was sent four days later, a more reasonable assumption is that the receipt was sent belatedly.[31]

Not too long after the imperial decree had been issued and the example and manual had been sent to all regions, an order from Grand Vezir was sent to the local administrators of each region. The order required them to immediately send the first completed register (of any single village or quarter) to Istanbul as a sample. The reason was that if no registers were sent to the Porte until after completion of the entire survey for that site, the government would not learn of errors in the registers, if any, until then. Sending them all back would be difficult and would delay establishment of the new tax system. Thus, the order was designed to check whether the registers were being properly compiled in each area. The order also stipulated that, to avoid improprieties, the survey work should not all be left to the *kaza* chiefs and *muhtar*s of villages, and if any suspicion was raised during the survey, the Porte should be contacted immediately.[32]

Knowing that the 1840 survey had a number of discrepancies of content and format, the order to require local officials to submit a sample, and to inquire if they had questions, reflects the firm intention of the Porte to standardize the register.

Commencement of the income survey was thus announced to the entire Tanzimat reform region. However, as will be explained in the following sections, the Porte continued to add a series of decisions on the survey in a haphazard manner. The Porte seemed to have no long-term vision for the survey, nor even a clear plan on how to complete it.

The New Manual and the Model of a Register

The example and manual initially distributed were very simple. Thus, once the survey had begun, various questions about technicalities unavoidably arose. After the Grand Vezir's order, for example, specific questions were

---

[31] A.MKT. 26/67 (gurre Ş 1261, 5/8/1845).

[32] A.MKT. 24/19; A.MKT. 25/80 (11 B 1261, 16/6/1845, a letter from Mehmed Şerif Paşa, governor of Sivas).

posed to the Porte about how to record the revenue of a merchant who has been doing business for one year after having moved from one *kaza* to another, and how to record the property in his hometown.[33] The most serious question was to what extent income was to be accounted for — in other words, whether necessary expenses should be deducted from the income?

Mehmet Paşa, the *kaymakam* of Kütahya, sent to the Porte a report (*mazbata*) compiling questions from people and his answers, which were based on the first completed register. He also sent a proposal letter, in which he argued that if the necessary expenses, such as seed for reproduction and wages, could be deducted from the income, the concealment of income could be avoided.[34]

Immediately, these works of Mehmet Paşa were highly appreciated. After adding several articles at the Accounting Council (*Meclis-i Muhasebe*), the report was examined at the Supreme Council and recompiled in the form of a memorial (*lâyiha*). It was then printed as a manual and distributed to local administrators to be used in other regions. On the other hand, Mehmet Paşa's proposal on the deduction of expenses was rejected. This was because the intention of the survey was to carry out a fair taxation, not to collect remaining expenses as taxes.[35]

We could find neither the original copy that Mehmet Paşa submitted nor the printed manual. But two copies of the memorial based on the report of Mehmed Paşa are at the Prime Ministry Ottoman Archives. Judging from the paragraphs in red ink, one is the draft and the other is the fair copy.[36] The red ink is believed to have been used when corrections and additions were made at the Accounting Council.

The new manual consists of 26 questions and answers. The length of articles varies, but overall is rather long. The questions are mostly specific. The most typical question was, "Should the profit a taxpayer made in an inquired situation as income be filed? If so, how? "

---

33 A.MKT. 25/54 (5 B 1261, 10/7/1845, a *mazbata* from the Committee of Public Works of Elviye-i Selâse).

34 İrade Mesâil-i Mühimme 65 lef 2.

35 A.MKT. 32/34; İrade Mesâil-i Mühimme 65 lef 2.

36 The draft: A.DVN. 13/44. The fair copy: İrade Mesâil-i Mühimme 65 lef 1. Both texts are the almost same except for minor differences. The draft was published with the transcription by Adıyeke, *op. cit.*, pp. 797-823.

Other hypothetical questions are the following:

-Should the income of a non-taxpayer be filed?
-How should properties of religious endowments be handled?
-Should the property of an orphan ward be filed?
-If the location of a water mill and the location of the residence of its owner are different, how should they be filed?
-If one's property covers more than one *sancak*, how should it be filed?
-If the property owner has deserted, or is not present due to military service, how should this be handled?
-Should useless livestock be filed?
-Should they survey a former nomad who has settled down but has not yet started farming, and currently makes a living by stock farming?
-Should fruits and vegetable harvested from the garden attached to one's own house be filed?
-If nobody in the village can write, and a scribe would have to be hired, what should be done?

Of these 26 questions and answers, the most noteworthy in relation to the proposal by Mehmet Paşa is the issue of the deduction of expenses, which was listed last.

Even though in Mehmet Paşa's report, on which the manual was based, one could deduct seeds and wages from income, the actual manual approved absolutely no deductions of this kind; they should be filed as income.[37] This issue of a deduction or not was probably the most serious question Mehmet Paşa had faced in the actual surveying process. As for himself, Mehmet Paşa had decided to allow a deduction in order to avoid the concealment of income. Yet, considering the gravity of the issue, we believe, he made that proposal just in case. Nonetheless, the proposal was rejected at the Supreme Council, its reference to that deduction in the report was modified, and, after adding a few articles, it was finally printed as the manual to be distributed. Still, it is quite intriguing that almost the whole content of Mehmet Paşa's report was adopted by the Porte.

Furthermore, a model of a register (*defter nümûnesi*) was created following the manual at the Supreme Council, and was also printed for

---

[37] İrade Mesâil-i Mühimme 65 lef 1, lef 2.

distribution.[38] This five-page register shows specific forms with proper nouns made anonymous and all numerical figures expressed with zeros.

The above decision at the Supreme Council was addressed to the Sultan by the Grand Vezir, and an *irade* to approve the decision was issued.[39] Two letters of order were sent from the Grand Vezir to local administrators. One was to inform them of the decision to conduct the survey without any deduction of expenses.[40] The issuance of one independent order reflects how serious the issue of deductions was.

The other order was to announce the sending of the manual and register model and to urge local administrators to submit the first completed register as a sample accordingly. Fascinatingly enough, whereas at the beginning of the survey a huge number of examples were printed, this time the manuals were sent only to high-ranking local administrators, who were prohibited from handing them over to *kaza* chiefs and *muhtars*.[41] The reason was to avoid any unnecessary confusion from misunderstanding or a lack of understanding. In other words, this manual was a hypothetical Q & A collection for local administrators only.

The accurate dates of sending the above manuals, register models, and orders are not clearly known. But, based on the dates of reports from local administrators acknowledging receipt and promising to send the sample register back immediately, these were sent in early July of 1845[42] at the latest.

Although the register model and manual had gone into specific detail, not all questions were answered. For instance, the governor of Rumeli

---

38 The printed version of this register has not been found yet, but the original handwritten copy is preserved in İrade Mesâil-i Mühimme 65 lef 4. Part of this document is in "Appendix III" of the present volume. See also Güran, "19. Yüzyıl Temettüat Tahrirleri," pp. 82-85.

39 İrade Mesâil-i Mühimme 65 lef 5.

40 İrade Mesâil-i Mühimme 65 lef 5.

41 İrade Mesâil-i Mühimme 65 lef 3.

42 A.MKT. 25/58 (Bilecik, 7 B 1261, 12/7/1845); A.MKT. 25/83 (İzmid, 11 B 1261, 16/7/1845); A.MKT. 26/54/1 (Rumeli, 11 B 1261, 16/7/1845); A.MKT. 26/7 (Siroz, 17 B 1261, 22/7/1845); A.MKT. 26/10 (Ankara, 19 B 1261, 24/7/1845); A.MKT. 26/11; A.MKT. 26/11/1 (Tırhala, 19 B 1261, 24/7/1845); A.MKT. 26/34 (İslimye, 23 B 1261, 28/7/1845); A.MKT. 26/41 (Menteşe, 25 B 1261, 30/7/1845); A.MKT. 26/42 (Menteşe, 25 B 1261, 30/7/1845).

Province immediately sent a letter of inquiry regarding certain problems the manual could not answer.[43]

Also, discontent about the decision to disapprove deductions deepened in all regions. In Ankara, town notables — mostly farm owners — strongly demanded that the seed expense be deducted from income. Although they were persuaded in the end, the Committee of Public Works in Ankara reported to Istanbul that they had reached a compromise only after agreeing to put notes on seeds in the register.[44]

According to a report by Mehmed Şerif, the governor of Sivas, one Sivas notable named Hacı Ali Bey, though he had been involved with the survey, was dissatisfied as to the estimated income figure concerning expenses. He insisted to the governor at the council that one could not make 50 *kuruş* of income from just one milk cow. The governor brought yogurt from the market and found out that a farmer can get one bowl of yogurt from one cow, which was sold for 40 *para*; the cow could be milked for six months. According to this calculation, the farmer annually gets 180 *kuruş* from one cow. The governor asked Hacı Ali Bey why 50 *kuruş* was not satisfactory. He explained: "In exchange for 3 *kıyye* of butter (=1,282 grams) is worth 12 *kuruş*, a cow can be leased to a person who assists a farmer in return for a share of the crop. But, to keep a cow, the farmer needs three truckloads of straw for six months, costing him 45 kuruş. Thus, in order to earn 12 kuruş, the farmer has to spend 45 *kuruş*." People at the council remained speechless for a while.[45] Moreover, Mehmet Şerif reported that values of foodstuffs and livestock were examined and decided in a similar manner. Although the manual stipulated not to consider expenses in estimating income, this was not always enforced in actuality.

Meanwhile, when Hacı Ali Bey conducted a survey in his own residential quarter and submitted a register to the governor, he claimed his income as a mere 1,400 *kuruş*. The governor pointed out that that figure could not even be enough for his annual tobacco money and told him to correct it. Hacı Ali Bey reluctantly revised it to 2,000 *kuruş*. Actually, though,

---

43 İrade Meclis-i Vâlâ 1290. On the inquiries, see A.MKT. 25/90 (12 B 1261, 17/7/1845) and A.MKT. 27/23/1 (25 B 1261, 30/7/1845).

44 A.MKT. 25/52 (5 B 1261, 10/7/1845). The answer of the government, which received the register of Ankara with notation: A.MKT. 26/37 (24 B 1261, 29/7/1845).

45 A.MKT. 26/70 (gurre-i Ş 1261, 5/8/1845).

he had had more than 1,000 *kese akçe* of interest income from real estate, but did not declare even one-fifth of it. Perhaps this was an extreme case. Yet, it is an unavoidable fact that not approving deduction of expenses contributed to the concealment of income.[46]

Inspection of Sample Registers and Submission of the Total Slip

Immediately after the imperial decree to conduct the survey was issued, local administrators were instructed to submit the registers of villages or quarters, where the survey had been completed first in the *sancak*. The author has already mentioned that Mehmet Paşa, the *kaymakam* of Kütahya, submitted a sample register along with the proposal. While new manuals and register examples were being distributed, the survey had already begun and as of July 1845 at least some sample registers were on their way to Istanbul. The sample register had to be enclosed with the report to the Porte notifying the submission of the register and questions about the survey. According to those reports, some had separately submitted first registers of villages and quarters one by one.[47] That was probably due to different occupations in urban and rural areas. In other words, because of the different types of data they were sending, just to be on the safe side they sent both types of the register as a sample.

Samples were first checked at the Supreme Council. Samples with a problem were sent to the Department of Imperial Finance for rechecking. If the sample was cleared after referring to the register model and manual,

---

46 A.MKT. 26/70 (gurre-i Ş 1261, 5/8/1845).

47 A.MKT. 26/36 (Amasya: Kışlacık Village and Saraçhane Quarter, 5 B 1261, 10/7/1845); A.MKT. 26/23 (Bilecik: Günveren Village, 11 B 1261, 11/7/1845); A.MKT. 25/94 (Konya, 13 B 1261, 18/6/1845); A.MKT. 25/96 (Aydın, 13 B 1261, 18/6/1845); A.MKT. 26/ 4 (Kesriye: Dimbeni Village, now Dentrohori in Greece 17 B 1261, 22/7/1845); A.MKT. 26/6 and 26/6/1 (Hamid: Fazlullâh Quarter of Isparta and Çunur Village, 17 B 1261, 22/7/1845); A.MKT. 26/47 (Ankara: Gicik Village, 18 B 1261, 23/7/1845); A.MKT. 26/87 and 26/87/1 (Üsküp: Sopişte Village, 18 B 1261, 23/7/1845); A.MKT. 26/68 (Selânik, 23 B 1261, 28/7/1845). When the governor of Rumeli had submitted five registers of the *kaza* of Manastır as samples, the Supreme Council replied that registers should have been submitted *kaza*-by-*kaza*. A.MKT. 26/89 (Manastır: Sarıca-i Sagir Village, Barakova [Barakovo] Village, İstrejeve [Strejevo] Village, Çernober Village, Gradişte Village, 7 Ş 1261, 11/8/1845)

confirmation of conformity to the manual was recorded in the register and then it was sent back to the individual *sancak* along with the Porte's reply.[48]

If the register was found to be problematic, specifics were described on the other side of the report, which had been enclosed in the register, in red ink at the Department of Imperial Finance.[49] Examples of problems were: income figures from stock farming were not written, the 1261 product was recorded in addition to that of 1260 even though 1261 was not necessary, the land rent income that was to belong to landowner and the crop income to tenant were not recorded separately, sons' incomes were not included in the father's in the same household, or the total income figure was not correct.

Not every problematic register was sent to Istanbul. When registers had been sent from the survey site to the center of the region, and a problem was found at that time, they were directly sent back to the village for re-surveying.[50] Therefore, we still find problematic register samples among those submitted to Istanbul in spite of their having been checked before submission. This is probably because the submission of the sample register coincided with the receipt of the register model and a new manual in an untimely manner. We also found one unique case, submission of a register that copied the register model exactly, like a lithographic copy.[51]

After a mistake or problem in the form was pointed out, sample registers were also sent back to *kaymakam*s in order to correct and

---

48 A.MKT. 26/23/1 (Bilecik, 19 B 1261, 24/7/1845). "*Manzûr-ı nezâret-penâhîleri buyuruldukdan sonra iktizâsının iş'âr buyurulması; Ta'lîmâta muvâfık idüği derûn-ı deftere dahi şerh verilmiş olduğu; Cevâb-nâme yazılup defter i'âde olunmuşdur. Fî 19 Receb sene 61.*"

49 A.MKT. 26/36 (Amasya, 5 B 1261, 10/7/1845); A.MKT. 26/36/1 (Amasya, 24 B 1261, 29/7/1845); A.MKT. 26/9 and 26/9/1 (Bolu); A.MKT. 26/67 (Kırkkilise: Karahızır Village, now Chernodab in Bulgaria, gurre Ş 1261, 5/8/1845); A.MKT. 26/89 (Manastır: Sarıca-i Sagir Village, Barakova [Barakovo] Village, İstrejeve [Strejevo] Village, Çernober Village, Gradişte Village, 7 Ş 1261, 11/8/1845); A.MKT. 27/56 (Tırnova, 27 Ş 1261, 31/8/1845); A.MKT. 27/68 and 27/68/1 (Niş, 14 Ş 1261, 18/8/1845).

50 A.MKT. 25/80 (Sivas, 11 B 1261,16/7/1845).

51 A.MKT. 26/9/1 (Bolu). It said, "*Zikr olunan nümûnede sıfır ile geçilen yalnız hâne ve numarada olmayup mahsûlât u hayvânât mâddelerine dahi ol vechile sıfır vaz' olunmuş ve nümûne-i mezkûre ta'lîmât-ı ihtâriyye ve teshîliyye olarak litoğrafiya gibi 'aynının tersîmi demek olmadığı bedîhâtdan bulunmuş olmağla hâne ve numara rakkamlarının dahi usûlü vechile terkîmi tabî'at-i maslahat iktizâsından idüği.*"

re-submit.[52] However, observing the submitted examples, some *kaymakams* might have submitted another register from a different village or quarter as the new sample register instead of submitting the corrected register.[53]

It is important to note, however, that when a correction is demanded, only the issue of form is involved — whether or not the register is in line with the manual. In contrast, apparently the content of survey data was not strictly inspected. In Istanbul the object of inspection was to determine whether or not the register was following the standard form. The checking of survey content was entirely up to the officials at the survey site.

In this manner, the first completed register submitted as a sample was, valid or not, eventually returned to the region via a review in Istanbul. The survey was implemented on a full-scale basis towards the *kaza*-by-*kaza* submission of the register. Yet, people who were from the center of the province or *sancak*, not local village officials, often conducted the actual survey. For example, villages subject to the city of Manastır were divided into six parts. Six new scribes from Manastır were appointed, following the new manual, since the villages had no scribe. Next, six more officials were assigned from those under the governor Ziya Paşa, making pairs of two officials. The salary of scribes was paid from *emval sanduğu* (the coffers of the province). The *defterdar* was in charge of surveying *kazas* around Manastır. Following Manastır's example, *kazas* were also divided into six parts for survey.[54] Those methods remind the author of the method adopted in Edirne in the 1840 survey.

Meanwhile, as the inspection of submitted sample registers progressed, the Supreme Council decided on August 13 to ask for submission of the total slips — all tax payments of 1260 and total income of 1261— of all *kazas*. For tax reform, it was imperative that the central government should know tax payments of the previous year and annual income, but it would be too time-consuming to tally registers after all of them had arrived from individual regions. For the same reason the initial plan of the Minister of Finance was abandoned, that the ministry would make a fair copy of each of

52 A.MKT. 27/42 (Varna, 23 Ş 1261, 27/8/1845); A.MKT. 30/1 (Alâiye: Sirke Village, 21 L 1261, 23/10/1845); A.MKT. 30/1/2 (6 L 1261, 8/10/1845).

53 İrade Mesâil-i Mühimme 74 lef 3 (5 Ş 1261, 9/8/1845, Ya'kûtiyye Quarter of Amasya, and Şerefder Village of the *kaza* of Varay). See also A.MKT. 26/36 (Amasya: Kışlacık Village and Saraçhane Quarter, 5 B 1261, 10/7/1845).

54 A.MKT. 27/23/1 (Manastır, 25 B 1261, 30/7/1845).

the submitted registers before tallying. The Supreme Council decided that *kaza*-by-*kaza* total slips would be prepared in advance in each *kaza* and those would be submitted to Istanbul together with the register. The form of the total slip was also decided: the printed examples would be sent to local administrators.[55]

The Grand Vezir conveyed the decision of the Supreme Council to the Sultan. Once the *irade* was issued, orders addressed to local administrators were drafted and sent with the printed example of the total slip.[56] Unlike the manual, the example of the total slip was distributed to all officials down to the lower ranks, such as *kaza* chiefs.[57]

In the meantime, before the total result was tallied, the president of the Supreme Council, Sadık Rifat Paşa, proposed compilation of a register to contrast the total revenue and total expenditure of the Ottoman Empire.[58]

In the beginning of his memorandum (*müzekkire*), Sadık Rifat Paşa stated the goals of this survey. One goal was to examine the degree of tax burden in all the regions and to implement fairer tax rates. Another goal was to help increase the revenue of the Empire and cover expenditures such as military spending. In previous correspondences with local administrators, including the imperial decree, the authorities had emphasized implementation of fair taxation as a purpose. But the actual objective was expected to be an increase in financial benefit to the government, i.e., a tax increase. Yet, this second goal had never been stated in public —for fear, of course, of angry reaction from the people.

In any case, after the survey, the registers by *kaza* were gradually sent in sacks to Istanbul. In Ankara, after those responsible had closely examined the gathered registers of the quarters and investigated some questionable ones at the Ankara council, those responsible presented the registers, with the total slips, of all town locations except the Armenian quarters. Three sets of the registers were made. The first one was stored at local survey sites and the second was stored at the coffer of Ankara Province. The third one was sent off without making a fair copy, stating that there would not be any more

55 İrade Mesâil-i Mühimme 70 lef 1 (9 Ş 1261, 13/8/1845).
56 İrade Mesâil-i Mühimme 70 lef 2; A.MKT. 27/35 (Bursa, 21 Ş 1261, 27/8/1845); A.MKT. 27/70 (Rumeli, gurre N 1261, 3/9/1845); A.MKT. 27/74 (Tırhala, 3 N 1261, 5/9/1845); A.MKT. 28/5 (Konya, 11 N 1261, 13/9/1845).
57 For example, A.MKT. 27/75 (Yenişehir, 3 N 1261, 5/9/184).
58 İrade Mesâil-i Mühimme 73 lef 1.

income.[59] Slowly, registers of *kaza*s along with total slips started to come to Istanbul.[60]

The submission of registers was actually not very successful. Even in October of 1845, many *kaza*s had not yet submitted registers. As stated in the imperial decree for the commencement of the survey, a new taxation based on the survey result was supposed to begin from the financial solar calendar of 1262 (1846). For this reason, the Supreme Council, assuming that the delay of submission was due to the making of fair-copy registers, decided to prompt local administrators to submit the total slips before the originals.[61] A new order was issued to instruct them to submit total slips to the Ministry of Finance and the Supreme Council and then, eventually, the original registers.[62]

Some *sancak*s, immediately reacting to the order, submitted total slips. But many more *sancak*s could not even do that. We noted many excuses for the delay in reporting order receipt to the Porte; for example, a lack of scribes in rural regions, or the register was not properly compiled, therefore necessitating a repeat of the survey. If the register had not reached the center of the *sancak*, it was of course impossible to compile a total slip.[63]

---

59 A.MKT. 27/63 (Ankara, selh-N 1261, 2/10/1845); A.MKT. 27/63/1 (Ankara, selh-i Ş 1261, 2/9/1845). The original of the total slip (*icmâl pusulası*): A.MKT. 27/63/2. Considering this fact, those registers were stored in local regions as well. Thus, there is some chance that Temettuat registers may turn up at places other than the Prime Ministry Ottoman Archives in Istanbul.

60 A.MKT. 28/14 (Ankara: Tabaklı, Konur, 14 N 1261, 5/9/1845); A.MKT. 28/64 (Karahisar-ı Sahib: Geyikler, N 1261, 9/1845); A.MKT. 28/65 (Karahisar-ı Sahib: Homa, N 1261, 9/1845); A.MKT. 29/63 (Hüdavendigâr: Gemlik, 25 L 1261, 27/10/1845); A.MKT. 29/63/3 (Hüdavendigâr: Domaniç, Pazarcık, Yarhisar, Harmancık, Mudanya, Gemlik); A.MKT. 30/8 (Konya: Saideli, 5 Za 1261, 5/11/1845); A.MKT. 31/34 (Konya: Akşehir, Beyşehir, Kaşaklı, 13 Z 1261, 13/12/1845); A.MKT. 35/16 (Nevşehir, 9 S 1261, 8/2/1846); A.MKT. 35/29 (Silistre: Hırsova, 11 S 1262, 8/2/1846); A.MKT. 35/61 (Konya: Gaferyad, 15 S 1262, 12/2/1846); A.MKT. 35/86 (Silistre: Maçin, 18 S 1261, 15/2/1846); A.MKT. 35/94 (Hüdavendigâr: Lefke 19 S 1261, 16/2/1846).

61 A.MKT.MVL. dosya 1, no. 73 (7 L 1261, 9/10/1845); A.MKT. 29/42 (Silistre, 21 L 1261, 23/10/1845).

62 A.MKT. 29/42 (Silistre, 21 L 1261, 23/10/1845); A.MKT. 30/42 (Edirne, 13 Za 1261, 13/11/1845).

63 A.MKT. 29/41 (Konya, 21 L 1261, 23/10./1845); A.MKT. 29/91 (Üsküp, 3 Za 1261, 3/11/1845); A.MKT. 30/6 (Niş, 5 Za 1261, 5/11/1845); A.MKT.

One major reason for delay was the inclination to conceal income. If any evidence of concealment was exposed in the center of the *sancak* before submitting the register to Istanbul, a re-survey was obligatory.[64] The author has already explained the case of local notable Hacı Ali Bey in Sivas. Sometimes the whole *kaza* was guilty. For instance, in the *kaza* named Anduğu in Nevşehir, a new scribe was appointed to conduct a re-survey. He learned that the 133,117 *kuruş* initially claimed as *kaza* income was actually 602,371 *kuruş*, an almost 80% income concealment. In another example, *kaza* income figures in the register of Zile and Tokat were considerably lower than those of other *kazas*. *Kaza* chiefs and members of *kaza* council were summoned to Sivas, the center of the province, to be cross-examined. They continued to insist that they had no additional income. Thus, officials had no choice but to submit those registers to Istanbul. Since officials in Istanbul could not check the content of the register, a number of suspicious cases of income concealment like those seemed to have gone unchecked.

Total Survey Result

According to the initial plan, tax collection based on the 1845-46 survey results was to begin from 1262 in the financial solar calendar. As the first date of that calendar, March 13, 1846, approached, however, the survey was not complete. Moreover, they could not even decide how the survey result should be incorporated into tax collection.

For this reason, the Supreme Council decided to conduct a test on their tax reform program in the *sancaks* of Kocaeli and Gelibolu, designated model districts of the Tanzimat reform. Various opinions were exchanged at the Supreme Council as to how the taxation should be implemented. Later, those opinions were compiled in the form of a memorial (*lâyiha*).[65]

The memorial consisted of the following ideas:

30/83 (Rumeli, 22 Za 1261, 22/11/1845).

64 A.MKT. 26/70 (gurre-i Ş 1261, 5/8/1845); A.MKT. 29/41 (Konya, 21 L 1261, 23/10/1845); A.MKT. 30/6 (Niş, 5 Za 1261, 5/11/1845); A.MKT. 35/16 (Nevşehir: Anduğu, 9 S 1261, 8/2/1846); A.MKT. 38/30 (Nevşehir: Anduğu, 21 Ra 1262, 19/3/1846).

65 İrade Mesâil-i Mühimme 102 lef 10.

- An across-the-board 20% tax will be imposed on income of every taxpayer.
- Tax will be imposed according to the population and income on a *kaza*, *sancak* or province basis.
- An amount of 50 *kuruş* per person in every *kaza* will be imposed. Then this amount will allocated according to the individual capacity for the tax burden.
- Taxes will be collected based on a taxation table, which will be made according to immovable property, property, and livestock owned by the individual taxpayers.
- An annual amount of 50-60 *kuruş* per household in every administrative unit will be imposed. This amount will then be allocated and distributed according to capacity for the tax burden.

Just as we constantly argue over the best taxation system in the present day, Supreme Council members also expressed numerous opinions, and failed to reach any agreement even at this stage. Finally, they agreed to test all of the above ideas in the *sancaks* of Kocaeli and Galibolu and then pick the best alternative.[66]

In March 1846, two lists were made — a list of *kazas* whose register had arrived to the Porte and a list of total income of 1261 and all tax payments of 1260 in *kazas* whose total slip had arrived.[67] The purpose of compiling those two lists was believed to be to shed light on the progress of the survey in the first month, *Mart*, of 1262. The former list (see Table 1) suggests has an amazingly large number of *kazas* with unsent registers. Delay was particularly conspicuous in the European region. The registers submitted from there included those of only eight *kazas*[68] and the Tatar tribe of the *sancak* of Silistre in Silistre Province, meaning that absolutely no registers had been submitted from the four provinces of Niş, Üsküp, Selânik and Vidin and the three *sancaks* of Yanya, Avlonya, and Delvine called Elviye-i Selâse, where Tanzimat reform had been introduced only in 1845.

66 İrade Mesâil-i Mühimme 102 lef 11.

67 İrade Mesâil-i Mühimme 102 lef 5, lef 4. These lists are non-dated. It is reasonable, however, to consider that the lists were compiled in March 1846, as they include *kazas* from which the registers were sent in February but do not include ones from which the registers were sent in March.

68 Rusçuk, Cum'a-i Atîk, Şumnu, Hırsova, Umûr-ı Fıkh, Maçin, Silistre and Çartak.

Table 1: The Number of *Kazas* Whose Registers had Arrived by March 1846

Name of province	Name of *sancak*	Number of *kazas* having sent registers
<European Region>		
Silistre	Silistre	9
<Asian Region>		
Hüdavendigâr	Hüdavendigâr	18
	Bilecik	10
	Karahisar-ı Sahib	5
	Kütahya	14
Bolu	Bolu	18
	Viranşehir	15
	Kastamonu	23
	Kocaeli	24
Ankara	Ankara	14
Sivas	Sivas	12
	Bozok	7
	Divriği	1
Konya	Konya	23
Aydın	Aydın	4
Total		188

Source: İrade Mesail-i Mühimme 102 lef 5

By contrast, relatively more *kazas* had submitted their registers from the Asian region. Yet, the only regions with conspicuously smooth progress in surveying were the Hüdavendigâr and Bolu Provinces and some *sancaks* at the center of Ankara and Konya, followed by Sivas Province. In other words, progress showed a remarkably local dispersion and register submission was smoother in the Asian region than in the European region. Particularly striking is that no registers were sent from Erzurum and Diyarbakır Provinces, where implementation of the Tanzimat had occurred from 1845 on.

Looking at the latter list of total income and total tax payments in *kazas* whose total slips had arrived (see Table 2), the list is similar to the former one in that total income and tax payments are listed by province, *sancak* and *kaza*, divided into the European region and the Asian region. But this list records total numerical values, and the total income and tax payments of

Table 2: The Number of *Kazas* Whose Total Slips had Arrived by March 1846

Name of province	Name of *sancak*	Number of *kazas* having sent total slips
<European Region>		
Vidin	Vidin	10
Silistre	Silistre	7
	Varna	11
<Asian Region>		
Hüdavendigâr	Hüdavendigâr	17
	Bilecik	10
	Karahisar-ı Sahib	5
	Kütahya	1
Bolu	Bolu	18
	Viranşehir	15
	Kastamonu	23
	Kocaeli	24
Ankara	Ankara	15
	Kangırı	23
Sivas	Sivas	16
	Bozok	10
	Divriği	1
Konya	Konya	15
	Nevşehir	11
	Hamid	20
Aydın	Aydın	13
	Denizli	10
Total		275

Source: İrade Mesail-i Mühimme 102 lef 4

sancak are also indicated when total slips of all the *kazas* were submitted. According to this list, a number of *kazas* had submitted the total slip before submitting the register, complying with the above-mentioned order. At the same time, other *kazas* had submitted the register but not the total slip as Silistre and Çartak from the *sancak* of Silistre. The submission of the total slip signifies the completion of a survey; thus, in the European region, the survey was completed in submitted only the thirty *kazas* — the twenty-eight *kazas* of the Table 2 with *kazas* of Silistre and Çartak where the total slip was unsent but the register was submitted. As for the *sancaks* of Vidin and Varna, the total income and tax payments of *sancak* are indicated in the list, suggesting that at the very least the survey had been completed even though the register was not submitted.

In the Asian region, the total slips had been submitted from 247 *kazas*. The total slip was not submitted but the register was, from one *kaza* in Hüdavendigâr and thirteen in Kütahya. Thus, the survey had been completed in a total of 261 *kazas*. In the *sancaks* of Bilecik, Bolu, Kastamonu, Kocaeli, Bozok, Hamid, and Denizli, where the number of total slips are shown, the survey was completed. The areas where all the work had been completed were limited to the *sancak* of Bilecik in Hüdavendigâr Province, and the *sancaks* of Bolu and Kastamonu in Bolu Province. Incidentally, as expected, no total slips were found from Erzurum and Diyarbakır Provinces, underscoring a serious lag in survey performance in eastern southeastern Anatolia.

In any case, total slips submitted by March 1846, were all tallied up. The survey result and debates over it were drafted as a three-article report at the Supreme Council. The report was presented at the meeting of the General Council (*Meclis-i Umûmî*) on March 22.[69]

According to the report, debate on the total result went on as follows:

First, the annual tax payments and total income were clarified by the Census Office (*Cerîde Muhâsebesi*)[70] from the total slips, and their pros and cons were evaluated under the supervision of the Supreme Council. Depending on the individual, the tax payment per income of 100 *kuruş* had a wide range of dispersion from 3 to 70 *kuruş*. It also became clear that the taxation rate estimated from the submitted registers was 14.5%, on average, and the rate would have been 20% if re-estimated after the submission of all registers. The tax payment per person in comparison to the male population in the Tanzimat reform region was also estimated. The total male population, Muslim and non-Muslim, was approximately 4,178,000. The total tax payment was approximately 356,000 *kese akçe*. After subtraction of the number of minors, the annual tax payment per adult was 64.5 *kuruş*.[71]

As the result of the inspection of registers, the tax rate per annual

69 İrade Mesâil-i Mühimme 102 lef 1 (24 Ra 1262, 22/3/1846).

70 On *Cerîde Muhâsebesi*, see Ali Akyıldız, *Tanzimat Dönemi Osmanlı Merkez Teşkilâtında Reform (1836-1856)*, Istanbul, 1993, pp. 101-2, 113.

71 İrade Mesâil-i Mühimme 102 lef 1(24 Ra 1262, 22/3/1846).

income had a dispersion of 1.5% to 55% depending on location. Of course, a 50% or 60% tax rate is far too high for residents to pay. Residents in those places were believed to have concealed their income. To realize a fair taxation system, the Supreme Council considered the idea of reducing the tax to 15% in heavily taxed areas and raising it in lightly taxed areas. However, after also considering the general trend that taxation is light in the European region and heavy in the Asian region, the Supreme Council judged putting a heavier tax burden on only one side was undesirable. Another idea was to implement an across-the-board standardization, after having reduced tax in heavily taxed areas, to make up for the loss. Another opinion was that at the end of the fiscal year, when the revenues and expenditures of the Ottoman Empire were clearly presented — in other words, after the necessary revenue amount was precisely estimated — then certain measures could be adopted. The tax reform was originally planned to start from 1262 in the financial solar calendar, but the first month of 1262 had already begun. In the meantime, the Supreme Council decided to await the test results in the *sancaks* of Kocaeli and Gelibolu, designated tax reform model districts. Finally, at the very least, they decided to collect tax in 1262 as had been collected in the previous year.[72] They also decided to instruct those members of the Committee of Public Works assigned to supervise the survey to return to Istanbul.[73]

As one can see from the above decisions at the Supreme Council, the survey continued after March of 1846 and the tax reform was eventually postponed for another year. The debate over how the tax system should be implemented went on even after April. Opinions were sought by the Grand Vezir concerning implementation of the tax reform in the model *sancaks* of Kocaeli and Gelibolu.[74]

By reading the reply letters from regions where the submission of registers had been long delayed, we could see that urgings for sending registers and total slips continued.[75] Local administrators continued to send

---

[72] İrade Mesâil-i Mühimme 102 lef 1.

[73] İrade Mesâil-i Mühimme 102 lef 1.

[74] A.MKT. 40/24 (24 R 1262, 7/4/1846); A.MKT. 40/24/1 (22 R 1262, 19/4/1846).

[75] A.MKT. 38/40 (Tekirdağ, 23 Ra 1262, 21/3/1846); A.MKT. 40/45 (Saruhan, 19 R 1262, 24/4/1846); A.MKT. 40/83 (Samakov, 21 R 1262, 18/4/1846); A.MKT. 40/99 (Üsküp, 25 R 1262, 22/4/1846); A.MKT. 40/81 (İzmir, 28 R 1262, 25/4/1846).

the register long after April. In some areas, the survey was still going on in June.[76]

Setbacks in the Income Survey

As seen in the previous section, implementation of the tax reform was postponed until the financial calendar year 1263 (began in March, 1847) or later. We find no evidence, however, of a tax system reform near that point in time.

Nevertheless, in July 1847, a group-by-group table of *sancaks* was created to rectify unfair tax burdens. It was made from income and tax payment rates in accordance with the necessity for a tax hike or tax cut.[77] According to the table, areas subject to tax reduction were the eight *sancaks* of Ankara, Kangır, Kastamonu, Sinop, Bolu, Viranşehir, Amasya and Biga; areas subject to tax increase were the fourteen *sancaks* of Konya, Hamid, Teke, Divriği, Bilecik, Vidin, Tırnova, Niş, Köstendil, Manastır, Kesriye, Silistre, Varna and Vize; areas with no need to change tax payments were the six *sancaks* of Niğde, İçel, Bozok, Kayseri, Sivas and Samakov; and areas where tax adjustments were entrusted to the governor or *kaymakam* were the two *sancaks* of Aydın and Kütahya. Worth noting here, moreover, is that in some areas the Temettuat registers were not submitted,[78] thus postponing any tax measure temporarily. Those areas were the seventeen *sancaks* of Alâiye, Erdek, Kara-hisar-ı Sahib, Ayvalık, Yeni İl, Selânik, Siroz, Dırama, Sofya, Ohri, Tırhala, Üsküp, Prizren, Priştine, Kaymakamlık-ı Nevâhî-i Erba'a ma'a Silivri, Filibe and İslimiye.[79]

Remembering that, in the 1846 listing, the total income in *sancaks*

---

76 A.MKT. 37/56 (Konya: Güci/Fasıllar, 13 Ra 1262, 16/2/1846); A.MKT. 37/91 (Silistre: İsakçı, 17 Ra 1262, 15/3/1846); A.MKT. 38/30 (Nevşehir: Anduğu, 21 Ra 1262, 19/3/1846); A.MKT. 38/30/1 (Nevşehir: Anduğu, 17 Ra 1262, 15/3/1846); A.MKT. 39/14 (Aydın: Yenipazar, Ayasluğ, Kıran, 7 R 1262, 7/4/1846); A.MKT. 40/29 (Sivas: Kayseri, Karaguş, Zile, Tokad, Turhal, Gürün, Kangal, Aşudi, Yürükân, 25 R 1262, 22/4/1846); A.MKT. 43/57 (Niş: Ürgüp, 13 C 1262, 8/6/1846); A.MKT. 43/78 (İçel, 17 C 1262, 12/6/1846); A.MKT. 43/87 (Konya: Seydişehri, 17 C 1262, 12/6/1846).

77 İrade Mesâil-i Mühimme 147 lef 1 (14 Ş 1263, 28/7/1847, *mazbata* of the Supreme Court).

78 It said, "*temettü'ât defterleri olmadığına mebnî.*"

79 İrade Mesâil-i Mühimme 147 lef 2.

could be totaled only if the total slips from all the *kazas* had been collected, the survey was completed in the first thirty *sancaks* of the table. We believe that the survey was not completed in the last seventeen *sancaks*. Additionally, we note that *sancaks* belonging to Diyarbakır, Erzurum and Elviye-i Selâse, where the Tanzimat reform had been newly launched from 1845, were not in the table.

It seems, however, that actual tax reduction and tax increase did not precisely followed this table. Tax hikes, in particular, had to be carried out cautiously since strong opposition or angry reactions were to be expected. The Supreme Council decided to inquire if the area could bear the tax increase.[80] A list of *sancaks* indicating whether the area could take a tax hike or not was compiled. According to this list, *sancaks* needing tax reduction were Ankara, Kangırı, Kastamonu, Bolu, Biga and Viranşehir. Areas where they should inquire about a tax hike were Konya, Hamid, Teke, Alâiye, Divriği, Niş, Samakov, Sofya, Köstendil, Vidin, Tırnova, Manastır, Kesriye, Silistre, Varna, Filibe, İslimiye, Vize, Selânik, Siroz, Dırama and Bilecik.[81] Those areas include Samakov, which was subject to no change, and Alâiye, Selânik, Siroz, Dırama, Sofya, Filibe, and İslimiye, which were supposed to be subject to postponement. Those areas were probably presumed to be lightly taxed even without complete data from the income survey.

We cannot say whether the survey was still going on as of 1847 in areas where it had not been completed. We observe, however, that few registers belonging to provinces such as Erzurum and Selânik[82] are on the *kaza*-by-*kaza* list of regional distribution of the registers now stored at the Prime Ministry Ottoman Archives. Of course, we cannot assume that all the

80 İrade Mesâil-i Mühimme 147 lef 1, lef 3.

81 İrade Mesâil-i Mühimme 147 lef 2, lef 3.

82 Öztürk, "Temettuat Tahrirleri," pp. 569-75; *Yozgat Temettuat Defterleri,* pp. 53-4. According to the list, the province-by-province number of *kaza* whose registers were completed are Ankara, 42; Aydın, 96; Bolu, 96; Cezayir-i Bahr-i Sefid, 8; Edirne, 31; Erzurum, 5; Hüdavendigâr, 59; Konya, 67; Niş, 12; Rumeli, 21; Selânik, 3; Silistre, 23; Sivas, 61; Üsküp, 9; Vidin, 10. See also Table 1 of "Introduction" of the present volume. If we compare them with Table 2 of this chapter, the progress after March 1846 will be clear. We could not find any *kaza* of Diyarbakır Province in either list, but the execution of the survey in Diyarbakır is confirmed by the document: A.MKT. 24/60 (11 Ca 1261, 27/5/1845).

registers up to current times have been handed down, but we believe that a large number of registers were abandoned in an incomplete condition in many regions.

In fact, it seems that the Porte gave up completion of the survey entirely in 1848. In July 1848, one report was presented from the Accounting Council to the Supreme Council concerning the taxation experiment conducted in the *sancaks* of Kocaeli and Gelibolu. According to the report, they were supposed to come up with one appropriate standard of taxation out of the four alternatives: tithe, number of households, population, and income. For accurate taxation, however, it was imperative to have appropriate knowledge of immovable property and income. The Accounting Council could not find any method of realizing that and therefore abandoned the idea of surveying the data. In the end, the Accounting Council decided the easiest compromise was to approximate the capacity for tax burden at each area and impose taxes accordingly.[83]

In this manner, the Porte not only abandoned the plan of the recent survey completely, but also had come to believe that it was impossible to figure out all individual property and income. Consequently, the noble goal of the Tanzimat reform, fair taxation according to individual income, was never realized. The enormous survey results of individual income, said to have covered more than 1.1 million households,[84] were kept in dead storage and not used for actual taxation. Never again did the Ottoman Empire try to conduct a simultaneous survey of individual income.

Conclusion

As part of the series of Tanzimat reform programs, the comprehensive income surveys of the Ottoman Empire were carried out with the goal of introducing a fair taxation system relative to property as well as gathering complete data on individual income and property. The first survey in 1840 ended in failure, however, and then the newly established survey system did not work either, simply because it was implemented by *muhassıls*. As the *muhassıl* system collapsed, the survey came to a standstill. Forms and

83 İrade Mesâil-i Mühimme 176 lef 1 (17 Ş 1264, 19/7/1848).

84 "Introduction" of the present volume, p. 8. See also, Güran, "19. Yüzyıl Temettüat Tahrirleri," p.79.

articles of the survey were never standardized, and the contents of the registers lacked credibility.

When the survey was conducted again in 1845, to the local administrators were distributed a large number of examples and model registers, trying to avoid previous mistakes. The Porte had the first completed register in each *sancak* submitted to Istanbul as a sample. They were attempting to implement a uniform survey, with a manual to consult.

Despite these efforts, the survey made little progress and showed large local dispersions. The survey system was often inadequate due to manpower shortages in rural regions. Although no one openly rebelled against the survey, concealment of income was rampant because of the refusal to allow deductions on expenses when surveying income.

According to the initial plan, tax reform was to be launched in 1846 following the income survey. Completion of the whole survey process was impossible, however, within a single year. Thus, the Porte decided to put the total income and tax payment figures of all *kaza*s and *sancak*s ahead of individual registers. On top of that, nothing had been decided about how tax would be collected based on the survey results, and this made postponement of tax reform necessary.

They did succeed in clarifying the degree of tax burden by *sancak*s based on the total tally. Yet, tax reform was never carried out, and the idea of surveying individual income and property was finally abandoned. A massive amount of gathered data ended up in storage and has hardly been used.

Thus, the Temettuat registers have been passed on as unique historical data in Ottoman history. Only the closest attention will make possible the use of these data, as other materials cannot confirm them. As the author has already pointed out, the "income" in these registers includes expenses, and thus even a large income figure does not necessarily reflect the scale of individual profits but, instead, might merely indicate the scale of individual economic activity. Furthermore, the Porte admitted to rampant income concealment by the taxpayers and to the data's lack of credibility.

When using the Temettuat registers as historical sources, the researcher must be especially cautious and not readily take individual numerical values as valid sources. The initial purpose of the income survey and creation process of the registers must be kept in mind at all times.

Chapter 2

Samokov: An Ottoman Balkan City in the Age of Reforms

Svetla IANEVA

1. Setting the Scene

The city of Samokov is located in the central part of the Balkan provinces of the Ottoman Empire, 62 km south from Sofia, on the main road from the Ottoman capital to Macedonia, Bosnia and Albania. It is situated in a high valley (900m above sea level), with excellent pastures, surrounded by mountain crests, near the river Iskar and its affluent Bistritsa. The local climate is cool, the average annual temperature being 7.3° C with average annual temperature variations of 20.7° C.[1]

The economic and social development of the city is to a large extent influenced by the specific geographical and climatic conditions of the Rila mountain area, favourable to timber industry, stockbreeding and the crafts related to them. Decisive for its economic prosperity are the nearby iron-ore deposits. Samokov has been for centuries a prominent center of ore mining, metallurgy and metal working. The name of the city itself comes from the metal industry: *samokov* means a hammer that forges by itself. It designates the special mechanism through which iron was drawn in bars. Additional favourable natural conditions are the hot mineral springs, especially those in

1 "Samokov," *Encyclopaedia Bulgaria,* Vol. 6, Sofia, 1988, pp. 20-22.

the villages of Bane-i Köstençe (Bania-Kostenets) and Bane-i Has (Sapareva Bania). The population of some of the villages around Samokov belonged to the category of *reaya*, with special status under the Ottoman system: their occupations included falconer (*doğancı),* pass-guard (*derbentci*), miner (*madenci*) and coal miner (*kömürcü*), and so forth.

All these conditions contributed also to the development of the city of Samokov into the center of a administrative district, *kaza*, in the eighteenth century belonging to the *sancak* of Sofia and later, in the beginning of the Tanzimat period, into a center of *kaymakamlık*, governed by a *kaymakam,* belonging to Niş Province.

Existing data on the Samokov population are fragmentary and contradictory. Travellers have estimated 3000-4000 people in 1794 (Louis Auguste Félix Beaujour),[2] 7000-8000 in 1807 (Louis de Zamagna),[3] 5000-6000 in 1812 (Antoine-François d'Andreossy),[4] and 4000-5000 in 1836 (Dr. Ami Boué).[5] According to nineteenth century Bulgarian authors, the numbers were even greater, 12,000 in K. Fotinov's *Geography* (1842) and 9000 according to I. Bogorov in 1846, one-third of them Turks, a few hundred Jews, and the rest Bulgarians. According to Hr. Semerdjiev's calculations, in the second half of the nineteenth century a total of 14,500 inhabitants in the city included 1650 Christian households comprising 8500 people, as well as 5000 Turks and 1000 Jews and Gypsies.[6] The same author, following the local tradition, asserts that part of the Jewish population of Samokov came to this area around 1550-1600 from Thessaloniki and that later Jewish families arrived from other Balkan regions as well. Thus the rich Jewish merchant family Arie, originally from Vienna, came from Vidin via Sofia in the last decade of the eighteenth century,[7] while the Kuyumcı

---

2 B. Tsvetkova (ed), *Frenski patepisi za Balkanite XV-XVIII v.*, Sofia, 1975, p. 405.

3 B. Tsvetkova (ed), *Frenski patepisi za Balkanite XIX v.*, Sofia, 1981, p. 31.

4 *Ibid.*, p. 69.

5 *Ibid.*, p. 395.

6 Hr. Semerdzhiev, *Samokov i okolnost'ta mu: prinos kam minaloto im ot turskoto zavoevanie do osvobojdenieto*, Sofia, 1913 (rep. 1986), p. 116. According to later censuses, the local population was 9970 people in 1880, 9658 people in 1887 and 9568 people in 1892: "Samokov," *Encyclopaedia Bulgaria*, p. 23.

7 N. Danova, *Konstantin Georgiev Fotinov v kulturnoto i ideino-politicheskoto razvitie na Balkanite prez XIX vek.*, Sofia, 1994, p. 84.

family from Macedonia was invited to settle down in the city in the first quarter of the nineteenth century because of the fine goldsmiths among its members.[8]

The words of a local notable, Yasim Bey, dating from around 1860, cited in the memoirs of Bohor Kuyumcıoğlu, collected and reported by Hr. Semerdzhiev, give us an idea of the most developed branches of local economy in the mid-nineteenth century: "There are three things which cannot be bought with money in Samokov: an *abacı* shop in the street, a mine, and the title of *emir* (commander)."[9]

Samokov was indeed famous for its metal industry. Iron produced in Samokov was among the best reputed for quality and was traded all over the Ottoman Empire. Much of the local output, not only raw material (i. e., the iron bars) but also finished metal products (nails, horse-shoes, horse-shoe nails, knives, axes, ship anchors, pickaxes, hammers, spades, etc.), was ordered and delivered as directed by official state commands. The ironware was produced under government contract and control and ordered in definite quantities with fixed sizes, kind, volume and purpose. The iron industry flourished during the sixteenth, seventeenth and eighteenth centuries and was declining by the end of the eighteenth and during the nineteenth century.[10]

The biggest and most famous trading street in Samokov was the *Abacı* Market. *Aba* craft, making stout coarse woolen cloth, already developed in the eighteenth century, experienced a relatively late boom in the city during the 1840s and later, employing numerous master-craftsmen and an auxiliary labor force, who worked in specialized workshops as well as at home. Their product was destined for massive export to distant markets in Bosnia, Ioannina, Albania, and the fairs of Macedonia, Serbia and Uzundzhovo [11] and presented the characteristics of a proto-industry. According to existing research, other developed local crafts with exportation potential were making woolen braid lace (*gaytancılık*), spinning goat hair (*mutafçılık*), and tannery work, as well as the shoemaking (*pabuşçuluk*) and saddle making (*sarraçlık*)

---

8 Hr. Semerdzhiev, *op. cit.*, p. 118.

9 *Ibid.*, p. 195.

10 Hr. Semerdzhiev, *op. cit.*, pp. 195-206; St. Andreev & E. Grosdanova, *Iz istoriyata na rudarstvoto i metalurgiyata v balgarskite zemi prez XV-XIX vek.*, Sofia, 1993, pp. 115-25.

11 Hr. Semerdzhiev, *op. cit.*, pp. 207-13.

that were carried on to a lesser degree and only in neighbouring regions.[12]

The city of Samokov was also an important cultural and intellectual center. Schools in Samokov, for both Muslims and Christians, were well appointed and well attended. The percentage of literate people in Samokov's Bulgarian population is claimed to be one of the highest among the Bulgarians in the Empire as a whole. In the mid-nineteenth century, the city had one public and three private Bulgarian schools. The public school had a library. The education of women by local nuns also developed. Eminent Bulgarians, men of letters and teachers, such as Iosif Bradati, Aleksi Velkovich Popovich, Ioakim Karshovski, Neofit Rilski, and Zahari Krusha, worked in Samokov. The first Bulgarian printing press started functioning in Samokov in 1828.[13] The proximity of the Rila monastery was favourable to the cultural and intellectual development of the local Christian population. In the eighteenth and nineteenth centuries, a school of painting, represented by three local families, the Zograf (since 1770),[14] the Obrazopisov (since 1810 to 1820) and the Molerov (since 1810), developed in Samokov. Most of the painters followed a traditional training, but some of them also studied abroad, in Italy and Russia, in the second half of the nineteenth century.[15]

Samokov was also one of the important centers of Muslim culture in the Balkans. In the seventeenth, eighteenth and nineteenth centuries, 10 local authors wrote and compiled at least 26 pieces of work. Copying activities were also developed; for the same period, 45 copyists with 203 volumes have been identified. The most active local men of letters were Ahmed el-Keşfi Efendi (d. 1747), Şeyh Hasan Efendi, Mücellid-zade Şeyh El-hacc İbrahim Efendi, and Ahmed Efendi İhtimani. In 1842-1843, the trustee (*nazır*) of the pious foundations in Samokov, Mehmed Hüsrev Paşa, incorporated the existing smaller libraries and created a large and famous library maintained by pious foundations. One of the richest in the Balkans, it contained not only Arabic, Persian and Turkish books but also volumes in French and other European languages.[16]

---

12 *Ibid.*, pp. 213-21.

13 N. Danova, *op. cit.*, pp. 82-83.

14 Its most famous representatives were Zahari Zograf, Dimitar and Stanislav Dospevski.

15 Hr. Semerdzhiev, *op. cit.*, pp. 222-30.

16 St. Kenderova, "The Town of Samokov: A Center of Creative Activities, XVIII.—Beginning of the XIX Centuries." Paper presented at the International Symposium on Islamic Civilisation in the Balkans, Sofia, 21-23

Architectural monuments from the Ottoman period in Samokov include the Big Fountain with the Earring (1662); the Bairakli (Bayraklı) Mosque;. and Christian churches of the Assumption (1772), Presentation of the Blessed Virgin (1835), and St. Nicolas (1861).

2. The Temettuat Registers of Samokov

The Prime Ministry Ottoman Archives of Turkey in Istanbul preserve 18 Temettuat registers for 1260H (1845) from the city of Samokov (*nefs-i Samoko kasabası*), belonging to the *kaymakamlık* of Samokov, Province of Niş. Sixteen of them register the incomes and taxes by city quarters (ten Muslim and six Christian quarters),[17] one reports the incomes and respective taxes of the Jewish population of the city,[18] and the other lists those of the Gypsies (Muslim and non-Muslim) inhabiting the city of Samokov and the villages belonging to the *kaza* of Samokov.[19]

The term *hane* is used as the unit of registration and taxation, and in these registers seems to correspond to "household." At the end of each register of the six Christian quarters, after the number of *hane,* the *perakende,* people with provenance from other places, are listed without a proper number; they were more or less temporary residents in the city of Samokov. The households are represented by their heads, whose full names and primary professional occupations are given.

Samokov Temettuat registers indicate not only the total annual income

April, 2000.

17 ML.VRD.TMT. no. 11199, 11206, 11207, 11213, 11214, 11216, 11217, 11227, 11233, 11236, 11238, 11239, 11249, 11250, 11252, 11258. A comparison with other contemporary sources, like a register of the population survey (*nüfus defteri*) from 1261H /1845 (NBKM OO, D506) and the account register (*muhasebe defteri*) from 1258H /1842 (NBKM OO, D687), both from Samokov, suggests that the quarter (*mahalle*) as a fiscal unity doesn't necessarily correspond to the respective city territorial quarters. Both the Temettuat registers and the population register list 605 Muslim households, but 23 of them are registered as residents of a *mahalle*, named Keşkek in the population register, that does not appear in the Temettuat register. In the account register from 1842, on the other hand, the number of non-Muslim *mahalle* varies from six, as in the Temettuat register, to seven.

18 ML.VRD.TMT. no. 11244.

19 ML.VRD.TMT. no. 11197.

of each household but also the approximately evaluated incomes from professional activities of the head of the household as well as, in some cases, those of the other economically active members of the household (sons, sons-in-law, brothers, etc.), and the annual incomes from all the immovable properties such as workshops and stores, water mills, inns, meadows and fields in the city territory, as well as livestock. The possession by Samokov urban residents of out-of-town properties in surrounding villages and in other *kazas* is also noted, although these properties and their incomes and taxes are not described in registers, but probably in those of the respective places.

In addition to annual incomes for each household, the annual tax for the previous year, or the reason of its absence, is indicated, together with other rubric taxes (*rüsumat-ı saire*) due, in the case of Samokov, for iron production and the fiscal category of the non-Muslim *cizye* taxpayers. At the end of each register the total annual income (*temettuat)* of the quarter (*perakende* included), or of the community for Jews and Gypsies, as well as the total amount of the taxes and other taxes (if any), are summed and registered. They are attested by the signatures of the first and the second headmen (*muhtars*) of quarter and of the *imam* for the Muslim quarters.

3. Population

The Muslim quarters of the city of Samokov (Hoca Sefer, Abdülcebbar, Tekye, Şeyh, Cami-i Atik, Cami-i Cedid, Nazır Cafer, Kurşunlu, Musalla, Mehmed Cavuş) number 605 households, as is shown in Table 1. The six quarters Koca Papas, İskır Kenarı, Palas, Leşker, Mandal and Pasban (Pazvant) indicated as part of the *Varoş* (which usually indicates, as a fiscal term, the community of the Christian population[20]) number 841 households and 174 *perakende* (1015 entries altogether). According to the registers, the number of Jewish households in Samokov is 45 and of Gypsies is 43 (of which 42 are Muslim and one is *zimmi*). The city of Samokov thus presents a varied ethnic and religious composition. All the *perakende,* as well as 54.8% of the households in the city registers, are Christian; 39.5% of the households are Muslim, 2.9% Jewish, and 2.8% Gypsy.

---

20 Sv. Ivanova, "Danachnoto oblagane na naselenieto v balgarskite gradove i formiraneto na negovite instituzii (XVII-XVIII vek)," *Izvestiya na darzhavnite arhivi*, no. 65, 1993, pp. 91-94.

Table 1: Names of Quarters and the Number of Households

Quarters		Number of households	Number of *perakende*	Total
<Muslim Quarters>				
1	Hoca Sefer	81		81
2	Abdülcebbar	72		72
3	Tekye	86		86
4	Şeyh	95		95
5	Cami-i Atik	38		38
6	Cami-i Cedid	56		56
7	Nazır Cafer	33		33
8	Kurşunlu	56		56
9	Musalla	54		54
10	Mehmed Çavuş	34		34
<Christian Quarters>				
11	Koca Papas	127	22	149
12	İskır Kenarı	89	15	104
13	Palas	123	18	141
14	Leşker	113	18	131
15	Mandal	159	44	203
16	Pasban	230	57	287
<Jewish Community>				
17	Yahudiler	45		45
<Gypsies>				
18	Taife-i Kıbtiyan*	43		43
Total		1534	174	1708

*Gypsies who were living out of the city are excluded.

Calculation of the city's population using these household numbers is difficult. Registers are not explicit as to size and composition of households, since this is not the purpose of the fiscal registration. We can assume by indirect data, however, that the size of a household is more or less large.

The number of *cizye* payers within a single non-Muslim family, which ranges from one to six per household, could be a clue. More than 60% of these households have one *cizye* payer per household; about 21% have two; 44 have three; nine have four; three have five; and two households have six *cizye* payers each. Among the *perakende*, in 53 cases no *cizye* payer is indicated, which probably means they do not pay this kind of tax in Samokov. But usually (111 cases) one *cizye* payer per *perakende* is registered; in eight cases, two, and in two cases three, are registered. In these 10 cases, a *perakende* staying in Samokov is believed to be composed of more than a single man, that is, fathers are accompanied by sons, brothers, and the like, or even by full households.

The number of breadwinners in one household could also show the size of a household. In 14.5% of the registration of household incomes, for both Muslim and non-Muslim households, not only the heads of households but one, two, or even three other persons are mentioned as having their own professions; they are sons, sons-in-law, brothers, uncles, and so forth, of the heads of the households. Of these cases, 32 are of more than two breadwinners in a household.

Although this indicates the existence of larger households, the data cannot be considered systematic and representative enough for a precise evaluation of the size and composition of the households. Estimates of the Samokov population are therefore only approximate. Thus, if we try to speculate about the Samokov population in 1845, we have no certain way to determine it; by assuming five as the standard number of people in a household, however, we can calculate as follows: (1534 *hane* x 5 people) + (8 x 2) + (2 x 3) + 164 possibly single = 7866. This suggests that somewhat fewer than 8000 people, at a minimum, were living in Samokov. If we consider the households with more than two breadwinners registered, many of which also coincide with households having numerous *cizye* payers, as possibly larger households, our estimate of population could grow to between 8000 and 8100.

The registered names of the heads of households suggest the places of provenance of some Samokov urban residents. They came from such surrounding villages as Rayova (Raiovo), Lozen, Diren (Dren), Yarlova (Iarlovo), Vakarel, Dosbeg (Dospei), Belçin, Ak İskır (Beli Iskar), Diragoşin (Dragushinovo), İzlakoçan (Zlokuchene), Okol-i Zir (Dolni Okol), Okol-i Bala (Gorni Okol), Popogian (Popovyane), Çamurlı (Shishmanovo), Bane-i Has (Sapareva Banya), and Köstence (Kostenets); from İhtiman; from neighbouring regions such as Breznik, İznebol (Tran), Razlog, and Pernik; and from Sofia or the rural area around it, for example, İştip (Shtip). Most Samokov *perakende* also came from surrounding villages that belonged to the *kaza* of Samokov, such as Rayova, Ak İskır, Kara İskır, Köstençe, Kovaçefçe (Kovachevtsi), Belçin, Çamurlı, Yarlova, Vakarel, Lozen, Diragoşin, Tacilar (Venkovets), Okol-i Zir, Dosbeg, Bane-i Has, and

İzlakoçan, as well as from the town of İhtiman. A few came from neighbouring regions: Razlog, Radomir, Boboşa, Borovan (in the *kaza* of Radomir), Dikanya-i Zir (Dolna Dikanya, in the *kaza* of Radomir), and Breznik. Two *perakende* are indicated as *Şop* (people from the rural region around Sofia) and three others are *Sofyalı* (people from Sofia). Some interesting cases of provenance present a worker of manufacturing of woolen braid lace (*gaytancılık*) from Karlovo (the most reputed center of this industry at the time) and a assistant doctor (*hekim kalfası*), Nikolaki, indicated as *Selanikli* (from Thessaloniki).

Some Samokov *perakende* seem to already have permanent residence in the city since they own immovable properties there, such as meadows (5 cases) and workshops (10 cases), as well as livestock (21 cases). Other contemporary sources also confirm this; in a Temettuat register of the Pasban Quarter, preserved in the Oriental Department of the National Library in Sofia, [21] the *perakende* are already registered not only with proper numeration but also with a consecutive household number from the beginning of the register, following the general household numeration.

4. Socio-professional Structure and Incomes

An analysis of the socio-economic and income structure of Samokov society shows that the most developed economic activity in the city was manufacturing and trade. 62.9% of the heads of households were engaged in this section, and more than 70% of the local revenues registered were from them. The iron industry had traditionally been developed, but already in the nineteenth century was in decline in comparison to previous times although nevertheless still providing more than 29% of the local revenue and engaged 131 full-time miners (*maden amelesi*), 7.7% of the heads of households in the city.[22] The most significant incomes in this sector belonged to the

[21] NBKM OO, D 598.

[22] We should bear in mind that many of the people engaged in mining (*madenci, kömürcü*, etc.) were living also in the surrounding villages. For example, 36% of the heads of households in the villages of Iovan and Dosbeg are indicated in the local Temettuat registers as coal miners (*kömürcü*): ML.VRD.TMT. no. 11200 and no. 11201. Some years earlier (1840) the proportion in Banya Kostenets (Bane-i Köstence) was registered as even larger, 51%, and in Mahalata, 75%. D. Dimitrova, "Statistitcheski danni ot

Table 2: Occupations of Heads of Households

Types of occupation	Number	%
Religion and education	52	3.0
Administration and military	85	5.0
Agriculture and stockbreeding	51	3.0
Manufacturing and trade	1074	62.9
Transporter	60	3.5
Laborer	135	7.9
Others	251	14.7
Total	1708	100.0

owners of iron enterprises (*ashab-ı fabrika*). Their incomes varied between 10,640 and 37,435 *kuruş*.[23] Average incomes of miners' households were 40 to 100 times less.

In addition to mining,[24] more then 60 different craftsmanship existed in Samokov. The most developed local crafts, with a particularly diversified intra-branch structure, were in the textile manufacturing — for example, coarse woolen cloth maker (*abacı*), tailor, dyer, draper, skullcap maker (*takkeci*), woolen braid lace maker (*gaytancı*) — as well as metalwork (knife maker, blacksmith, iron heel maker, gunsmith, wheel maker, farrier, tinsmith, goldsmith). Another developed craft sector was construction, represented by *dülgerlik* (carpenter), *çeşmecilik* (fountain founder), *taşçılık* (stonemason), *doğramacılık* (carpenter), and so forth. Clothes and shoe manufacturing provided the biggest portion, almost half, of all revenues from craftsman activity in the city and engaged nearly 44% of all craftsmen who were heads of households.

Among Christian craftsmen, the most popular were textile industries

1840 godina za madandzhiiskite sela Banya Kostenets i Mahalata, Samokovsko," *Izvestiya na natsionalniya istoritcheski muzei*, no. 2, 1978, pp. 223-46

23 These are gross revenues. After the reduction of the tax (*rüsumat-ı saire*), the net incomes of the *ashab-ı fabrikas* can be estimated as 8375 *kuruş* on average, if we exclude the income of an *ashab-ı fabrika,* who was a *kaymakam* at the same time.

24 The administrator of mines, that is, *maden müdürü*, secretaries, scribes and other clerks, although closely related to this economic sector, is excluded from this part of the analysis and considered as part of the administration sector in the city.

(every fifth Bulgarian craftsmen in this register is *abacı*), construction, furriery, some metalwork, painting, shoemaking, and tavern keeping. Muslim craftsmen had almost a monopoly on the local tannery, saddle making, iron heel making and farrier work. They were the almost exclusive providers of other city services too: all the barbers, and keepers of public baths, coffeehouses, and sweet shops, were Muslim. Samokov Jewish craftsmen occupations included not only tinsmith (*tenekeci*), a typical craft for Balkan Jews, but also draper (*çuhacı*), textile merchant (*bezzaz*), and sandal maker (*çarıkçı*). Gypsies were primarily coal miners (*kömürcü*), as well as wooden spoon and bowl makers, blacksmiths and tinsmiths.

At the same time, it is worth noting that more than one-fifth of Samokov manufacturing were mixed; that is, members of different ethno-confessional groups in the city practised them. In the Samokov Christian population, craftsman activities predominated, representing the main professional occupation of more than 70% of the economically active Christian urban residents. In the Jewish population, crafts and trades also predominated, while among Muslims no single occupational sector clearly predominated.

An important number of heads of households were listed as *kalfa* (assistant), *çırak* (apprentice), *işçi* (worker), *hizmetkar* (servant), *tabi* (attendant), and so forth, numbering more than 22% of all the cases registered, which gives evidence of a notable presence of auxiliary and wage labor in the Samokov manufacturing and trade sector.

If we consider the fact that only occupations of heads of households are systematically registered and younger members of the households are more likely to be employed in the auxiliary and wage labor force, we might conclude that wage labor had a more important presence in Samokov. Sometimes, however, when heads of households are indicated simply as *işçi* (worker), we do not know whether they were wage workers or independent master-craftsmen.

An important differentiation of incomes can be observed in the mid-nineteenth century among the craftsmen of Samokov. The master craftsmen's incomes varied between 60 *kuruş* (for a tailor) and 3150 *kuruş* (for an *abacı*). The lowest average income of a craftsman's household was less than one-twentieth of the highest one. The biggest differentiation of income among craftsmen from the same manufacturing branch can be observed in textiles. Average incomes were higher in services (*hizmetkar*) and food supply and lower in metalwork and construction. Some relatively profitable occupations were butcher, candle maker, painter, draper, and *abacı* craft, while tailor, cook, and dealer in second-hand wares seem to have been less profitable.

As for the occupations of heads of households in Samokov who practised a trade, shopkeepers such as grocery, greengrocery, herbalist and haberdasher predominated. Most small shopkeepers were Christian and Jewish, whereas Muslims were more often reported as *tüccar* (merchant), *tuzcu* (salt seller), *celep* (farm animal dealer), and the like, although grocers and greengrocers were quite numerous too. Gypsies engaged in trade were all horse dealers (*cambaz*). The differences in the incomes of small shopkeepers (for example, greengrocer, haberdasher) and of merchants (*tüccar, celep*) were notable. The average income of a household in trade exceeded those in the manufacturing sector (except for the iron industry) and was also higher than the average household income for all occupations in the city, apart from administration.

The transportation sector, in which about 3.5% of the heads of households are engaged, provided less than 1.5% of the total revenues of the city. About 60% of the people who worked in transportation were Muslim and the rest were Christian. Some Samokov transporters (*kiracı*) were employed in the transportation of local iron and metalwork towards distant markets and the Ottoman capital.

The agricultural and stockbreeding sector represents the main profession of only 3.0% of the heads of household, and Christians were traditionally predominant (90%). The incomes in this group of occupations were low, making up only 1.2 % of the total revenue of the city.

Military and administrative occupations (5.0% of heads of households registered) were exclusively Muslim. On the other hand, educational and religious professions (3.0% of the heads of households registered) showed a relative parity among the different ethno-religious groups, except that Gypsies were entirely absent. As for the differentiation of incomes in these occupational sectors, the biggest differences appear in the administration sector. The modest income of a court scribe (80-120 *kuruş*) naturally cannot be compared to the revenues of a mine administrator (*maden müdürü*), whose income reached nearly to 4500 *kuruş*. But the income of a mine administrator is even less than that of a *kaymakam*, which exceeded 100,000 *kuruş* On the other hand, the least differentiation at a city level could be observed in the incomes of people who are engaged in the agricultural and stockbreeding sector (50 to 430 *kuruş*) and of wage workers (50 to 500 *kuruş*, with one exception).[25]

An important general finding from the analysis of urban revenue distribution in the Samokov population is the polarisation of income levels, with a heavy concentration in the low levels of income. Even excluding households that had no registered taxable revenues whatsoever, nearly 40% of the remaining households had incomes of fewer than 200 *kuruş*. This large low-income group encompassed most of the *perakende*; many households with heads listed as disabled, old or invalid; persons engaged in stockbreeding, transportation and mining; all the apprentices; most of the journeymen and wage workers; and even a few master craftsmen.

At the opposite extreme, those with incomes exceeding 10,000 *kuruş* and reaching even more than 100,000 *kuruş*, we found only 10 households, representing the owners of iron enterprises and the *kaymakam*. Even after a reduction of the value of the iron due to the state, indicated in the rubric tax (*rüsumat-ı saire*), the net incomes of these households would remain quite large, in most cases ranging from more than 5000 to 90000 *kuruş* and more.

The group of incomes between 1000 and 10,000 *kuruş*, indicating a prosperous economic situation, is also quite limited, approximately 3% of the cases registered in Samokov Temettuat registers. This group, however, is more diverse in its socio-professional composition: more than half of the heads of these households are master craftsmen and about 30% are shopkeepers and merchants, while the rest are inn-keeper (*hancı*), representatives of mining administration and religion, and a few people living on rents.

In the levels of modest and average incomes, from 500 to 1000 *kuruş*, most are master craftsmen and shopkeepers; others are representatives of administration, the army or religion, or owners of farms (*ashab-ı çiftlik*).

---

[25] The occupation of a head of household is sometimes not indicated in the register. The incomes of some of these came from trade or from land properties in surrounding villages, and thus are mentioned in the registration of incomes. For household heads listed as disabled, old, invalid, or minor, on the other hand, part of the income came from other members of the household, whose professions are usually not reported. In both cases we have followed the main principle of registration and identification through the head of the household when drawing up the tables.

Table 3: Socio-professional Structure and Incomes

(1) Religious and Educational Section

Occupation	Number of households	Total income	Lowest income	Highest income	Average of income
derviş (dervish)	2	0	0	0	0
daskal (teacher)	2	460	200	260	230
hafız (mosque attendant)	3	1490	0	765	496.7
haham (Jewish rabbi)	1	0	0	0	0
hatib (preacher)	1	300	300	300	300
imam (prayer leader)	5	1280	150	470	256
keşiş (Christian monk)	5	1130	0	1010	226
---*keşiş hizmetkarı*	1	80	80	80	80
kelya(?) *hizmetkarı*	1	0	0	0	0
metropolit (bishop)					
---*metropolit hizmetkarı*	1	0	0	0	0
muallim-i sıbyan (teacher)	1	468	468	468	468
müezzin (prayer caller)	3	760	80	560	253
mütevelli (trustee of *vakıf*)	1	220	220	220	220
müderris (madrasah teacher)	1	290	290	290	290
papaz (priest)	15	5400	100	730	360
seyyid (descendant of Prophet)	1	1190	1190	1190	1190
şeyh (sheikh)	3	0	0	0	0
talebe-i ilim (madrasah student)	5	590	0	330	118
Total	52	13658			262.7

(2) Military and Administrative Section

Occupation	Number of households	Total income	Lowest income	Highest income	Average of income
asakir-i mansure (soldier)	9	750	0	490	83.3
asakir-i nizamiye (soldier)	27	890	0	370	33
asakir-i nizamiye binbaşı (commander of army)	1	530	530	530	530
beglikçi hizmetkarı (chancery officer)	1	0	0	0	0
çavuş (sergeant)	1	0	0	0	0
emir (commander)	3	0	0	0	0
ihtisapçı (supervisor of market)	1	520	520	520	520
kaymakam (head official of *kaymakamlık*)	1	114800	114800	114800	114800
katip (clerk)	7	2510	220	700	358.6
katib-i mahkeme (clerk of court)	1	390	390	390	390
kavvas (archer)	4	1395	0	1025	348.8

maden katibi (clerk of mine)	2	1365	570	795	682.5
maden müdürü (administrator of mine)	5	9555	770	4490	1911
maden yazıcısı (scribe of mine)	1	680	680	680	680
mahkeme muhzırı (officer of court who summoned persons)	2	200	80	120	100
muhtar (headman of quarter)	5	3125	540	745	625
mukayyid-i nüfus (census registrar)	1	530	530	530	530
nüfus nazırı (census inspector)	1	1660	1660	1660	1660
pasban (watchman)	2	270	90	180	135
paşa hazinedarı (accountant of *paşa*)	1	0	0	0	0
paşa katibi (clerk of *paşa*)	1	0	0	0	0
sa'i (foot messenger)	1	180	180	180	180
teroğlanı (assistant of *cizye* collector)	2	430	80	350	215
timar me'muru (*timar* officer)	1	940	940	940	940
yazıcı (scribe)	2	410	180	230	205
yevmiyeci (daybook registrar)	2	380	120	260	190
Total	85	141510			1664.8

(3) Agricultural and Stockbreeding Section

Occupation	Number of households	Total income	Lowest income	Highest income	Average of income
ashab-ı çiftlik (owner of farm)	4	1810	450	900	603.3
bahçevan (gardener)	1	300	300	300	300
çoban (shepherd)	30	4880	50	430	162.7
seyis (horse keeper)	9	675	60	120	75
sığırtmaç (herdsman)	5	660	90	210	132
---*sığırtmaç hizmetkarı*	2	210	80	130	105
Total	51	8535			167.4

(4) Manufacturing, Trade and Service Section

Occupation	Number of households	Total income	Lowest income	Highest income	Average of income
abacı (maker of coarse woolen cloth)	42	27845	120	3150	663
---*abacı işçisi*	68	12805	50	1060	188.3
---*abacı kalfası*	15	2220	50	360	148
---*abacı çırağı*	6	240	0	180	40
ashab-ı fabrika (owner of iron enterprise)	9	186820	10640	37435	20757.8

aşçı (cook)	3	245	55	110	81.7
---*aşçı hizmetkarı*	1	55	55	55	55
attar (herbalist)	10	4336	105	1900	433.6
bakkal (grocery)	59	27198	130	2490	461
---*bakkal hizmetkarı*	1	110	110	110	110
berber (barber)	10	1710	50	350	171
---*berber kalfası*	1	90	90	90	90
---*berber çırağı*	1	0	0	0	0
bezzaz (textile merchant)	3	1280	360	550	426.7
bıçakçı (knife maker)	1	150	150	150	150
boyacı (dyer)	17	7925	120	2060	466.2
cambaz (horse dealer)	6	1830	250	470	305
celep (cattle dealer)	7	11077	920	2643.5	1582.4
---*celep hizmetkarı*	1	270	270	270	270
çamurcu dülgeri (mortar worker)	3	360	90	150	120
çarıkçı (sandal maker)	1	385	385	385	385
çarkçı (wheel maker)	1	120	120	120	120
çerçi (haberdasher)	11	5207	75	1660	473.4
çeşmeci (fountain founder)	14	4080	110	610	291.4
---*çeşmeci işçisi*	1	90	90	90	90
---*çeşmeci kalfası*	3	280	80	110	93.3
çubukçu (tobacco pipe maker)	2	220	110	110	110
çuhacı (draper)	4	3880	430	2170	1293.3
debbağ (tanner)	21	8890	150	940	423.3
---*debbağ işçi*	9	1525	75	450	169.4
---*debbağ kalfası*	20	2940	70	310	147
---*debbağ çırağı*	2	60	0	60	30
değirmenci (miller)	14	2360	85	430	168.6
---*değirmenci hizmetkarı*	1	90	90	90	90
dellal, tellal (broker)	2	240	90	150	120
dikçi (stitcher)	1	100	100	100	100
doğramacı (carpenter)	4	910	150	320	227.5
dülger (carpenter)	98	24260	50	560	247.6
---*dülger kalfası*	10	970	50	160	97
---*dülger çırağı*	2	0	0	0	0
duhancı (tobacco seller)	2	400	110	290	200
eskici (dealer in second hand wares)	11	1590	100	280	144.6
fahimci (coal dealer)	22	5540	110	460	251.8
fıçıcı (barrel maker)	6	1395	85	490	232.5
fırıncı (bakery)	15	5225	80	1140	348.3
---*fırıncı hizmetkarı*	3	350	80	150	116.7
fişekçi (cartridge maker)	1	320	320	320	320
gaytancı (maker of woolen braid lace)	2	1100	350	750	550

---*gaytancı hizmetkarı*	4	575	100	210	143.8
---*gaytancı çırağı*	2	0	0	0	0
haffaf (shoemaker)	2	1040	510	530	520
hallaç (wool comber)	3	1735	410	720	578.3
hamamcı (keeper of public bath)	2	650	120	530	325
hancı (inn-keeper)	13	8456.5	200	1846	650.5
---*hancı hizmetkarı*	4	480	10	150	120
hatab kesici (wood chopper)	2	200	70	130	100
hekim (physician)	1	140	140	140	140
---*hekim kalfası*	1	250	250	250	250
helvacı (sweet maker)	1	100	100	100	100
kahveci (coffee seller)	2	260	110	150	130
---*kahveci tabi'i*	2	185	60	125	92.5
---*kahveci çırağı*	1	60	60	60	60
kalaycı (tinsmith)	3	840	80	670	280
kantarcı (steelyard maker)	2	230	50	180	115
kapamacı (dealer of ready-made clothing)	1	210	210	210	210
kasap (butcher)	5	3955	430	1760	791
---*kasap hizmetkarı*	14	1910	75	310	136.4
kemaneci (violin maker)	1	220	220	220	220
kovaç (blacksmith)	17	4380	80	670	257.7
---*kovaç işçisi*	2	190	60	130	95
---*kovaç kalfası*	1	80	80	80	80
kunduracı (shoemaker)	1	240	240	240	240
kuyumcu (goldsmith)	3	590	90	350	196.7
---*kuyumcu kalfası*	1	230	230	230	230
küleci (?)	1	80	80	80	80
kürkçü (furriery)	14	4995	120	750	356.8
---*kürkçü işçisi*	2	375	135	240	187.5
---*kürkçü çırağı*	1	50	50	50	50
maden amelesi (mine worker)	131	29960	75	715	228.7
meyhaneci (tavern keeper)	53	29894	40	2870	564
---*meyhaneci hizmetkarı*	3	350	100	150	116.7
mısırcı (corn seller)	2	135	60	75	67.5
mumcu (candle maker)	4	4155	250	2380	1038.8
---*mumcu kalfası*	1	80	80	80	80
muytab (goat woolen cloth maker)	13	4265	120	790	328.1
---*muytab işçisi*	11	1600	80	300	145.5
---*muytab kalfası*	2	250	100	150	125
mücellit (book binder)	2	780	200	580	390
nakkaş (decorator)	5	4170	340	1410	834
nalband (farrier)	26	7565	170	810	291
---*nalband kalfası*	10	1310	80	190	131
---*nalband çırağı*	4	120	0	120	30

nalçacı (iron heel maker)	1	180	180	180	180
---*nalçacı kalfası*	1	130	130	130	130
pabuşçu (shoemaker)	14	5550	80	910	396.4
---*pabuşçu işçisi*	5	1615	100	980	323
---*pabuşçu kalfası*	7	860	65	190	122.9
---*pabuşçu çırağı*	8	130	60	70	65
---*pabuşçu eskici*	2	290	110	180	145
saatçi (watch maker)	2	190	70	120	95
sarraç (saddler)	3	1002	260	382	334
---*sarraç kalfası*	1	100	100	100	100
semerci (packsaddle maker)	2	1050	200	850	525
---*semerci kalfası*	1	120	120	120	120
sepetçi (basket maker)	3	410	50	300	136.7
sırçacı (glass maker)	1	400	400	400	400
simitçi hizmetkarı (*simit* seller)	1	95	95	95	95
şişeci (bottle maker)	1	120	120	120	120
tablakar (itinerant vendor)	1	175	175	175	175
tahmisçi (roaster of coffee)	1	498	498	498	498
takyeci (skullcap maker)	15	9455	210	1720	630.3
---*takyeci işçisi*	1	100	100	100	100
tarakçı (comb maker)	2	345	95	250	142.5
taşçı (stonemason)	1	240	240	240	240
tenekeci (tinsmith)	1	0	0	0	0
teraş (shaver)	1	200	200	200	200
terzi (tailor)	31	10440	100	2060	336.8
---*terzi eskici*	2	120	40	80	60
---*terzi işçisi*	15	2110	60	280	140.7
---*terzi kalfası*	2	280	100	180	140
---*terzi çırağı*	3	80	0	80	26.7
topaviçar (gunsmith)	2	760	210	550	380
tuzcu (salt seller)	1	710	710	710	710
tüccar (merchant)	7	3540	150	1420	505.7
tüfenkçi (gunsmith)	5	2090	110	920	418
yemişçi (greengrocer)	7	665	40	150	95
Total	1074	520483.5			484.5

(5) Transporter

Occupation	Number of households	Total income	Lowest income	Highest income	Average of income
arabacı (transporter)	38	8045	80	980	211.7
hintocu (coachman)	1	0	0	0	0
kiracı (transporter)	20	2740	80	380	137
koçucu (coachman)	1	100	100	100	100
Total	60	10885			181.4

(6) Laborers

Occupation	Number of households	Total income	Lowest income	Highest income	Average of income
aylak (laborer)	1	460	460	460	460
amele (worker)	3	800	90	410	266.7
çırak (apprentice)	1	70	70	70	70
hademe (servant)	2	440	120	320	220
hizmetkar (servant)	101	13255	50	500	131.2
ırgad (day-laborer)	11	1430	50	280	130
işçi (worker)	2	180	70	110	90
mezarcı (gravedigger)	1	100	100	100	100
saraydar (steward)	1	75	75	75	75
tabi (servant)	12	4177	75	1190	348.1
Total	135	20987			155.5

(7) Others

	Number of households	Total income	Lowest income	Highest income	Average of income
dilenci (beggar)	2	0	0	0	0
deceased	2	0	0	0	0
non-indicated	24	9256	0	1365	385.7
exempt	1	0	0	0	0
disabled, old, invalid	127	9680.5	0	1428.3	72.2
minor	78	2635	0	800	33.2
poor	14	80	0	80	0
woman, widow	3	430	90	230	143.3
Total	251	22081.5			88.0

As for the structure of household incomes, in about 30% of Samokov households the revenues from the main economic activity of the head of the household were supplemented by income from meadows, other immovable properties, and livestock. In 90% of the cases, however, these incomes were only of secondary importance compared to the revenue from the main professional activity. Whereas at the lower levels the incomes of the economically active population were almost entirely based on professional revenues, at average and higher levels of income this population presents a more diversified income structure, with varied and sometimes multiple sources. In the higher categories of income, that part of the income coming from urban immovable properties, meadows, and livestock grows and tends to approach the level of the professional revenue. In the category of highest revenues, the biggest portion of household income is usually due to revenues from local iron enterprises, with the exception of a *kaymakam*, whose remuneration for administrative services usually exceeds the iron industry revenues. The structure of the household incomes of the economically non-active urban residents from all levels of income is, in contrast, based mainly on rents from immovable properties.

The sources studied, though they do not have systematic data, indicate some general characteristics of the economic activities of the population of Samokov at the micro-level of the household. As already mentioned, about 14% of the households have more than one member whose profession and respective income are indicated; apart from the heads of household, these are sons, sons-in law, brothers, fathers, uncles, and so forth. These cases were typical (about three times more common) for Samokov *abacı*. In their households it was also more common that all members of the household with registered incomes from an economic activity exercised the same craft, *abacılık*. More often than in other households, their number was multiple, with three, four, and even six people practising this craft. Thus, for example, Hacı Tone Deyanoğlu from the Palas Quarter was practising the *abacılık* together with his three sons, as expressly indicated in the register.[26] They had all, clearly, adopted their father's profession. Hacı Kostooğlu Todor, in whose household six *cizye* payers were registered, is indicated as practising the same craft in his own workshop together with his brothers (the revenues of two of them being registered among the revenues of his household).[27] In

26 ML.VRD.TMT. no. 11236, p. 18.
27 ML.VRD.TMT. no. 11206, p. 21.

addition to indicating the larger size of these families and the greater number of economically active people in them, this kind of information also demonstrates a greater frequency of transmission of the craft through generations as well as its role as a family activity. In these cases the *abacı* household had economic unity, employing all the male members of the family. It is impossible to have any information from our source on the economic activities of women and minors who were members of the household and who could also have participated in this family production, as characteristic for proto-industries, which *abacılık* in the city is shown by other sources to have been.

Table 4: Income by Quarters and their Tax

	Quarters	Number of households	Total income (*kuruş*)	Average income (*kuruş*)	Total *vergi* (*kuruş*)	Average of *vergi* (*kuruş*)	Other taxes (*kuruş*)
1	Hoca Sefer	81	32025	395.4	1150	14.2	11800+
2	Abdülcebbar	72	143010	1986.3	1350	18.8	32673+
3	Tekye	86	16288	189.4	1374	16.0	
4	Şeyh	95	22002.5	231.6	1243	13.1	
5	Cami-i Atik	38	41395	1089.3	1180	31.1	22011+
6	Cami-i Cedid	56	42901	766.1	1434	25.7	16355+
7	Nazır Cafer	33	94275	2856.8	1250	37.9	60781+
8	Kurşunlu	56	13615	243.1	950	17.0	
9	Musalla	54	26740	495.2	650	12.0	11800+
10	Mehmed Çavuş	34	6985	205.4	416	12.2	
11	Koca Papas	149	58259	391.0	9324	62.3	6240*
12	İskır Kenarı	104	26648	256.2	4225.5	40.7	3615*
13	Palas	141	57147	405.5	9344.3	66.3	5400*
14	Leşker	131	28455	217.2	3920	30.0	3795*
15	Mandal	203	44025	216.9	7177.8	35.6	5685*
16	Pasban	287	64547.5	225.0	10158.8	35.4	9420*
17	Yahudiler	45	11443	255.0	1500	33.3	1290*
18	Taife-i Kıbtiyan	43	8370	195.7	1530	35.6	30*
	Total	1708	738131	432.2	58177.4	34.1	

\+ *rüsumat-ı saire* (total 155420 *kuruş*)
* *cizye* (total 35475 *kuruş*)

5. Taxes

The Temettuat registers of Samokov provide us with information on taxation of the local urban population with the special tax (*vergi-i mahsusa*), the additional rubric tax (*rüsumat-ı saire*, concerning only a few cases), and the *cizye* (for non-Muslims). The amount of the *vergi-i mahsusa* and the *rüsumat-ı saire* for every household, and the *cizye* category of every individual non-Muslim adult male urban resident, are indicated in the registers, as well as the total amount of *vergi-i mahsusa* and *rüsumat-ı saire* due by every quarter. These data allow us to estimate the total of these impositions at a city level, to observe their amount to the incomes registered, and to look at internal distribution of the taxes among the taxpayers.

The *vergi-i mahsusa* collected in the city of Samokov represents 7.9% of the total local revenues registered in the Temettuat registers. To estimate the actual ratio of taxation, however, we would have to exclude the revenues from iron production from the total amount of the Temettuat incomes indicated in the registers, because they were subject to a different category of taxation, *rüsumat-ı saire.*[28] After this reduction, the average ratio of *vergi-i mahsusa* in the city can be estimated at 11.0% to the tax dutiable incomes.

The average ratio of *vergi-i mahsusa* to total income in the Muslim quarters was 4.8% and shows considerable variation: specifically, 6.7% in Musalla, 5.7% in Şeyh, 5.8% in Mehmed Çavuş, 8.4% in Tekye, 6.3% in Cami-i Cedid, 7.0% in Kurşunlu, 7.9% in Cami-i Atik, 7.7% in Hoca Sefer, 11.6% in Nazır Cafer, and only 1.4% in Abdülcebbar.

The average ratio of *vergi-i mahsusa* to total income for Samokov non-Muslims was 15.7%. It was lowest in Jewish households, 13.0%. In the

[28] The amount of the sums due by the possessors of the iron enterprises, the *ashab-ı fabrika,* to the state treasury are indicated in our registers under the rubric *rüsumat-ı saire.* According to an *irade* from the seventh of July, 1843 (11 Receb 1259H), in the Tanzimat period there was an attempt to replace the delivery of a fixed amount of iron required, or of its equivalent in money, by the collection of the equivalent of one-tenth (the tithe) from the production plus the respective duty tax, or, as a whole, the equivalent of one-fifth of the production. *Dokumenti za balgarskata istoriya,,* Vol. 3, pp. 277-79. The case reflected in our source, however, seems to correspond to the old practises instead.

other Samokov non-Muslim quarters, the ratio of *vergi-i mahsusa* to total income was quite uniform: 15.7% in Pasban, 16.0% in Koca Papas, 16.4% in Palas, 16.3% in Mandal, and 15.9% in İskır Kenarı. Its proportion went lower only in the Leşker Quarter at less than 13.8%. The average ratio of *vergi-i mahsusa* to total income in the Samokov quarters indicated as part of the *Varoş* (corresponding to the community of the Christian urban residents) was thus 15.8%. *Vergi-i mahsusa,* as part of the incomes registered, was highest for Gypsies at 18.3%. As a whole, taxation in the Muslim quarters (Gypsies excluded) was less than one-third of that in the non-Muslim ones.

Samokov Temettuat registers also give us the opportunity to estimate the *cizye* taxation of the non-Muslim population. As is well known, the *cizye* tax was collected from the male non-Muslim population in three categories: superior *(alâ)*, 60 *kuruş*; middle *(evsat)*, 30 *kuruş*; and inferior *(edna)*, 15 *kuruş*. The Temettuat registers indicate the number and kind of *cizye* categories for each non-Muslim household, describing لا for *alâ,* ط for *evsat,* نا for *edna,* which allows us to estimate the total number of non-Muslim *cizye* taxpayers and to calculate the amount of the *cizye* tax paid in each household, quarters or communities and in the city of Samokov as a whole. The *cizye* tax represents between 9.5% (the Palas Quarter) and 14.6% (the Pasban Quarter) of the incomes registered in the respective non-Muslim quarters (13.3% in the Leşker Quarter, 10.7% in the Koca Papas Quarter, 13.6% in İskır Kenarı, 12.9% in the Mandal Quarter, and 11.8% for the Jewish), an average of 12.2% (12.2% for Christians and 11.3% for Jews). Together with the *vergi-i mahsusa, cizye* taxation in the different non-Muslim quarters represents a range of between 24.4% (Jewish) and 30.3% (Pasban Quarter) of the incomes registered. The total average fiscal taxation of the non-Muslim population at the city level can thus be estimated as 27.9% from the incomes (24.4% for Jewish and 28.1% for Christian urban residents).

As for the internal distribution of *vergi-i mahsusa* among the taxpayers in the quarters or communities, the registers confirm repartition of a total sum (portion) within the community after evaluation of the economic circumstances of every taxpayer. In the non-Muslim quarters especially, taxes due from individual households were almost never round sums; for example, figures such as 19 *kuruş* 32 *para* or 54 *kuruş* two *para* were usual. Incomes don't seem to have been the only criteria for allotment of the *vergi-i mahsusa,* for not only at a city level but also at the level of the quarters, equal incomes were taxed at different amounts. Movable and immovable properties owned (even when not a source of revenue), perhaps together with the household's number of economically active members, seem to have influenced evaluation of economic potential.

6. Immovable Properties and Farm Livestock

Land Area

Approximately every fourth Samokov household had a piece of land within the territory of the city. In all cases except two, these were meadows. Small meadows (*çayır*), giving less than five cart (*araba*) of production annually, were most typical, representing more than 73% of all cases and nearly 90% of the land possessions of the non-Muslim population of Samokov. Almost half the meadows of the Muslim population of Samokov, on the other hand, were registered as giving between five and more than 20 cart of production (26% gave between 10 and more than 20 cart). Meadows, as part of Samokov urban residents' possessions, provide evidence that raising cattle, rather than agriculture, was a source of revenue for these households, usually only a secondary source, to judge by the importance of the annual income from the meadows registered. Some Samokov urban residents participated in the ownership of summer pastures (*yaylak*). In Samokov Temettuat registers, 12 such cases are registered, most of them joint ownership between two and seven partners.

Table 5: Meadows (*çayır*) Owned by Urban Residents

	0-5	5-10	10-20	20+	Total (*araba*)
Muslim	107	44	31	22	204
Christian	232	19	6	1	258
Jewish	1	1			2
Total	340	64	37	23	464

Workshops and Stores

Samokov Temettuat registers consecutively register, as part of the immovable property of the urban residents, the private workshops, shops, taverns, inns, water mills and similar structures belonging to the local population. Their value is not mentioned, but the record indicates whether the owner (or members of the household) were making personal use of them or were renting them to other people; if the latter, rents were registered as part of the annual incomes of the household. Nearly half (48%) the workshops and stores registered were used directly by their owners or by household members (sons, sons-in-law, brothers, etc.). The rest (52%) were rented to other craftsmen or shopkeepers.

Nearly 80% of the owners of private shops in Samokov had one workshop, or a part of a workshop, registered among their immovable properties. Most of such owners were craftsmen and shopkeepers. Representatives of other professional and social groups were slightly more common among the owners of two or of multiple workshops. Concentration of property on Samokov workshops was relatively rare; the 21 owners with more than two shops possessed 73 shops in common, or less than 20% of this kind of urban property.

Among the 374 private workshops and stores registered in the Temettuat registers,[29] 280 (75%) belonged to local craftsmen and shopkeepers. The internal distribution of the workshops in these professional groups was, however, quite unequal. Most Samokov craftsmen and shopkeepers did not possess a private working space registered among their properties. Even if we consider that almost 20% of the craftsmen were in professions whose exercise does not require a specific workshop (e.g., masons, fountain-makers, or coal dealers), the proportion of Samokov craftsmen without a private shop still remains considerable. Nearly half of the Samokov craftsmen without a private workshop were registered in the local Temettuat registers as apprentices, journeymen, or wage workers. We can assume the rest were master craftsmen working on their own in hired workshops. Of the craftsmen and shopkeepers, 194 had one workshop (or a part of a workshop) registered among their immovable properties. More than 70% of them were using it for the practise of their craft or trade. The rest

[29] In 23 of the cases, a joint ownership of workshops was registered. It refers to 11 shops (ten with two co-owners each and one with three). Thus the total number of private shops in Samokov could be estimated at 374. In the great majority of cases of joint ownership of workshops (all except four), the owners did not possess other workshops and, therefore they are among the people with one workshop in our table.

were renting their workshops at moderate rents, from 40 to 100 *kuruş* in most cases. Only about 2 % of all Samokov craftsmen and a few shopkeepers were owners of more than one workshop. The majority of these had only two shops.

At the same time, Samokov Temettuat registers show a very thin stratum of well-to-do craftsmen and shopkeepers who are owners of multiple shops. The additional shops were rented to other members of the professional group and were a significant source of complementary revenues for their owners. For the majority of Samokov craftsmen and shopkeepers, owners of this kind of immovable property, the workshop represented an essential component of their properties and means of production, giving them greater economic independence.

Samokov Temettuat registers include, as part of the household's sources of revenue, seven cogwheels for the production of woolen braid laces (*gaytancı çarkı*). All belonged to local Bulgarians. Four were used by their owners or members of the household (two of them in partnership), and three were rented. The incomes from the cogwheels are considerable, that is, between 450 and 1800 *kuruş* annually, and the rents are from 250 to 550 *kuruş* per year. Thus Samokov Temettuat registers reaffirm their importance as a rich source for study of the local economy and society, testifying to the development in this city of braid lace making, a relatively new and quite profitable branch of the woollen textile manufacturing. The registers also suggest the possible place from which this craft was "imported." As previously mentioned, one of the registered *perakende* was a maker of woollen braid laces from Karlovo, the most famous center of this craft, from which this craft was most probably brought to Samokov.

Another kind of immovable property registered in Samokov Temettuat registers is the water mills. Most of them had one millstone, but water mills with two, three, four, and even six stones were also registered. Of the local urban residents, 28 owed proper water mills and 15 others took part in joint ownership. Among them Muslims were predominant. Every fourth water mill was rented to other people.

Samokov Temettuat registers thus draw the picture of a quite differentiated local society as far as ownership of these kinds of urban immovable property is concerned.

Property of Urban Residents in Surrounding Villages

Samokov Temettuat registers list 73 urban residents with property in surrounding villages; of these, 65 are Muslim. One is *perakende*. Urban residents that own out-of-town properties thus represent about 11% of Samokov Muslim households and less than 1 % of the Christian ones. None of the Samokov Jewish or Gypsy inhabitants had property in the surrounding villages.

As for the location of the out-of-town properties, 40 Samokov urban residents owned properties around İhtiman, 11 in the village of Çamurlı, three in Köstence, one in Bane-i Köstence, one in Rayovo, one in Solo (?), one in Dosbeg, one in Vakarel, two in Karlilar (Polyantsi), seven in Bane-i Has (all the preceding villages belong to the Samokov District), three in non-indicated villages of the *kaza* of Dubniçe (Dupnitsa), two in the *kaza* of Köstendil, and one in the *kaza* of Pazarcık. These properties were registered, described and taxed in the respective villages, and therefore information as to type, size and revenues was not usually given in Samokov Temettuat registers. In some cases it was only mentioned that the property concerned was a farm (*çiftlik*); more than half of these cases were in Bane-i Has Village. The farm belonged to well-to-do Samokov Muslim urban residents, including the *kaymakam,* two owners of farm and one mine administrator.

The social and professional characteristics of Samokov urban residents who own out-of-town properties are diverse: 24 craftsmen, five shopkeepers, five merchants, eight miners, five servants, one minor in age, two students, a woman, three old or invalid, five designated as owners of farms, three related to cult and religion, four engaged in different levels of local administration (from the *kaymakam* to a *muhtar* of a quarter), two mine administrators, three owners of iron enterprises, and two whose occupations are not indicated. As for economic status, judging from the incomes and urban properties registered in Samokov Temettuat registers, craftsmen and shopkeepers who are owners of properties in surrounding villages seem to belong to the middle strata, merchants up to the middle and upper merchant "classes," miners and servants have modest incomes and properties. In contrast, officials in local or mine administration and the owners of farms have important incomes and other properties registered.

Table 6: Kind of Livestock and their Number

Kind of animal	Number	Income	Per capital income
Cow (*karasığır, inek*)			
Milch Cow	114	2280 *kuruş*	20 *kuruş*
Barren	424		
Heifer	213		
Ox	112		
Calf	150		
Steer	33		
Buffalo (*manda*)			
Milch buffalo	92	3680 *kuruş*	40 *kuruş*
Buffalo-barren	35		
Buffalo-heifer	18		
Buffalo-calf	4		
Buffalo-steer	4		
Sheep (*koyun*)			
Milch Sheep	49	196 *kuruş*	4 *kuruş*
Sheep	15		
Lamb	5		
Horse			
Baggage horse (*bargir*)	183		
Stallion (*tay*)	5		
Mare (*kısrak*)	11		
Donkey (*merkep*)	5		
Hen (*tavuk*)	3		
Beehives (*kovan*)	60	180 *kuruş*	3 *kuruş*
Total		6,336 *kuruş*	

Livestock

Livestock owned by each Samokov household were registered in the Temettuat registers with their number and the approximate income from their products. These incomes were usually 20 *kuruş* annually from a milch cow, 40 *kuruş* from a buffalo, four *kuruş* annually from a milch sheep and three *kuruş* from every beehive.

While families in the surrounding villages (Iovan, Dosbeg, etc.) had mostly small livestock such as sheep, goats, lambs, and kids,[30] Samokov urban residents, according to the Temettuat registers, primarily raised cattle.

30 As shown in ML.VRD.TMT. no. 11200 and no. 11201.

Other livestock were donkeys, hens, bees, and horses; the latter were owned by both Muslims and Bulgarians as well as by Gypsies, but in the greatest numbers (from three to even seven) only by some of the well-to-do Muslims. Less than half of all the urban households had livestock, usually only a cow, which was often accompanied by a heifer or a calf. Livestock possessed by Muslims were usually numerous and varied, and in contrast were most rare in Jewish people, present in only eight of the 45 Jewish households in the city. All professional groups in Samokov, craftsmen as well as shopkeepers, miners, merchants and people related to cult and administration, had some livestock.

Since the Samokov population owned more meadows than arable land in the city territory, livestock were not important as a source of labor. For almost all households, the animals seem to have been only a complementary, secondary source of revenues (for milk, cheese, butter, meat, etc.). Only for the transporter (*arabacı*), who usually were registered with a pair of oxen, was the ownership of these animals closely related to the main professional activity and probably essential for its exercise.

Conclusion

The Temettuat registers of Samokov from 1845 contain valuable data for the study of the local society. As a tax register they do not, and cannot, provide precise information on the number of the local population and on the structure of the households, but they allow us some approximate estimates in these fields together with a quite precise evaluation of the ethno-confessional and socio-professional composition of the local urban society. Samokov from the mid-1840s thus appears as a city center quite varied in its ethno-confessional composition, having a population of nearly 8000 people (Christians, Muslims, Jews and Gypsies) and an extremely diversified occupational structure, including a dominant manufacturing sector (more than 60 different crafts and industries). Samokov Temettuat registers are particularly explicit and detailed in the registration of immovable properties and livestock belonging to the urban residents. The exact correlation between the household incomes indicated and the *vergi-i mahsusa* on the other hand is not quite clear. Apart from the incomes, movable and immovable properties owned (even when they were not a source of revenues) seem to have influenced the evaluation of the economic potential of the household and the respective rate of taxation, as the number of economically active household members may have done as well. The redistribution of the tax portions among the tax units within the quarter additionally disguises this correlation. The registers show nevertheless considerable variations in the incomes and in the properties of the urban residents, testifying thus to the existence, already in the mid-1840s, of an advanced socio-economic differentiation of the local society.

Chapter 3

Tatarpazarcığı: Socio-economic Condition of Muslim Urban Residents

Mahir AYDIN

1. The Social Panorama of Tatarpazarcığı

In the year 1845, Tatarpazarcığı was a small town belonging to the *sancak* of Filibe (now Plovdiv) within the Edirne Province of the Ottoman Empire. The town's present name is Pazardzhik in the Republic of Bulgaria. This town was located, in the Ottoman Era, on the trade route ranging from Edirne, Filibe to Sofia, and on the banks of the River Maritsa. Tatarpazarcığı, extending to near the outskirts of the Dospat Yaylası, had a natural feature that makes the area suitable for agriculture. Although the centre of town was located on the upper bank of the River Maritsa, the villages belonging to it were located in marshy areas, not far from each other on both sides of the river.

Evliya Çelebi, an Ottoman traveller of the 17th century, noted that this settlement area was once a small village that took its name from a Tatar tribe settled here during the reign of Sultan Murat I. During the reign of Süleyman the Magnificent, the importance of this area increased because of campaigns against the Austrian front, and several settlement policies were applied by the Grand Vezir Makbul İbrahim Paşa; this resulted in the small village's development into a small provincial town, Tatarpazarcığı.[1]

---

1 Evliya Çelebi, *Seyahatname*, Vol. 3, Istanbul, 1314, pp. 986-88.

Table 1: Names of Quarters and the Number of Households

	Quarters	Number of households	ML.VRD.TMT
1	Akmescid	12	6354
2	Ayasbey	120	6342
3	Bostan	59	6364
4	Boyacıbali	6	6341
5	Cami-i Atik	13	6352
6	Çıksalın	42	6321
7	Divan-ı Sefer	36	6312
8	Hacıkılıç	45	6346
9	Hacısalih	61	6324
10	İbrahimpaşa	64	6336
12	İmaret	29	6356
11	Karaterzi	59	6319
13	Katipyusuf	100	6350
14	Musalla	65	6295
15	Naibhamza	61	6314
16	Ortacami	21	6340
17	Ökçebasan	109	6318
18	Sadihoca	83	6347
	Total	1102	

The Quarters of Tatarpazarcığı

In the Ottoman understanding of urbanization, quarters (*mahalle*) have a significant place. Usually, quarters are formed by people who are acquainted with each other and have common needs and interests. This formation, occurring particularly around a mosque or church, is also a kind of lifestyle in which common cultural assets are preserved and maintained.[2]

In the period studied, Tatarpazarcığı was composed of more than 26 quarters. According to Evliya Çelebi this number had been 16,[3] which means that within a period of 200 years the number of quarters increased from 16 to at least 26. This is understandable because Tatarpazarcığı is a rich small town, not only in terms of agriculture but also of commerce and

2 Özer Ergenç, "Osmanlı Şehrindeki 'Mahalle'nin İşlev ve Nitelikleri üzerine," *Osmanlı Araştırmaları*, no. 4 , 1984, p. 69.

3 Evliya Çelebi, *op.cit.*, p. 986.

stockbreeding. But unfortunately a part of the Temettuat registers of the city quarters have not yet been found. Temettuat registers extant in Prime Ministry Ottoman Archives, and used in this study, are the registers for 18 Muslim quarters only (Table 1). Five more Muslim quarters, at least two non-Muslim quarters, and one Gypsy quarter could also be verified by attributions in the present Temettuat registers we have.

For example, the Karaserver Quarter is mentioned in the report of a shop rented by a son of Haffaf Hacı Hasan Abdi, who is in the register of the Musalla Quarter. According to the registration, the son rented the shop from a resident of the Karaserver Quarter, Ayşe Hanım, wife of Mustafa.[4] In this way we have also determined quarters of İbrahimpaşa-yı Kefere, Kiremitçi, Mahmud-ı Atik, Okçular, Oruçluv and Varoş.[5] But because the information about these seven quarters is scanty, our sample will be the 18 Muslim quarters that have their own Temettuat registers.[6]

The muhtars *(Headmen) of Tatarpazarcığı*

According to the Temettuat registers, Tatarpazarcığı had *muhtar*s, who were responsible for residents of the quarters and their security and also kept a watch on non-residents visiting the quarter; the *muhtar* system was newly established at that time.[7] In 17 registers out of 18, we find that a first and a second *muhtar* served in the quarters of Tatarpazarcığı. The Boyacıbali Quarter, which had no *muhtar* because of an insufficient number of households, is the one exception.

Most of the *muhtar*s of Tatarpazarcığı belong to various professional groups, such as herbalist, barber, butcher, farrier, wool comber, shoemaker,

4 "*Dükkan-ı mezbur Karaserver Mahallesi sakinlerinden Mustafa'nın zevcesi Ayşe Hanım'dan icare olunmuş olduğu,*" ML.VRD.TMT. no. 6295, hane 13.

5 The word *varoş* means the Christian community in general and therefore cannot indicate a quarter of normal scale at all. Because registers for the Christian Bulgarian quarters do not exist, information about Tatarpazarcığı is limited to that of the Muslim Turkish community.

6 The Register of a Gypsy quarter, the Yenimahalle Quarter, is in existence. but information from the register could not be included for this paper. ML. VRD. TMT 6349.

7 As for the *muhtar* institution, which was established by a decree of Sultan Mahmud II, see Musa Çadırcı, *Tanzimat Döneminde Anadolu Kentleri'nin Sosyal ve Ekonomik Yapıları*, Ankara, 1991, pp. 38-40.

sandal maker, carpenter, candle maker, coffer seller, tanner, hardware dealer, tile seller, wool merchant, and tax collector (*tahsildar*). Some *muhtars*, like *imam*, do not pay their tax: however, other *muhtars* do pay. Of these, the first *muhtar* of the Musalla Quarter pays the highest tax, 195 *kuruş*, and the second *muhtar* of the İbrahimpaşa Quarter pays the lowest, five *kuruş*.

The unanimous opinion of the notables determined whether a resident of the their quarter, including *muhtar*, would pay tax or not. The notables of the Akmescid, Katipyusuf, and Ortacami Quarters unanimously decided that the *muhtars* of these quarters did not have to pay the tax.[8] While the burden of tax is usually the same for first and second *muhtars*, the Musalla Quarter is an exception. Although the first *muhtar* pays 145 *kuruş* in taxes, the second *muhtar* pays no tax at all because of his position as *muhtar*.[9]

Imams *in Tatarpazarcığı*

Mosques in the Muslim quarters did not serve solely as places of worship, they also undertook the complexities of social service in their adjacent buildings. Every Muslim quarter in Tatarpazarcığı had its own mosque and the *imam* of the mosque, as a notable of the quarter, registered in the first column in Temettuat registers. In the non-Muslim quarters, priests of churches played the same function. In Tatarpazarcığı, Mehmed Efendi, son of İsmail Efendi, the *imam* of the Cami-i Atik Quarter, is recorded as the *reis-i ulema* (chief of religious members) of the city.[10]

İmams usually paid no tax at all. This was also decided unanimously by the notables of the quarters.[11] We find that *imams* were sometimes poor and had no income (for example, those of the Musalla and Akmescid Quarters), and they made a living by the support of the quarter residents.[12] The annual income of *imams* varied between 15 and 400 *kuruş* for different

8 It is said , "*mahalleli ittifakıyla.*" ML.VRD.TMT. no. 6340, 6350, 6354.

9 It is said originally that "*Mahalle-i mezburun muhtarlık hizmetinde bulunmuş olduğundan vergisi olmadığı....,*" ML.VRD.TMT. no. 6295.

10 ML.VRD.TMT. no. 6352.

11 For the Akmescid Quarter, it is said originally that "*Efendi-i mumaileyh mahalle-i mezburun imamı olduğundan vergi tahsil etmedikleri.*" ML.VRD.TMT. no. 6354. For a few of the other examples refer to: ML.VRD.TMT. no. 6318, 6319, 6364.

12 Originally said, "*şunun bunun ianesiyle geçinmekte olduğu,*" ML.VRD.TMT. no. 6295, 6336, 6354.

quarters.[13] We also witness that some *imams* held a variety of jobs, such as wool trade, soap trade, brokerage, or sandal trade. Others were preacher (*hatip*), with a wage six or seven times their normal earnings as an *imam* in other quarter mosques.[14] The *imams* of the Bostan, Musalla, Ökçebasan and Katipyusuf Quarters were teaching in primary schools in their quarters, and the *imams* of the Naibhamza and İbrahimpaşa Quarters were doing the same task ad interim. The Çıksalın Quarter had a madrasah, and the *imam* of the quarter was also working as a professor there.

The Mosques in Tatarpazarcığı

Although we are able to find the exact names of the imams, we cannot do the same for the mosques themselves. In the present 18 Temettuat registers, we find the names of only 16 mosques, some deriving from a quarter's name and some not. Of the 16 mosques, 11 bear the same names as their quarters: Ayasbey, Atik, Çıksalın, Divan-ı Sefer, Hacıkılıç, Hacısalih, İmaret, Musalla, Ortacami, Ökçebasan, and Sadihoca. The other five mosques are Çarşı Camii,[15] Güllük Camii,[16] Hamam Camii,[17] Paşa Camii[18] and Saraçhane Camii.[19]

In addition to the 16 mosques, an Armenian church was in the Musalla Quarter. It is registered that the people belonging to this Armenian church paid 50 *kuruş* a year to the *imam* of the Musalla Mosque.[20]

---

13 The incomes of the *imams* were 15 *kuruş* in Divan-ı Sefer, 250 *kuruş* in Naibhamza, 300 *kuruş* in Hacısalih, 540 *kuruş* in Ökçebasan, 190 *kuruş* in İbrahimpaşa, 400 kuruş in Ortacami, 300 *kuruş* in Karaterzi, 360 *kuruş* in Çıksalın, 200 *kuruş* in Ayasbey, 160 *kuruş* in İmaret, 100 *kuruş* in Bostan, 400 *kuruş* in Sadihoca, 170 *kuruş* in Hacıkılıç, 350 *kuruş* in Katipyusuf, 200 *kuruş* in Cami-i Atik, and 100 *kuruş* in Çarşı Camii; the *imams* of Musalla and Akmescid quarters have no incomes at all.

14 *İmam* of the Divan-ı Sefer Quarter has an additional income of 100 *kuruş* from working as *hatip* besides his regular income of 15 *kuruş* as *imam*.

15 ML.VRD.TMT. no. 6336, hane 1, hane 2; defter 6342, hane 50, hane 77; no. 6356, hane 4; no. 6352, hane 60.

16 ML.VRD.TMT. no. 6340, hane 16; no. 6342, hane 62.

17 ML.VRD.TMT. no. 6312, hane 15.

18 ML.VRD.TMT. no. 6324, hane 28; no. 6340, hane 9; no. 6342, hane 59; no. 6350, hane 6.

19 ML.VRD.TMT. no. 6364, hane 53; no. 6352, hane 47.

20 ML.VRD.TMT. no. 6295.

The Population of Tatarpazarcığı

The 18 quarters of Tatarpazarcığı had 1,102 households, including 1,031 complete households with a male population (*erkek hanesi*), 39 incomplete households without males (*kadın hanesi*), and 32 composed only of children (*çocuk hanesi*). In these *çocuk hanesi*, some children without parents were registered under the protection of a stepfather, uncle, brother-in-law, or grandmother.

To estimate total population from the number of households, we have multiplied the number of households by five and the number of *kadın hanesi* by three, and have taken the number of *çocuk hanesi* as is. Based on the present registers, the total estimated population of the 18 quarters is 5,304, as shown in Table 2.

To estimate for the quarters whose registers were not preserved, the calculation method will have to be somewhat ingenious. We know of at least seven quarters in the town, of which we assume five are Muslim and two, non-Muslim. To multiply this number by 60 (the average number of households per quarter in the 18 quarters) gives 420 as the estimated number of households in the seven other quarters. We therefore estimate their population as 2100, though the so-called Varoş Quarter, which was the general term of Christian quarters, could be assumed to have a much larger population. Yenimahalle, where Gypsies dwelled, had 98 households and a population of about 490.[21]

As a result, we estimate a total population for the town of Tatarpazarcığı of at least 7894, combining the confirmed number 5304 of the 18 quarters, the estimated number 2100 of seven additional quarters, and 490 gypsies.

Notables in Tatarpazarcığı

When we check the population of Tatarpazarcığı, we find 20 established families, which are known with their family names in the area. These families are: Anberzâdeler, Baçdarzâdeler, Bekir Ağazâdeler, Davulcuzâdeler, Genç Ağazâdeler, Hacı Süleyman Ağazâdeler, Halil Efendizâdeler, Hoca Mehmedzâdeler, Hüseyin Beyzâdeler, İbrahim Beyzâdeler, Kavanozzâdeler, Manavzâdeler, Mirhanzâdeler, Molla Alizâdeler, Pir Ağazâdeler,

[21] ML.VRD.TMT. no. 6349.

Table 2: Number of Households and the Estimated Population

	Quarter	Total number of households	Male households	Female households	Children only	Estimated population
1	Akmescid	12	12	0	0	60
2	Ayasbey	120	108	5	7	562
3	Bostan	59	59	0	0	295
4	Boyacıbali	6	5	1	0	28
5	Cami-i Atik	130	126	1	3	636
6	Çıksalın	42	40	0	2	202
7	Divan-ı Sefer	36	35	0	1	176
8	Hacıkılıç	45	45	0	0	225
9	Hacısalih	61	51	9	1	283
10	İbrahimpaşa	64	62	2	0	316
12	İmaret	29	28	1	0	143
11	Karaterzi	59	59	0	0	295
13	Katipyusuf	100	93	1	6	474
14	Mussalla	65	45	17	3	279
15	Naibhamza	61	59	1	1	299
16	Ortacami	21	19	0	2	97
17	Ökçebasan	109	105	1	3	531
18	Sadihoca	83	80	0	3	403
	Total	1102	1031	39	32	5304

Süleymanzâdeler, Taktakzâdeler, Talip Ağazâdeler, Tayyib Ağazâdeler and Yakup Ağazâdeler.

Ali Bey from Hüseyin Beyzâdeler was the owner of rice cultivation. Forefathers of Hüseyin Beyzâdeler and İbrahim Beyzâdeler were in the Ottoman military service. We know that people in the Ottoman society were not addressed at random. Instead, those from military ranks were called *bey*, those from the religious or bureaucratic professions were called *efendi*, and those whose fathers or grandfathers were members of the army, but who themselves were men of religion or bureaucracy, were called *beyefendi*. This is true for Tatarpazarcığı. We find 19 men with the title of *bey*, 88 with *efendi* and five with *beyefendi* in the 18 Temettuat registers.

2. The Commercial Life of Tatarpazarcığı

Occupations in Tatarpazarcığı

Because of its geographic location and opportunities as the focus of its hinterland, Tatarpazarcığı was important not only for agriculture but for commerce as well. The Temettuat registers list almost every kind of occupation of those days. Of 1102 heads of household included in the 18 quarters, the occupations of 887 are identified. Most of them were in manufacturing or commerce.

Among the varieties of occupations, as many as 70, the job of servant (*hizmetkar*) appears most frequently, with 160 people listed. Considering that this term could be used in a somewhat general meaning, however, it is more accurate to say that the farriers (*nalband*) rank first with 63 people. This gives important clues about the importance of transportation with animals in this area. We also find 57 people dealing in the rental of animals for transport (*kiracı*). The registers record 182 horses and five donkeys in central Tatarpazarcığı; the economic logic behind the number of the farriers can be understood only because the above-noted skilled workers provided service for well over 90 villages governed by the center.

Looking at additional occupations with numbers over 10, we see 62 tanners; 57 barbers; 43 grocers; 41 tobacco sellers; 37 mat makers; 33 stitchers; 26 soap sellers; 24 wool combers; 23 shoemakers; 20 each of coffer sellers, candlemakers, hair rope makers and saddlers; 15 wool merchants; 14 transporters by horsecart; 12 brokers; 12 carpenters; and 12 daily workers.

With this variety in mind, and looking at the overall annual income for each field, the economic output in Tatarpazarcığı appears to be satisfactory. Amongst the occupations with the highest income, one inn-keeper, probably an exceptional case, comes first with 10,000 *kuruş*. A *hizmetkar* (servant) comes second with 1,200 *kuruş*, the rest in order as a grocer, a head of the rice cultivation plant (*çeltik kahyası*) and a tax collector (*mültezim*) with 800 *kuruş*; a wool comber and greengrocers with 650 *kuruş;* and a steward of the rice cultivation plant (*çiftlik kahyası*), a broker, a farrier, a pack saddle maker, and a wool merchant with 600 *kuruş* each. Occupations with the least annual earnings are saddlers with 40 *kuruş*, and coffee sellers, butchers, farriers, and tax collectors with 50 *kuruş* each. These data do not account for a person's total income, however, as many workers were known to take second jobs for sustenance. For example, a number of herbalists, barbers, horse cart hirers, wool combers, hair rope makers, and tile makers are meanwhile no less involved in agriculture. Beside these, some people had two professions, for example, grocer and head of the rice cultivation plants (*çeltik kethüdası*), barber and *muhtar*, or shoemaker and *imam*.

A list of occupations, with the number of people in them and their maximum and minimum incomes, is shown alphabetically in the table 3.

Commercial Buildings in Tatarpazarcığı

In Tatarpazarcığı, occupations were practiced in places called *dükkan* (shops) in the market places. Not only *dükkan* but also *oda* (rental room) and *mahzen* (storeroom) are mentioned in the registers as market or manufacturing places producing income, as demonstrated below.

The Tatarpazarcığı Temettuat registers report that 734 shops were used by the 1102 households of the 18 Muslim quarters.[22] We can identify 75 occupational types, using 684 shops, out of the 734 shops total (see Table 4). Among them, the highest numbers are: 81 grocery shops, 57 tobacco sellers, 50 farriers, 35 wool combers, 34 soap sellers, 31 hardware dealers, and 30 hair rope makers. At the other extreme, a shop each, are these: cook, cattle dealer, pottery maker, tobacco pipe seller, *kaftancı* (wardrobe maker), silk manufacturer, bookbinder, tinsmith, oil seller, and yogurt seller. Although these numbers do not show the total of shops used for specific occupations, we can get a general image of the economic activities of the city.

At the same time, the different amounts of rent indicate the economic

---

[22] Of the 734 shops, 100 were rental property, rented from shop owners or administrators of pious foundations (*vakıf*) by craftsmen or tradesmen as their workshops. The rest could be assumed to be the private property of said households, and 153 of them were also let out for rent by owners; the rest were either run by their owners or kept closed. This counting is vague because a shop could be recorded in the entry of both owner and tenant. Also, because we don't know the number of shops owned or rented out by non-Muslim residents, we cannot know the total number of shops in Tatarpazarcığı. Even so, the investigation of these 734 shops gives us some image of the variety of economic activities in Tatarpazarcığı.

prosperity of each occupation. The highest rents include a coffee grinder's place *(tahmishane)*, 813 *kuruş*; a grocery shop, 700 *kuruş*; and a coffeehouse, 400 *kuruş*. Among the shops with the lowest rents are those of the wool comber, three *kuruş*; grocery and farrier shops, six *kuruş* each; and *abacı* shop, seven *kuruş*. The substantial difference in grocery shop rents is probably due to differences in location, grandeur and incomes.

Apart from the shops mentioned above, Tatarpazarcığı has other commercial places, like inns, storerooms and halting places.

We have the names of four inns, Uzunhan, Büyükhan, Yenihan, and Küçükhan, and can confirm four more inns for which names are not known. The rooms in these inns were called *oda* and let for rent, and their number was 161 as best we could determine. They were occupied by transporters, potters, *kapamacı* (ready-made clothing business), *dibekçi* (mortar manufacturer), horse dealers, hair rope makers, and so forth.

Tatarpazarcığı also has a market called Arasta and known as Ordu Pazarı (a military market) in general. This commercial place located in the Çıksalın Quarter is not mere coincidence, for Tatarpazarcığı grew from a small village into a town, as we have said earlier, due to the military campaigns against Austria. Indeed, the Divan-ı Sefer Quarter also emerged that way (*divan-ı sefer* literally means "a meeting place for the campaign").

The leather business was important in Tatarpazarcığı thanks to the prosperous stockbreeding sector. Therefore, a tannery (*debbağhane*) where animal skins were processed had a significant place in the area. According to the registers, Tatarpazarcığı had a big tannery. Of a total 37 storerooms, 24 were attached to the tannery. However, four of these were either not available for use or closed for five to ten years.

Thus, according to the present 18 registers, the commercial places belonging to individuals, other than 734 shops, comprise eight inns, 37 storerooms, four inns, and 161 rental rooms.

Table 3: Occupations of Heads of Households and their Annual Incomes

Occupations	Minimum (*kuruş*)	Maximum (*kuruş*)	Number
arabacı (transporter by horsecart)	100	400	14
arzuhalci (writer of petitions)	---	150	1
aşçı (cook)	100	300	4
attar (herbalists)	125	500	2
avcı (hunter)	---	200	2
bakkal (grocery)	150	800	43
bekçi (night watchman)	100	230	9
berber (barber)	120	550	57
bıçakçı (knife maker)	---	---	1
cambaz (horse dealer)	250	350	2
camcı (glazier)	---	400	1
cerrah (surgeon)	---	200	1
çarıkçı (sandal maker)	150	300	4
çarşıpasbanı (market sentry)	200	250	2
çeltik kahyası (head of the rice cultivation plant)	350	800	9
çeltik yamağı (apprentice to the *çeltik* kahyası)	150	200	3
çerçi (peddler)	---	150	1
çiftlik kahyası (steward)	250	600	3
çoban (shepherd)	---	300	1
çubukçu (tobacco pipe seller)	---	120	1
debbağ (tanner)	100	500	62
dellal (broker)	100	600	12
dikici (stitcher)	130	400	33
dilenci (beggar)	---	---	3
dinkçi (felt maker, *aba* finisher)	280	360	2
doğramacı (carpenter)	150	300	12
duhancı (tobacco seller)	100	450	41
dülger (carpenter)	155	220	3
ekmekçi (baker)	---	150	1
eskici (dealer in second-hand wares)	100	250	6
gündelikçi (daily worker)	100	350	12
hademe (servant)	150	500	2
haffaf (shoemaker)	100	550	23
hallaç (wool comber)	120	650	24
hamamcı (keeper of a public bath)	180	300	2
hancı (inn-keeper)	250	10,000	5
hasırcı (mat maker)	100	335	37
hizmetkar (servant)	100	1,200	160
kahveci (coffee seller)	50	350	20
kasap (butcher)	50	400	6

katip (clerk)	450	500	2
keresteci (timber dealer)	250	300	5
kerpiççi (seller of sun dried bricks)	---	150	1
kiracı (transporter)	90	500	57
kiremitçi (tile maker)	200	500	2
korucu (warden)	120	180	2
kovaç (blacksmith)	---	400	1
kömürcü (coal dealer)	---	200	1
mahzarcı (scrivener)	250	300	2
mektep hocası (teacher of primary school)	100	150	2
mumcu (seller of candles)	---	400	1
muytab (hair rope maker)	100	450	20
mültezim (tax contractor)	---	800	1
nalband (farrier)	50	600	63
natır (attendant in a woman's bath)	---	300	2
perakendeci (retailer)	---	400	1
sabuncu (soap seller)	100	500	26
sarraç (saddler)	40	500	20
semerci (maker of packsaddles)	150	600	8
süpürgeci (maker/seller of brooms)	---	200	1
tahsildar (tax collector)	50	120	3
tahtacı (sawer)	200	400	5
terzi (tailor)	120	300	5
tömbekici (seller of water pipe tobacco)	---	150	1
tulumbacı (fire engine man)	---	225	1
tüfekçi (gunsmith)	200	300	5
uncu (flour dealer)	---	300	1
yapağıcı (wool merchant)	150	600	15
yaşyemişçi (greengrocer)	120	650	5
yoğurtcu (yogurt seller)	---	150	1
Total			887

Table 4: The Number of Shops in Tatarpazarcığı, with their Annual Incomes[23]

Kind of shops	Lowest rent (*kuruş*)	Highest rent (*kuruş*)	Number of shops
abacı (maker of coarse woolen cloth)	7	120	16
arabacı (transporter by horse cart)	16	100	7
arpacı (barley dealer)	40	70	3
aşçı (cook)	---	---	1
attar (herbalists)	25	80	12
aynacı (mirror maker)	---	30	1
bakkal (grocery)	6	700	81
berber (barber)	16	150	21
bezci (cloth seller)	25	80	7
bezir (dealer in linseed oil)	---	5	1
bezzaz (textile merchant)	10.5	100	11
bıçakçı (knife maker)	---	20	4
boyacı (dyer)	20	250	6
bozacı (maker/seller of *boza*)	13	230	9
buzhane (ice house)	25	33	3
celep (cattle dealer)	---	---	1
çanakçı (seller of pottery)	---	50	1
çarıkçı (sandal maker)	25	75	6
çerçi (peddler)	---	55	2
çömlekçi (potter)	15	40	9
çubukçu (tobacco pipe seller)	---	---	1
çuhacı (draper)	15	120	3
dellal (broker)	20	120	8
derici (leather dealer)	40	70	2
dikici (stitcher)	16	110	18
doğramacı (carpenter)	57.5	115	14
dökmeci (founder)	---	25	2
duhancı (tobacco seller)	20	180	57
ekmekçi (baker)	92	250	3
eskici (dealer in second-hand wares)	---	80	3
fıçıcı (cooper)	30	37.5	2
fırın (bakery)	55	150	7
gaytancı (maker of woolen braid lace)	40	45	2
haffaf (shoemaker)	20	120	22
hallaç (wool comber)	3	110	35

[23] We have listed pairs such as *arpacı* (barley dealer) and *zahireci* (cereal dealer), *dikici* (stitcher) and *terzi* (tailor), and *silahçı* (weapon makers) and *tüfekçi* (gunsmith) separately in accord with the notations in the registers.

hars (?)	20	220	2
hasırcı (mat maker)	---	30	2
kaftancı (wardrobe maker)	---	40	1
kahveci (coffee seller)	100	200	3
kahvehane (coffee house)	12.5	400	28
kalpakçı (seller of fur caps)	85	100	2
kasap (butcher)	40	120	14
kazzaz (silk manufacturer)	---	100	1
keresteci (timber seller)	50	100	6
kovaç (blacksmith)	50	130	5
kömürcü (coal dealer)	---	30	2
kuyumcu (goldsmith)	20	120	5
kürkçü (furrier)	10	110	21
meyhane (tavern)	12.5	225	7
mumcu (candle seller)	15	120	7
muytab (hair rope maker)	10	100	30
mücellid (bookbinder)	---	50	1
nalband (farrier)	6	110	50
nalbur (hardware dealer)	9	150	31
natırbaşı (head attendant in ladies bath)	---	40	2
sabuncu (soap seller)	25	350	34
sarraç (saddler)	30	100	14
sermeci (packsaddle maker)	15	30	4
silahçı (gunsmith)	---	35	4
simitçi (seller of *simit*)	25	250	6
şerbetçi (sherbet seller)	13.5	20	3
tahmishane (coffee grinding house)	30	813	4
tahtacı (sawyer)	14	---	7
takkeci (skull cap seller)	---	25	2
tarakçı (comb seller)	30	160	6
tenekeci (tinsmith)	----	150	1
terzi (tailor)	10	120	14
tömbekici (seller of water pipe tobacco)	---	---	1
tüfekçi (gunsmith)	---	20	5
uncu (flour seller)	---	100	2
yağcı (oil seller)	---	32	1
yapağıcı (wool merchant)	30	75	7
yaşyemişçi (greengrocer)	25	100	7
yoğurtçu (yogurt seller)	---	---	1
zahireci (cereal dealer)	100	120	2
Total			684

3. Agriculture in Tatarpazarcığı

Tatarpazarcığı was an important and productive area for agriculture because it was located on the both banks of the River Mariç. The most significant agricultural product, grown on wetlands, was rice, and it made the region prosperous. Several of the urban residents in the 18 registers were engaged in agriculture and had property in the countryside.

Table 5: Rich Landowners in Tatarpazarcığı

Names of rich landowners	Quarter	Size (*dönüm*)	Tithe Tax (*kile*)	Income (*kuruş*)
Mehmed oğlu Seyyid Ali	Akmescid	658	-	29,503
Hüseyin Bey oğlu Mahmud Beyefendi	Ayasbey	1,496	1,093	55,744
Hüseyin Bey oğlu Ali Bey	Ayasbey	338	689	39,336
Hacı Hüseyin oğlu Hasan Ağa	Ayasbey	284	420	23,319
Hasan Bey eşi Hatice İzzet Kadın	Ayasbey	207	156	3,759
Hacı Ali oğlu Hacı Mehmed	Cami-i Atik	66	159	22,597
Mehmed oğlu Ahmed	Cami-i Atik	75	32	9,534
Abdurrahman Efendi oğlu İsmail Hakkı Efendi	Cami-i Atik	36	36	1,974
İbrahim Bey oğlu Mehmed Beyefendi	İmaret	1,116	989	19,293
Abdurrahman Bey kızı Zülfikar Hanım	Hacısalih	998	828	17,482
Esad Efendi oğlu Mustafa Bey	Karaterzi	501	230	3,358
Yakup Ağa oğlu Mehmed	Musalla	252	30	3,558
Mehmed oğlu Mehmed	Musalla	75	36	2,334
Celal oğlu Abdülkadir Bey	Musalla	229	356	18,369
Hüseyin Paşa oğlu Ahmed Bey	Musalla	1,544	1,115	57,122
İbrahim Bey oğlu İsmail Bey	Musalla	1,248	1,115	76,929
Hacı İbrahim oğlu Ahmed Ağa	Musalla	678	383	35,196
Mahmud Ağa oğlu İsmail Ağa	Musalla	505	171	8,706
Abdullah oğlu Hurşid Ahmed	Sadihoca	102	218	24,690
Şakir Beyefendi	Sadihoca	153	325	10,915
Total		10,556	8,577	463,618

The Rich Landowners of Tatarpazarcığı

By examination of the registers, we identified rich landowners having large-scale lands used for rice agriculture, as of the year 1845, in Tatarpazarcığı. We noted that the annual income of people, in Table 5, was not totally from land; 20 to 30 percent was from other sources. It should also be emphasised, however, that the total annual incomes of these 20 persons made up nearly 60% of the total annual income, 795,529 *kuruş*, of Tatarpazarcığı. Two of these rich landowners were women.

Table 5 shows the rich landowners of the Tatarpazacığı. Residents of the Akmescid, Ayasbey, Cami-i Atik, İmaret, Hacısalih, Karaterzi, Musalla and Sadihoca Quarters have the most land available for agriculture, though they themselves live, or are registered, in the town. The Musalla Quarter takes first place with 4531 *dönüm* of land and the Ayasbey Quarter second place with 2325 *dönüm* of land. Ahmet Bey alone, son of Hüseyin Paşa from the Musalla Quarter, has 1544 *dönüm* of land in the villages of Tatarpazarcığı. The Musalla Quarter could be considered the wealthiest quarter in Tatarpazarcığı, with an annual income of 205,472 *kuruş*, and tithe 3,206 *kile*.

The Agricultural Areas Owned by Urban Residents of Tatarpazarcığı

We know that Tatarpazarcığı has a fertile soil, with various farm products, and that the crops grown here were taken to the surrounding settlements to be sold. Apart from the large-scale rice fields of the rich landowners, a number of agricultural areas were dispersed in 88 villages surrounding Tatarpazarcığı and owned by the urban residents as well.

The agricultural areas owned by urban residents in the villages of Tatarpazarcığı include fields (*tarla*), vineyards (*bağ*), gardens (*bahçe*), meadows (*çayır*), farms (*çiftlik*), marsh places (*sazlık*), groves (*koru*), and rice-fields (*çeltik* and *çorbalık*). Urban residents had 782 fields, 695 vineyards, 251 meadows, 30 gardens, 21 rice fields, 21 groves, four farms and one marsh place. We suggest that in these fields wheat, corn, and barley were grown, as was usual, and in the vineyards grapes were grown. But, because the registers we use belong to the town itself, we are unable to learn where and which products and on how many acres of land any particular crop was grown. (This kind of information would be recorded in the

Table 6: The Agricultural Areas in the Villages of Tatarpazarcığı Owned by Urban Residents

Kind of agricultural area	Number
Field (*tarla*)	782
Vineyard (*bağ*)	695
Meadow (*çayır*)	251
Vegetable garden (*bahçe*)	30
Rice field (*çeltik, çorbalık*)	21
Grove (*koru*)	21
Farm (*çiftlik*)	4
Marshy (*sazlık*)	1
Total	1805

Temettuat registers of relevant villages.) Nevertheless we can find some information concerning the gardens: for example, names of products such as vegetables, fruit, or wild apricot are mentioned, and the lands belonging to the same person could belong to several different villages.[24] As many as 251 meadow areas show the importance of stockbreeding in this area. As noted in the following chapter, urban residents owned 866 buffaloes, 730 sheep and 573 cattle.

Besides the above-mentioned agricultural areas, three other types of land used for agriculture are noted in the Temettuat registers. The first is *mezraa*, which means an arable field located outside a village. Use varies: *mezraa* were used as fields, meadows, vineyards, vegetable gardens, farms, or rice fields. Residents owned 14 of the *mezraa* plots surrounding Tatarpazarcığı, for the period studied. We cannot determine how many acres such units as these gardens, vineyards, or fields are composed of, since the

---

24 Although we were unable to determine what specific produce was grown in this area, we know that the following agricultural products were common: wheat, barley, millet, rye, oat, chickpea, common vetch, lentil, sesame, cow pea, cotton, flax, opium, tobacco, anise, mustard, rice, onion, broad bean, garlic, hemp, olive, date, lemon, orange and grape. Of these, grapes, onions, garlic and cow peas, as well as wine and *rakı* produced from grapes, were sold in the neighbouring settlement areas. See, Ahmed Arif Hikmet Beyefendi, *Rumeli Teftiş Defteri*, Istanbul Üniversitesi Kütüphanesi, T.Y., no. 2475, varak 6.

Table 7: The *Kıtas* for Rice Agriculture Owned by Urban Residents

Names of *kıta*	*dönüm*
Abdüllatif	100
Ada	78
Alişah	307
Bağçe	80
Baltacı	379
Bostancıbaş	101
Cedid	180
Çakmak	110
Çelebi Kadı	220
Hamam	106
İbrahim Paşa	342
İzlakoca	16
Kaynak	200
Manendli	257
Mutasarrıf	383
Müslim	185
Sabanlı	300
Sinan	775
Süleyman Paşa	230
Şehzade	150
Yakup	226
Zaim	89
Total	4814

Temettuat registers have no record of measure for the agricultural use of the *mezraas* mentioned above. We can only give their names: Aydınlı Mezraası, Baçdar Mezraası, Balabanlı Mezraas, Bitli Mezraası, Doyranlı Mezraası, Göncülü Mezraası, Kapucuk Mezraası, Kasımlı Mezraası, Kıpti Mezraası, Kırkoyun Mezraası, Müslim Mezraası, Sapanca Mecraası, Sarıca Mecraası, and Tutarköy Mezraası.

The second category is *kıta*, which means an area for rice agriculture. We find 22 *kıtas*, with 4,814 *dönüm* of land, owned by urban residents as of the year 1845. The place names of *kıtas*, and their measures, are as follows:

The third category is *nehir*, literally meaning river. The areas where rice is grown are called by the names of the rivers that irrigate them. As of the year 1845, these areas numbered eight. The lands watered by these rivers, named Çavuş, İbrahim Paşa, Karapınar, Kölemen Kuruçay, Sarcenik,

Tekfur, and Yellidere, have a total of 3,915 *dönüm*. Besides the normal rice agriculture, cultivation of a kind of rice called *çorbalık* (rice for making soup) is also practiced.

Rice is grown both on *kıta*s (inland fields) and by the rivers, covering a total of 8,729 *dönüm*. This sort of agricultural product, which needs wetlands, brings along with it a certain kind of animal, the water buffalo, which also lives on marsh places. It is therefore not surprising that the number of water buffaloes is high, as shown below.

Table 8: The *nehir* Where Rice Cultivation is Made

Name of *nehir*	*dönüm*
Çavuş	596
İbrahimpaşa	432
Karapınar	550
Kölemen	1,144
Kuruçay	79
Sarcenik	362
Tekfur	60
Yellidere	692
Total	3915

The dinks *(weaving houses) of Tatarpazarcığı*

Besides agriculture, stockbreeding is also an important means of subsistence for this region. In this respect, the crafts using animal products like wool — that is, hair rope making, felt making or weaving — are the major means of subsistence for the people of Tatarpazarcığı. Ahmet Arif Hikmet Beyefendi reported that the best socks are made in Sofia; four *zira* (unit of length) of *şayak* (homespun woolen cloth) are woven from one 300 grams of *yapağı* (a kind of wool); a woman knits a pair of socks a day; and people at ages from ninety to one hundred years make use of their time by weaving socks even when they are chatting.[25]

In ten villages we found a total of 13 *dinks* owned by the urban residents. *Dinks* are machines in which wool is made into felt by beating it with mallets. This activity contributes to the weaving sector, an important

[25] Ahmed Arif Hikmet Beyefendi, *op.cit.*, varak 10.

means of subsistence. Although it is essential that these *dinks* should be assessed according to the *tokmak* (mallet) unit calculation, in the Temettuat registers this detail is not always given. Nonetheless, we found that two *dinks* with four mallets in Yağmurlar village, a *dink* with four mallets in Tekfur village, and a *dink* with two mallets in Selahaddin village are owned by urban residents.

The villages with *dinks* are Hisarcık, İşterkova, Karailyaslı, Kasımlı, Selahaddin, Tekfur, Uğurcular, Vesicve, and Yağmurlar and Yassıca. Most of the villages have 1 *dink*, but Yağmurlar has two and Yassıca has three.

4. Stockbreeding in Tatarpazarcığı

We will examine three kind of livestock, water buffalo, cattle and sheep, that were raised in Tatarpazarcığı to be used for their meat, milk, wool or as a hauling force.

Water buffaloes (*manda*) are categorized as *sağmal* (milch), *kısır* (sterile), *koşum* (for carriage), *düğe* (heifer), *tosun* (young bull) and *fota* (skiffs); cattle (*karasığır*) include *öküz* (oxen), *sağmal inek* (milch cows), *kasır inek* (sterile cow), *dana* (calf), *tosun* (young bull), *düğe* (heifer/weaned), and *buzağı* (heifer/unweaned). The sheep (*koyun*) group includes *sağmal koyun* (milch sheep), *yoz koyun* (untrained sheep), and *kuzu* (lamb). In addition, horses and donkeys are used for carriages.

Unlike other regions of the Ottoman Empire, Tatarpazarcığı has no camels, goats or bees. On the other hand, because we cannot use the Temettuat registers belonging to the non-Muslim population, we do not know whether they bred pigs or not.

We have said above that rice agriculture was practiced on as many as 8,729 *dönüm* of land in Tatarpazarcığı. It is quite natural that water buffaloes, which live on wetlands, were bred on such fertile wetlands. Therefore, water buffaloes were of primary importance in their numbers and for every quarter owning them whose records we have.

As shown in Table 9, the number of water buffaloes of the Cami-i Atik Quarter comes first with 168, followed by the Ayasbey Quarter with 88. The total number of water buffalo owned by urban residents is 866. If we classify water buffaloes in six groups, we find 202 milch, 190 sterile, 76 harnessed for carriage, 27 young bull, 138 heifer and 233 skiffs. The annual

Table 9: Number of Water Buffaloes and Cattle in Tatarpazarcığı

	Quarters and number of households	Buffalo raising *hane*	buffalo number	Cattle raising *hane*	cattle number
1	Akmescid (12)	5	14	1	2
2	Ayasbey (120)	37	88	23	48
3	Bostan (59)	12	21	19	30
4	Boyacıbali (6)	3	6	-	-
5	Cami-i Atik (130)	58	168	29	50
6	Çıksalın (42)	7	20	14	38
7	Divan-ı Sefer (36)	17	52	9	14
8	Hacıkılıç (45)	17	39	11	17
9	Hacısalih (61)	19	36	10	22
10	İbrahimpaşa (64)	19	51	14	26
11	İmaret (29)	7	16	3	6
12	Karaterzi (59)	17	44	19	37
13	Katipyusuf (100)	34	79	28	48
14	Musalla (65)	19	52	29	26
15	Naibhamza (61)	23	49	22	45
16	Ortacami (21)	8	38	7	30
17	Ökçebasan (109)	20	37	39	74
18	Sadihoca (83)	28	64	26	60
	Total	340	866	303	573

income from milch buffaloes is most likely 60 *kuruş* each. The annual incomes from the others vary between 25 and 80 *kuruş*.

We also find that the *koşum* (harnessed buffaloes) were used in the *kiracılık* business, "hiring" (what now is called "transportation"), and of the occupations listed above, 57 people worked in *kiracı*. For instance, in the register of the Ortacami Quarter, a man whose annual income was 250 *kuruş* dealt in the "*kiracılık*" business using his buffaloes.[26]

Cattle breeding as well as water buffalo breeding occurred in Tatarpazarcığı and of course was one of the most important elements of agriculture and stockbreeding there. The number of cattle, 573, was considerable even though not as high as the number of water buffalo or sheep. However, whereas water buffaloes are seen in all quarters of Tatarpazarcığı, the same cannot be said for cattle. For instance, while there

26 ML.VRD.TMT. no. 6340, hane 12.

are no cattlebreeders in the Boyacıbali Quarter, the ratio, although low for the Akmescid Quarter, is 1:2 for the other quarters having cattle. In general, one-third of all households breed cattle in Tatarpazarcığı. The Çıksalın Quarter has the highest number of cattle.

We have classified all 573 cattle into seven groups: 92 oxen, 59 milch, 198 sterile cows, 39 young bulls, eight calves, and 177 heifers (both weaned and not yet weaned). Among cattle, milch cows produce the highest annual income. The annual income from a milch cow in Tatarpazarcığı varies between 15 and 80 *kuruş*, although 80 *kuruş* is exceptional. Income from normal cows are most likely to be recorded as 30 *kuruş*, which is just half of the income from water buffaloes.

Although not as important in terms of annual income as the water buffaloes and cattle, sheep are valued for their wool, the most essential material of the weaving sector. According to the registers, the annual income obtained from 730 sheep is five *kuruş* each from milch sheep and 2.5 *kuruş* from wild sheep. Sheep are second after water buffaloes in number and are classified as 450 milch sheep, 150 wild sheep and 130 lambs.

5. The Economic Condition of Tatarpazarcığı

Annual Income

Of the 1102 households of Tatarpazarcığı, 1052 have income. In the Temettuat registers to which we have access, the annual income of the 18 quarters is 798,599 *kuruş*. It is registered that 38,142 *kuruş* of tax was collected from a total of 1,102 households in previous year of the survey. The list below shows the total annual incomes of each quarter:

Looking at the Table 10, we see that the wealthiest quarter, with the highest income of 211,724 *kuruş*, is the Musalla Quarter. In terms of number of households, this quarter is just half of the Ayasbey Quarter, which is second in annual income with 161,145. These quarters are followed by the Sadihoca Quarter with an income of 82,275 *kuruş*. The quarters with the lowest incomes are Boyacıbali, 1170 *kuruş*; Naibhamza, 2740 *kuruş*; and Bostan, 11,775 *kuruş*.

As for the average income of household, the quarters of Akmescid, Musalla, and İmaret are richer than other quarters. The poorest are

Table 10: The Annual Incomes of the Quarters in Tatarpazarcığı

	Name of quarter	Number of households	Total annual income (*kuruş*)
1	Akmescid	12	50,494
2	Ayasbey	120	161,145
3	Bostan	59	11,775
4	Boyacıbali	6	1,170
5	Cami-i Atik	130	65,620
6	Çıksalın	42	10,936
7	Divan-ı Sefer	36	12,262
8	Hacıkılıç	45	12,217
9	Hacısalih	61	26,792
10	İbrahimpaşa	64	17,617
11	İmaret	29	41,714
11	Karaterzi	59	21,669
13	Katipyusuf	100	23,392
14	Musalla	65	211,724
15	Naibhamza	61	2,740
16	Ortacami	21	22,510
17	Ökçebasan	109	22,557
18	Sadihoca	83	82,275
	Total	1,102	798,599

Naibhamza, Naibhamza, Boyacıbali, and Bostan. The result is substantially affected, however, by the huge incomes of a few rich landowners, as seen in the previous section.

The Distribution of Income of Each Household

Table 11 shows the number of households in the order of their annual income and demonstrates that the distribution of their income, from 10 to 100,000 *kuruş*, is rather scattered.

We can assume between 100 *kuruş* and 400 *kuruş* as the average income of the households of Tatarpazarcığı, as 729 households, 69 % of the population, have incomes in that range. Of the 1052 households whose incomes are registered, 162 have incomes of from 101 to 150 *kuruş*. Their occupations are barber, peddler, servant, mat maker, broker and so forth. Those with incomes of 201-250 are in 145 households. Their occupations

Table 11: Distribution of Income

Annual income (*kuruş*)	Number of households
0-50	36
51-100	62
101-150	162
151-200	143
201-250	145
251-300	138
301-400	141
401-500	74
500-1,000	102
1,001-5,000	30
5,001-10,000	4
10,001-50,000	12
50,001-100,000	3
Total	1052

are shoemaker, head of rice-cultivation plant (*çiftlik kahyası*), farrier, carpenter, mat maker, gunsmith and so forth. Households with incomes lower than 100, the lowest-income group of the town, include probationers of stitchers or women who have been widowed and do not pay any taxes.

As incomes increase, the kinds of occupations often change, as might be expected. Occupations like timber seller, grocer, and innkeeper are registered with incomes of more than 400 *kuruş*. As seen before, rich landowners engaged in rice cultivation are the richest group, with incomes greater than 1000 and sometimes reaching 76,000 *kuruş* or more.

The Taxation in Tatarpazarcığı

Tax called *vergi-i mahsusa* (special tax) of the previous year of the survey, as seen in Table 12, amounts to only 38,142 *kuruş* for the whole of Tatarpazarcığı, in spite of its annual income of 798,599. Of 1052 households whose incomes are noted in the Temettuat registers, only 908 are shown as paying *vergi-i mahsusa*. That means 144 households were exempt from tax. In fact, *vergi-i mahsusa* in terms of annual income is at the ratio of 1:20, which is low compared with our time; nevertheless, we see that 14 % of urban residents do not pay any tax. Adding the number of households, 50,

Table 12: The Taxation of the Quarters in Tatarpazarcığı

	Quarter	Households	Tax payer	Tax exempt	Amount of tax (*kuruş*)
1	Akmescid	12	8	4	1,036
2	Ayasbey	120	109	11	9,990
3	Bostan	59	57	2	561
4	Boyacıbali	6	6	0	160
5	Cami-i Atik	130	116	14	2,743
6	Çıksalın	42	39	3	621
7	Divan-ı Sefer	36	28	8	880
8	Hacıkılıç	45	36	9	784
9	Hacısalih	61	40	21	1,232
10	İbrahimpaşa	64	48	16	561
11	İmaret	29	18	11	2,874
12	Karaterzi	59	51	8	1,692
13	Katipyusuf	100	76	24	2,035
14	Musalla	65	42	23	7,726
15	Naibhamza	61	52	9	1,010
17	Ortacami	21	15	6	974
17	Ökçebasan	109	97	12	800
18	Sadihoca	83	70	13	3,463
	Total	1,102	908	194	38,142

that have no income and thus no tax, we see that 194 out of 1102 households did not pay tax and 908 were subject to taxation.

The Ayasbey Quarter comes first both in number of households and amount of tax paid. The Musalla Quarter, with its well-off residents, comes second with a tax of 7,726 even though one-third of its households is tax exempt (due to the high amount of tax paid by the rest). At first, the sparsely populated Boyacıbali Quarter appears to be paying the least amount of tax, 160 *kuruş*, but the İbrahimpaşa Quarter actually pays the least, 561 *kuruş*, relative to its standard number of households.

The Distribution of the Tax of Each Household

Looking at the distribution of the *vergi-i mahsusa* to individuals (Table 13), tax amounts are clearly at a low level. Of the 908 taxpayers, 368, or one-third of the total, pay 10 *kuruş* or less, and 788 pay 50 *kuruş* or less.

Table 13: The Distribution of Tax

Tax paid (*kuruş*)	Number of people
1--10	368
11-20	215
21-30	96
31-40	70
41-50	39
51-100	67
101-150	24
151-200	12
201-300	5
301-500	3
501-1,000	6
1.001-2,000	2
2.001-2,500	1
Total	908

The tax figures vary from 1 to 2,500 per person. However, the mean average tax amount could be said to be 35 if a few taxpayers, whose extreme amounts reach to more than 2000, were removed from the calculation. The median average is, of course, less than 21 *kuruş*.

People who are tax-exempt in Tatarpazarcığı

A considerable number of people are exempt from the tax, even though it is a low amount. Within this category are *muhtar*, although not all of them; *imams* and *müezzins* (criers of the hour of prayer from the tower of mosque); as well as women parenting their children, orphans, the poor, the handicapped, the insane, members of religious sects, scholars, and the old.

Among the tax-exempt women parenting their children are more numerous than the other categories. Within these women, we find some whose incomes are as high as 3,836 *kuruş* [27] and yet who have comparatively low taxes. For instance, one woman with an annual income of 945 is charged a tax of only 12 *kuruş*.[28]

The *muhtars* had no definite tax-exemption despite the statement in the

27 ML.VRD.TMT. no 6295, hane 64.
28 ML.VRD.TMT. no 6342, hane 97.

Table 14: Tax-exempt People in Tatarpazarcığı

Group	Number of households
Women	69
Children	40
Poor people	39
People in charge of mosques	28
The handicapped	11
Members of religious sects	10
Teachers/scholars	9
muhtar (headmen)	7
The elderly	5
Total	218[29]

register that "the *muhtar* is tax-exempt because he is the head of the quarter, upon the unanimous decision of the residents of the quarter";[30] this was not a standard practice but only done by the consent of the residents. Hence, *muhtars* sometimes pay tax and sometimes do not, and the treatment of two *muhtars*, the first and the second *muhtars*, are not always the same in their quarter. For instance, we see that the *muhtars* of the Bostan, Cami-i Atik, Çıksalın, Divan-ı Sefer, İbrahim Paşa, Karaterzi and Sadihoca Quarters pay tax[31] whereas the first *muhtars* of the Hacıkılıç, Musalla and Ökçebasan Quarters pay but the second *muhtars* do not.[32] The opposite is true for the Ortacami Quarter.[33] On the other hand, *muhtars* of the Akmescid, İmaret and Katipyusuf Quarters do not pay any tax at all.

Another group not paying tax is *imams*, and they more commonly than *muhtars* are kept tax-exempt. Because of the clear statement in the register that "upon the unanimous decision of the residents, his tax is exempted

29 Twelve people are listed twice because they had two occupations. The actual number of households who did not pay tax is 194, as shown in Table 12.

30 ML.VRD.TMT. no 6295.

31 The amount of tax paid by the *muhtar* of the Divan-ı Sefer Quarter is 120 *kuruş*. ML.VRD.TMT. no 6312.

32 The amount of tax paid by the *muhtar* of the Musalla Quarter is 145 *kuruş*. ML.VRD.TMT. no 6295.

33 The amount of tax paid by the second *muhtar* of the Ortacami Quarter is 41 *kuruş*. ML.VRD.TMT. no 6340.

because he is the *imam* of the quarter,"[34] most *imams* do not pay tax despite the fact that they practice occupations such as sandal maker (*çarıkçı*) or soap seller (*sabuncu*) with annual incomes ranging from 170 to 807.5 *kuruş*.[35]

The same is true for *müezzins*. The *müezzin* of the Sadihoca Quarter, who is in the wool trade with an annual income reaching 500 *kuruş*, does not pay any tax at all.[36] However, some *müezzins* do pay tax, as for example the İbrahimpaşa Quarter totaling most up to 10.[37] People in the field of education, whether teachers or learners, are also tax-free,[38] by decision of the residents of the quarter. Besides those who attend madrasah, the primary school teachers[39] and students in the quarters living on others' support, which means with no income,[40] are also in this category.

Another group not paying the income tax is members of religious sects: the sheikhs of Nakşi[41] and Rifai[42], the keeper of Gazi Tekkesi[43] and the keeper of Hayran Baba Tekkesi[44] in the Ökçebasan Quarter, and dervishes.[45]

Among the tax-exempt children are those with no parents and depending on the support of others; those who are with their mothers, their grandmothers, or foster mothers but with no income; and those who are with their foster fathers or uncles. The decision about them is also made by the unanimity of the residents of the quarter.[46]

Among the tax-exempt people are also poor people who own no properties or land[47] and are unable to work. Beggars[48] are in the same category, again upon the unanimity of the residents of the quarters. Those

---

[34] ML.VRD.TMT. no. 6354.
[35] For the *imam* of the Cami-i Atik Quarter, see ML.VRD.TMT. no. 6352.
[36] ML.VRD.TMT. no. 6347.
[37] ML.VRD.TMT. no. 6336, hane 51.
[38] ML.VRD.TMT. no. 6352, hane 127.
[39] ML.VRD.TMT. no. 6352, hane 123.
[40] ML.VRD.TMT. no. 6318, hane 33.
[41] ML.VRD.TMT. no. 6342, 68; no. 6324, hane 20; no. 6319, hane 45.
[42] ML.VRD.TMT. no. 6318, hane 89.
[43] ML.VRD.TMT. no. 6318, hane 88.
[44] ML.VRD.TMT. no. 6318, hane 105.
[45] ML.VRD.TMT. no. 6324, hane 21.
[46] ML.VRD.TMT. no. 6347, hane 36, no. 6321, hane 27.
[47] ML.VRD.TMT. no. 6352, hane 95, no. 6350, hane 99, no. 6364, hane 36.
[48] ML.VRD.TMT. no. 6319, hane 47.

with permanent diseases,[49] insane people,[50] those whose fathers are insane and who have to look after them,[51] deaf people, and others[52] are also tax-exempt. The number of people who do not pay tax is given in Table 14.

Conclusion

In this survey, we have learned that Tatarpazarcığı, as a big provincial town, consisted of at least 26 quarters. With its market, shops, madrasahs, schools, mosques, inns, public baths, clock tower, fountains, and a church, it had the typical landscape of an Ottoman settlement.[53]

We understand that Tatarpazarcığı is a "barn of rice" economically above standard and owes this to the River Maritsa, on which it is situated, as well as some minor or major streams on both banks of the Maritsa. Being so wet and fertile, Tatarpazarcığı is suitable for breeding water buffalo and other kinds of cattle. Although cattle and sheep breeding are also done there, they have never reached the importance of water buffalo breeding.

Commercial life in Tatarpazarcığı is considerable, and the commercial liveliness is no less than in the other Ottoman settlements in Balkan and Anatolia. The town's geography—where it is situated and its characteristics of a "trade route"—play an important part.

---

49 ML.VRD.TMT. no. 6350, hane 85, no. 6342, hane 66.

50 ML.VRD.TMT. no. 6347, hane 83.

51 ML.VRD.TMT. no. 6346, hane 11.

52 For example, a fresh fruit seller with an annual income of 150 *kuruş* was exempted from tax, with the common consent of the people who lived in this quarter, because he was dumb. Refer to ML.VRD.TMT. no. 6340 , hane 8.

53 From the historical study of architecture, we knew the existence of 4 madrasahs, 7 primary schools, 2 soup kitchens (*imaret*), 5 convents (*tekye* and *zaviye*), 7 inns, 3 public baths, 1 caravanserai, and a castle in the town. Refer to Ekrem Hakkı Ayverdi, *Avrupa'da Osmanlı Mimari Eserleri,* Istanbul, 1982, pp. 114-5.

Chapter 4

Balıkesir: A Rural City in Social Economic Change

EGAWA Hikari

1. Setting the Scene

The city of Balıkesir is located in the northwest part of Anatolia in the Republic of Turkey. The Balıkesir Prefecture, today, is the nodal region of inland traffic, linking the three large cities of Istanbul, Bursa and Izmir. The Balıkesir plain spreads out in the center of the Balıkesir region, to the west of an alluvial plain formed by the tributary of the Susurluk River. Since the average annual temperature is 14.5 degrees Celsius and the soil and climate are suitable for agriculture, this region has an important role as a major food supplier for Istanbul.

The Balıkesir region was ruled by the Karesi Beyliği in the first half of the fourteenth century. After being annexed into the Ottoman Empire around 1345, it formed the *sancak* of Karesi at the end of fourteenth century. Under Ottoman rule, the administrative boundary of Balıkesir has changed several times. In the 1840s, when the Temettuat survey was executed, the city of Balıkesir was not only the center of the *kaza* of Balıkesir, but also that of the *sancak* of Karesi, of the Hüdavendigar Province.[1]

[1] For the historical details of the Balıkesir region, refer to the works of İsmail Hakkı Uzunçarşılı and Kamil Su. Uzunçarşılı, *Karasi Vilâyeti Tarihçesi*, Istanbul, 1925; *id.*, *Karasi Meşâhiri*, new ed., 3 vols, Balıkesir, 1991-2; Su,

In this chapter, Balıkesir will be investigated by way of the Temettuat registers of Balıkesir. From the historical viewpoint, Balıkesir is an important sample for defining transitions in the local societies of the Ottoman Empire in the nineteenth century.

The Temettuat registers of Balıkesir were first prepared in 1840. As already shown in Chapter 1 of this volume, the 1840 survey was conducted only in limited areas. Only a few registers from 1840 remain, but they include a variety of important information different from that of the 1845 survey.[2]

Documents[3] that are considered the manual for the 1840 survey present in concrete form the objectives of the survey and a model for entering the registers. This manual suggests that the survey in 1840 succeeded a procedure to survey the values of real estate and demographics that had already been tested by Mahmud II in the 1830s. The 1840 survey also aimed to know the individual income structure, to determine taxation amounts. For that reason, the 1840 registers specify each and every property, and assess both the value of movable and real properties and the total income of the individual.

Balıkesir ve Civarında Yürük ve Türkmenler, Istanbul, 1938.; *id.*, *XVII ve XVIIIinci Yüzyıllarda Balıkesir Şehir Hayatı*, Istanbul, 1937. For a short history of Balıkesir, see Aydın Ayhan and Mücteba İlgürel, *Tarih, Balıkesir Bir Kentin Kimliği*, Ankara, 1997, pp. 1-34; İlgürel, "Balıkesir," *İslam Ansiklopesidisi*, Vol.5, Türkiye Diyanet Vakfı: Istanbul, 1992, pp. 12-7. Also useful for study about Balıkesir are: *Kaynak*, the local magazine started in 1933, and Vital Cuinet, *La Turquie d'Asie: Géographie administrative statistique descriptive et raisonnée de chaque province de l'Asie-mineure*, Paris, 1894, pp. 247-99. In addition, the social analysis of this area based on Islamic court records (*şeri sicilleri*) of Balıkesir in the eighteenth century by Aynur Ünlüyol provided much valuable information for this study. Ünlüyol, *Şeriyye Sicillerine göre XVIII. Asrın İlk Yarısında Balıkesir (1700-1730)*, dissertation to Uludağ University, 1995 (unpublished). I would like to express my appreciation for her kindness.

2 This paper is mainly based on author's articles, published in Japanese: "The Tanzimat Reforms and Provincial Society: Analysis of the Temettü'ât Defteri in Balıkesir District (1840) from the Viewpoint of Land Possessions," *The Toyo Gakuho (The Journal of the Research Department of the Toyo Bunko)*, no. 79/2, 1997; "The Urban Society and Commerce-Industry of Balıkesir in the Middle of the Nineteenth Century: Especially from the Point of *Aba* Industry," *Ochanomizu Shigaku*, no. 42, 1998.

3 ML.VRD.TMT no. 17534.

The 1845 register, on the other hand, focuses on recording the income from both movable and real properties, and the economic activities of individuals, without recording the estimated values of their properties. These transitions of format from one set of registers to the other surely reflect the process of taxation reform, through trial and error, by the central government.

Balıkesir registers are also important because they have different sections for urban residents, villagers, and nomads.[4] This arrangement of the registers is useful for studying the socio-economic structure of the local societies as a whole.

Also important is that the Balıkesir region was the center of *aba* (coarse woolen cloth) production for the newly established armed forces, after the Janissaries (*yeniçeri*) had been dissolved in 1826. The military uniform reformation that occurred in the new army required the *aba* material, especially for winter clothes. This new demand made Balıkesir one of the centers of *aba* production in the nineteenth century. From this example, we can discuss how the government's industrial development scheme changed local society both economically and socially.

2. Structure of the City

The Temettuat register from the 1840 survey of Balıkesir contained records as follows. Each head of a family shows consecutive numbers called *hane*, and individual numbers called *numara*, on the first line. Underneath the first line was the name of the head of a family, plus personal appearance and nickname. Occupation was recorded either on the first line or next to the person's name. The third line listed the property of the head person, that is, total land dimension and estimated value of arable fields and vineyards, quantity and estimated value of urban buildings and movable property, and the types, quantity, and estimated value of livestock (*hayvanat*). On the last line were recorded the total estimated value of the person's livestock and real and movable property (*emlak*), the amount of income (*temettu*), and the tax

4 ML.VRD.TMT, no. 7225, 7226, 7227, 7228. The 7228 register entered the urban Muslim population; no. 7225 and no. 7226, nomadic population; no. 7227, people living in surrounding villages in the boundary of the *kaza* of Balıkesir. Registers for non-Muslim population unfortunately could not be found.

(*vergi*). As mentioned above, this description of the estimated value of each household's property, divided into *hayvanat* and *emlak*, is the distinguishing characteristic of the 1840 Temettuat registers.

Population

In 1840, the total number of Muslim households in Balıkesir was 1,562, as shown in Table 1. If this total is multiplied by a coefficient of five, which is generally used to calculate population in Ottoman studies, the result is 7,810. However, the heads of 103 of these 1,562 households were women, such as widows. Taking this into consideration, the Muslim population is estimated to be about 7,600. As for non-Muslim residents, the Temettuat registers containing records on them have not yet been discovered. The non-Muslim population at that time could be estimated, however, based on the census in 1831[5] and the *cizye* registers.[6] If the number of people subject to *cizye* is estimated at 600, about 3000 non-Muslims were residing in this region. The possible total population in Balıkesir city in 1840 is therefore approximately 10,000.[7]

Urban Institutions

In the same way as for other Ottoman cities, the infrastructure of Balıkesir was organized through the establishment of pious foundations. For example, the central institution of the city was the *vakıf* complex of Zağanos Paşa, founded by Zağanos Paşa, who was a Sultan's tutor and a commander at the

---

5 The male population of the *kaza* of Balıkesir as recorded in 1831 was as follows: 7,649 Muslim males, 756 non-Muslim males, 8,405 males in total (Said Muhib Efendi, *Memalik-i Şahanede 1247 Senesinde Mevcud Olan Nüfus Defteri*, İstanbul Üniversitesi Kütüphanesi, T.Y., no. 8867). Of this entire male population, most of the non-Muslim male population would have been residing inside the city of Balıkesir.

6 The non-Muslim male population subject to the *cizye* taxation was reported as 574 both in the 1842-3 (1258H) register and the 1850-1 (1267H) register (Kamil Kepeci–Cizye Muhasebesi Defteri, no. 3860, no. 3900). In the 1851-2 (1268H) register, the recorded number was 467 (*do.*, no. 3904).

7 Population census conducted after the year 1840, such as in 1842-3, 1845, and 1850 (Kamil Kepeci–Nüfus Defteri, no.6479), seems to have been carried out on the basis of the Temettuat register of 1840.

Table 1: Names of Quarters and the Number of Households

Names of Quarters	Number of households	Male households	Female households
Martlı	140	128	12
Yenice	38	34	4
Hacı İsmail	77	73	4
Mirzabey	58	53	5
Karaoğlan	93	92	3
Mustafa Fakih	80	77	3
Okçukara	47	47	0
Sahn-i Hisar	118	113	7
Börekçiler	47	46	2
Oruçgazi	128	114	14
Ali Fakih	1	1	0
Eski Kuyumcular	54	52	2
Umurbey	56	54	4
Şeyh Lütfullah	65	65	1
Salahaddin	96	91	5
Kassablar	166	156	11
Dinkçiler	89	84	16
Hacı Gaybi	34	35	4
İzmirler	69	65	4
Hacı İshak	75	79	2
Total	1562	1459	103

conquest of Constantinople in the fifteenth century. The complex of buildings was composed of a mosque, a soup kitchen (*imaret*), a roofed market (*bedestan*), and public baths (*hamam*).[8] Kamil Su described the area named after Zağanos Paşa, with its roofed market and ninety-two shops, as a most humming and attractive place in the seventeenth century. In the middle of the seventeenth century, however, fire destroyed this area. Kamil Su introduced the Islamic court records that showed reconstruction of the lost area.[9] Due to this reconstruction, the areas around the Sahn-i Hisar Quarter

[8] For detailed biographical information on Zağanos Paşa and his descendants, see Muharrem Eren, *Zağnos Paşa*, Balıkesir, 1994. Especially for his *vakıf*, see Ali Himmet Berki, "İslâmda Vakıf, Zağanos Paşa ve Zevcesi Nefise Hâtun Vakfiyesi," *Vakıflar Dergisi*, no. 4, 1958, pp. 19-37.

[9] Su, *XVII ve XVIIIinci Yüzyıllarda Balıkesir Şehir Hayatı*, pp. 16-7.

and the Zağanos Paşa Mosque most likely continued to be the political and economic center of the city even in the early eighteenth century.

Despite this, evidence related to the pious foundations is hardly ever found in the Temettuat registers of Balıkesir. Such entries as two shoe shops and three *aba* shops owned by a peasant who lived in the Martlı Quarter might be recorded as his *vakıfs*, but no record indicates to what purposes those shops were endowed. It is possible, however, to find some *vakıf* institutions through personal information about occupations. For example, descriptions such as "*imam* of the Hacı Ali Mosque" and "*imam* of the Zağanos Paşa Mosque" prove the existence of mosques in the area.

In addition to the mosques (*cami* or *mescid*) named after the city quarters, such urban institutions and prominent commercial buildings can be found in the Temettuat registers: Kandilli Camii, Kayabey Mehmed Şerif Camii, Yeşilli Camii, Hacı Hüseyin Mescidi, Köprübaşı Mescidi, İncioğlu Medresesi, Yeni Medrese, Zeytunlu Mektebi, Halil Ağa Hanı, Kolalıoğlu Hanı, Nebioğlu Hanı, Abacıhanı, Avret Pazarı, Pamuk Loncası, Fatma Sultan Vakıf Hamamı.

Among them, Avret Pazarı, where only females could shop, and *hans* (large commercial buildings or inns) evoke our imagination of the lively economic activities. Moreover, *lonca* was a gathering place for the guild. *Pamuk Loncası* (guild hall for cotton sellers) as well as *Abacıhanı* in Balıkesir are considered to be located around the complex of Zağanos Paşa. Therefore, having the complex of Zağanos Paşa as their center, the area around Karaoğlan, Mustafa Fakih, Salahaddin and Sahn-i Hisar Quarters could have continued to be the hub of commercial activities even in the middle of the nineteenth century.

As a building symbolizing the modernization of Balıkesir, the clock tower (*saat kulesi*) is significant. It was built in Balıkesir between 1828 and 1829, but the Temettuat register gives no description of it. Only a clockmaker who was living alone in the city and a rich merchant, Giridi-zade Hacı Yakub Bey, are slightly related to the clock tower, because the clock tower was constructed by a brother of Yakub Bey, Giridi-zade Mehmed Paşa.[10] It

[10] Giridi-zade Mehmed Paşa, who came from Balıkesir, constructed this clock tower during his term as governor of Silistre after his exploits in a war against Russia. He endowed a shop for this clock tower as a *vakıf* property. (Uzunçarşılı, *Karasi Meşâhiri*, Vol. 3, pp. 25-27; Mehmed Süreyya, *Sicill-i Osmani*, Vol. 4, Istanbul, 1996, pp. 1051-52)

became a symbol of Balıkesir in the second half of the nineteenth century.

As a matter of fact, since the middle of the nineteenth century, a number of immigrants moved into the territory of the Ottoman Empire, mostly from the Balkans and Caucasia. As a result, the population of Anatolian cities expanded, increasing the number of city quarters. Accordingly, the local administrators began establishing new administrative zones and constructing public facilities, such as the local administration building, barracks, a clock tower, and a telegraph office.[11] In a sense, construction of a new building for local administration, or a clock tower, was an indication of the dynamic changes of the urban societies. Indeed, in Balıkesir at the end of the nineteenth century the local administration building was built on the north side of the clock tower and the Agriculture Bank was placed on the west side. In addition, for the large population in the Martlı and Eski Kuyumcular Quarters, it is presumable that the area around the clock tower was developed as a new administrative zone along with the gradual development of the city since the early nineteenth century.

Another symbolic meaning of the clock tower is a transition in the concept of time. The clock towers in the modern period showed an evolution from "time for worship" to "time for labor." It could be understood as a change in the perception of time and also in lifestyle. The concept of "time" for labor might gradually infiltrate into Balıkesir with the growth of new industries such as *aba* manufacturing.

Urban Quarters and their Residents

The Temettuat registers of Balıkesir give us a clue to the physical structure of the city of Balıkesir in the nineteenth century, although the boundaries of quarters could not be known exactly. It is believed that the central city would have been the area enclosed by the quarters of Şeyh Lütfullah, Eski Kuyumcular, and Oruçgazi, with Sahn-i Hisar as the core district.

As for habitat segregation, data about the average estimated value of property and income for each household, by quarter, could be highly suggestive.

---

[11] Sevgi Aktüre, "Osmanlı Devleti'nde Taşra Kentlerindeki Değişimler," *Tanzimat'tan Cumhuriyet'e Türkiye Ansiklopedisi*, Vol. 4, Istanbul, 1985, pp. 896-99.

Table 2: Average Amount of Estimated Value of Property and Income per Household by Quarters

Names of Quarters	Average values of property (*kuruş*)	Average incomes (*kuruş*)	Total amounts (*kuruş*)
Martlı	552.1	476.3	1028.4
Yenice	355.3	347.4	702.7
Hacı İsmail	850.7	719.5	1570.2
Mirzabey	494.2	336.2	830.4
Karaoğlan	991.9	574.7	1566.6
Mustafa Fakih	1363.3	801.6	2164.9
Okçukara	939.0	897.9	1836.9
Sahn-i Hisar	679.5	93.0	1372.5
Börekçiler	904.8	701.9	1606.7
Oruçgazi	606.9	498.8	1105.7
Ali Fakih	3140.0	1450.0	4590.0
Eski Kuyumcular	1983.4	758.3	2741.7
Umurbey	799.5	535.7	1335.2
Şeyh Lütfullah	759.3	543.9	1303.2
Salahaddin	1329.0	702.6	2031.6
Kassablar	608.8	514.1	1122.9
Dinkçiler	290.7	335.2	625.9
Hacı Gaybi	844.4	729.5	1573.9
İzmirler	534.6	274.6	809.2
Hacı İshak	453.3	308.6	761.9
Average	772.5	553.8	1326.3

Table 2 shows the average amount of estimated value of property and income of each household in each urban quarter. The results indicate that the Ali Fakih Quarter has the highest total; however, this quarter had only one Muslim household registered, and was reported as predominantly a non-Muslim neighborhood in the eighteenth century, thus apparently an exception to the present discussion. The next highest quarters were Eski Kuyumcular, Mustafa Fakih, and Salahaddin Quarters. Of them, the Mustafa Fakih and Salahaddin Quarters had a long history of playing a central role in commercial activities. Most notably, many residents in the Mustafa Fakih Quarter were financially strong, owning properties in the city and the countryside. These quarters had bureaucrats, rich merchants, and also local notables such as the Giridi-zade Hacı Yakub Bey family.

The quarters with the lowest total amounts of average property and income included Dinkçiler, Yenice, Hacı İshak, and İzmirler. The Dinkçiler Quarter, for example, recorded sixteen widows. The outskirts of the city, called the Mirzabey Quarter, had five widows, and low total averages as well. Moreover, nine families in this quarter were renting houses. Therefore, these marginal quarters seem to have consisted of low-income singles, possibly relocated from outside the quarter.

Outsiders who relocated in the urban quarters were recorded on the last page of the Temettuat register of Balıkesir urban residents, which also contained information about the eleven ghost villages around the city.[12] For example, the village of Hacıömerler recorded that it had had eighteen households twenty years earlier but then became unable to pay tax due to a loss of population. Although ten years earlier five households still lived in the village, it was said that two of them decided to move out to the village of Çayırhisar and the other three eventually went to Balıkesir. Although it is hard to know the time transition process from the Temettuat register since it was recorded only once, historical changes in the outskirts of Balıkesir and the farming fields could be understood somewhat by looking at the context of the descriptions of register.[13] Young residents who relocated themselves from the local areas to the urban areas could have had houses for rent in the outskirts of the Balıkesir. That is because the register suggests that the people who rented houses were exempted from taxation.

Hence, Balıkesir at that time became larger in size due to the population increase, accepting the migration from surrounding villages. The city was experiencing modernization, which restructured its functional schema, transferring the administration to the south side from around the Mustafa Fakih Quarter, which had originally been the center of commerce and administration.

---

[12] This point will be analyzed in the following article: Egawa, "The Use of GIS to Locate Abandoned Villages Listed in the Temettuat Registers of Balıkesir County, Anatolia," Atsuyuki Okabe ed., *Islamic Area Studies with Geographic Information System*, 2004, London & New York, pp. 122-38.

[13] According to Aynur Ünlüyol, six out of the eleven ghost villages are mentioned as villages subjected to *avarızhane* in 1702-1703. Ünlüyol, *op.cit.*, p. 110.

Table 3: Working Situation of Heads of Households

Types	Number of households
Being at work	1331
Female head of household, like widow	103
Infant or the sick	81
No mention	47
Total	1562

Table 4: Occupations of Working Heads of Households

Types of occupation	Number of households	%
Religion and education	98	7.5%
Administration and military	53	4.0%
Agriculture	198	14.9%
Trade and manufacturing	737	55.6%
Physical labor	229	17.3%
Others	11	0.8%
Total	1326	100.0%

Occupational Composition of the Urban Residents

Table 3 shows the urban residents' working situation in Balıkesir. Of the 1,562 total households, 47 had no information provided for occupation, age, physical traits, and so on. Eighty-one families had records only for orphanage, old age, blindness, and so on. No description for their occupations was found for these 128 families, as well as 103 widows' households, making 231 households in all that lacked that information. The remaining 1331 heads of households could be considered being at work at the time of Temettuat survey.

Of the 1331 heads of households in the working population, 45 were registered as in the reserves (*redif*). Soldiers in the reserve were sometimes described with their other jobs, such as *imam* (prayer leader) or *börekçi* (pie maker), because they were serving temporarily. Considering this situation, those in the reserve are excluded from the category of "administration and military" occupation in Table 4, which explains the occupational structure of the urban area. In the case of urban residents having more than one occupation, each occupation is classified respectively in Table 4.

As for religious and educational positions, the register recorded scholars of Islamic law (*müfti*), madrasah teachers (*müderris*), primary school teachers (*muallim-i sıbyan*), *imam*, preachers (*hatib*), and prayer callers (*müezzin*). Administrative positions include the former *mütesellim* (magistrate) of *sancak*, headmen of quarters (*muhtar*), tax collectors (*tahsildar*), clerks (*kâtib*), and security officers (*zabıta neferi*).

As for local administration, the Tanzimat government organized the local councils for *eyalet, sancak* and *kaza*. Taxation officers (*muhassıl*) in the local councils played a central role in deciding the amount and distribution of taxation, which was the primary function of the local administrative agency. The local councils consisted of financial clerks (*mal kâtibi*), population and real estate clerks (*nüfus ve emlak kâtibi*), judges (*hakim*), scholars of Islamic law (*müfti*), security officers, and four representatives selected from among the local notables.

An example of the local council members recorded in the Temettuat register was "a *müfti* belongs to *kaza*, who is also a Fatma Sultan Madrasah's teacher (*kazanın müftisi ve Fatma Sultan Medresesi'nin müderrisi*)," mentioned at the head of the register of the Martlı Quarter. The amount of estimated value of his property was 1,997 *kuruş*, indicating that he was a wealthy man, but he was exempted from the taxation because of his double and administrative occupations.

The Temettuat register has a description of another specialist engaged in the population census, who was called *jurnal*. Musa Çadırcı reported that a person called *mukayyid* (registrar) or *jurnal* conducted fieldwork as a subordinate officer for the census services, established in 1831.[14] The *jurnal* mentioned in the register was a wealthy merchant who had developed well-balanced properties over the urban and local areas, such as *aba* shops, arable fields, livestock, and a share of a water mill in the suburban villages. In a sense, the central government selected a person who was cautious enough to watch over both urban and local areas to control the residents.

Mütesellim of *sancak* was highest in the hierarchy of the local administration of Balıkesir. The former *mütesellim*, Şerif Ağa, had the largest property in Balıkesir according to the register. Şerif Ağa's household was not registered in the urban quarter of Balıkesir, however, but as residing in the village of Köylüköy where his farm (*çiftlik*) was located. According to

---

[14] Musa Çadırcı, *Tanzimat Döneminde Anadolu Kentleri'nin Sosyal ve Ekonomik Yapıları*, Ankara, 1991, p. 48.

Uzunçarşılı, Şerif Ağa was from the *kaza* of Bigadiç and was a local notable who enjoyed being treated as head of the guards at the Sultan's palace (*kapıcıbaşı*). As far as the register shows, Şerif Ağa developed the largest property in the Balıkesir area, setting his base in villages, and attained the *mütesellim* position. Moreover, the register indicates that his brothers also owned rich farms (*çiftliks*). Thus, it is clear that Şerif Ağa's families were local notables who founded their financial base in the urban areas in Balıkesir as well as in the local areas. Giridi-zade Hacı Yakub Bey also owned a large amount of property, almost equivalent to Şerif Ağa. Yakub Bey was a brother of Giridi-zade Mehmed Paşa, who constructed the clock tower in Balıkesir mentioned above. Therefore, the Giridi-zade and Şerif Ağa families were the two leading local notables who had the highest total number of properties in the *kaza* of Balıkesir.

As for the people who are engaged in agriculture, we can cite farmer (*rençber*) households living in the city of Balıkesir. Their total number was reported as 198, which was 14.9% of the total. Of the 198 households, 134 had arable fields with two farming cattle (*sığır öküzü* or/and *camus öküzü*). This suggests that 67.7% of the *rençber* households were recognized as urban residents as well as landed farmers. The other 32.3% of the households did not have two farming cattle or arable fields. Instead, they survived through cooperative work or tenant farming. Because a tenant farming style called *ortakçılık* (sharecropping) was not recorded on the register, the actual circumstances of tenant farming is unknown.[15]

More than half of the working population, 55.6%, is engaged in trade and manufacturing. The various types of such occupations in Balıkesir are shown in Table 5.[16] This table also shows average income and estimated value of property for each occupation. The average of income, which was investigated through all types of occupations in trading and manufacturing, is 770.8 *kuruş* per household.

---

[15] In addition to *rençber*, some farmers could have existed in *ırgad* or *hizmetkâr* as tenant farmers. However, the register has no clear evidence for this speculation.

[16] In general, it is assumed that trading and manufacturing had three classes of workers, that is, master (*usta*), assistant master (*kalfa*), and apprentice (*çırak*). Some information was given for one tailor apprentice (*terzi çırağı*), one stitcher apprentice (*dikici çırağı*), one farrier apprentice (*nalband çırağı*), and three shoemaker apprentices (*pabuşçu çırağı*). On the other hand, no information for masters and assistant masters was provided.

If some types of occupation having only one member are excluded, the highest total amount of both the average income and the average value of property is as follows: two innkeepers (*hancı*) 10,924; eight merchants (*tüccar*) 10,657.1; twenty-two cloth merchants (*bezzaz*) 5,855.8; two clerks (*kâtip*) 5,050; seven headmen of quarters (*muhtars*) 4,378.1; twenty-seven herbalists (*attar*) 3,469.8; five cheap shoemakers (*haffaf*) 3875.5, and nine camel transporters (*deveci*) 2,787.8 *kuruş*. These wealthy occupations, excluding the administrative clerks and the headmen of quarters, seem to reflect Balıkesir's character as a city of inland trading and of active commerce and manufacturing. Moreover, because several nomadic groups were living around the city, many people engaged in the leather industries, saddle and horseshoemaking, and also in woolen textile manufacturing for goat and sheep's wool. Balıkesir had thirty-six households engaged in the *aba* business, one of the main manufacturing activities in the city. The total amount of the average estimated value of property and income of such households was 2,006.4 *kuruş*.

Table 5: Average Income and Estimated Value of Property by Occupation

(1) Religion and Education

	Num. of households	Income				Value of property
		Total	Max.	Min.	Average	
ders hocası (teacher)	1	0	-	-	0	530.0
hatib (preacher)	3	0	0	0	0	1308.3
imam (prayer leader)	36	3200	2500	0	88.9	1048.4
imaretçi (manager of soup kitchen)	1	325	-	-	325	375.0
muallim-i sıbyan (primary school teacher)	3	0	0	0	0	2060.7
müderris (teacher of madrasah)	12	0	0	0	0	1240.8
müezzin (prayer caller)	9	1350	750	0	150	741.1
müfti (scholar of Islamic law)	2	0	0	0	0	2158.5
kayyum (mosque keeper)	1	0	0	0	0	2025.0
mütevelli (*vakıf* trustee)	1	750	-	-	750	0.0
şeyh (sheikh)	3	0	0	0	0	362.0
talebe-i dini, tahsil-i ilim (student of religion)	20	2700	600	0	135	691.0
ulema	6	0	0	0	0	451.3
Total	98	8325			84.9	

(2) Administration and Military

	Num. of households	Income Total	Max.	Min.	Average	Value of property
askeri (military officer)	30	5025	2000	0	167.5	474.3
jurnal (census official)	1	2000	-	-	2000	4284.0
kabzmal-i mahalle (income collector of quarter)	6	3790	2040	300	631.7	1227.8
katip (clerk)	2	2600	2000	600	1300	3750.0
menzilci (manager of a government posthouse)	1	800	-	-	800	1075.0
muhtar-ı mahalle (quarter headman)	7	10925	3000	575	1560.7	2817.4
muhzır (officer of a court of justice)	1	400	-	-	400	150.0
müteselllim-i sabık (former magistrate of *sancak*)	1	0	-	-	0	39800.0
pasban (watchman)	1	500	-	-	500	275.0
zabıtada neferi (policeman)	3	900	400	200	300	123.3
Total	53	26940			508.3	

(3) Agriculture

	Num. of households	Income Total	Max.	Min.	Average	Value of property
bahçevan (gardener)	30	24320	2200	200	810.7	874.6
çiftlik kethüdası (manager of a farm)	1	0	-	-	0	2170.0
çoban (shepherd)	13	4650	700	0	357.7	707.0
rençber (farmer)	198	145025	2750	0	732.4	1136.0
sığırtmaç (herdsman)	1	400	-	-	400	125.0
Total	243	174395			717.6	

(4) Commerce and Manufacturing

	Num. of households	Income Total	Max.	Min.	Average	Value of property
<Food Section>						
arpacı (barley seller)	7	6300	1500	300	900	1048.4
attar (herbalist)	27	37950	3000	150	1405.6	2064.2
bakkal (grocer)	15	13050	2000	325	870	964.7
balcı (honey seller)	1	2040	-	-	2040	4582.0
börekçi (*börek* maker)	4	1450	400	250	362.5	198.8
değirmenci (miller)	2	1950	1200	750	975	888.5
ekmekçi (baker)	1	500	-	-	500	420.0
hubz tablakarı (bread vendor)	1	300	-	-	300	25.0
helvacı (sweet maker)	16	9850	1500	0	615.6	636.8
hoşabcu (stewed fruit seller)	1	250	-	-	250	63.0
kadayıfçı (*kadayıf* maker)	2	750	500	250	375	295.0
kahveci (coffee seller)	16	5500	650	0	343.8	260.5
kasap (butcher)	9	5125	1400	150	569.4	349.6
leblebici (raosted chickpeas seller)	2	1300	1000	300	650	674.0

macun satar (macun maker)	1	250	-	-	250	390.0
nohudcu (chickpea seller)	1	850	-	-	850	100.0
uncu (flour seller)	2	2000	1500	500	1000	777.5
<Textile Section>						
abacı (coarce woolen cloth maker)	36	35100	2700	0	975	1031.4
abacılar kethüdası (head of the *abacı* guild)	1	2500	-	-	2500	1670.0
bezzaz (cloth merchant)	22	44500	5000	500	2022.7	3833.1
boyacı (dyer)	2	2400	1800	600	1200	727.5
derzi, terzi (tailor)	36	19170	2300	0	532.5	546.9
derzi çırağı (tailor apprentice)	1	150	-	-	150	20.0
dikici (sewer)	55	28191	1750	0	512.6	377.2
dikici çırağı (sewer apprentice)	1	150	-	-	150	40.0
dinkçi (*aba* finisher)	4	2075	700	425	518.8	380.0
keçeci (felt maker and seller)	4	3400	2000	350	850	592.8
muytab (goat woolen cloth maker)	22	15300	1900	0	695.5	534.5
<Leather and Harness Section>						
debbağ (tanner)	119	100225	2750	0	842.2	847.7
demirci (blacksmith)	22	13300	1750	150	604.5	315.0
nalband (farrier)	26	24075	2400	325	926	647.6
nalband çırağı (farrier apprentice)	1	0	0	0	0	0.0
sarraç (saddler)	26	16500	1800	0	634.6	535.8
semerci (packsaddle maker)	9	4800	800	300	533.3	545.9
<Manufacturing and Processing Section>						
bıçakçı (knife maker)	2	800	800	0	400	280.0
borucu (pipe maker)	1	750	-	-	750	0.0
çakıcı (knife maker)	1	400	-	-	400	515.0
çakmakçı (flint maker)	2	1650	1000	650	825	1117.0
çıkrıkçı (latheman)	1	500	-	-	500	515.0
çizmeci (boot maker)	3	1450	650	300	483.3	904.7
çubukçu (pipestem maker)	1	300	-	-	300	110.0
destici (pitcher maker)	1	250	-	-	250	90.0
haffaf (shoes maker)	5	9650	4000	400	1930	1945.5
hallaç (cotton fluffer)	5	2850	1000	350	570	446.0
kalaycı (tinsmith)	17	9375	1000	150	551.5	536.0
kaltakçı (saddle maker)	1	400	-	-	400	65.0
kilci (clay seller)	1	800	-	-	800	310.0
kirişçi (catgut maker)	3	1700	750	450	566.7	213.7
kuyumcu (goldsmith)	2	800	400	400	400	253.0
mumcu (candle maker)	3	1850	1250	250	616.7	488.3
pabuşçu (shoemaker)	54	32025	1800	0	593.1	504.5
pabuşçu çırağı	3	300	150	0	100	321.7
saatçi (watch maker)	1	350	-	-	350	75.0

sandıkçı (chest maker)	2	2000	1400	600	1000	660.0
sandukacı (sarcophagus maker)	2	2075	1650	425	1037.5	1542.5
süpürgeci (broom maker)	1	500	-	-	500	515.0
urgancı (rope maker)	10	7600	1500	450	760	792.0
<Engineering and Building Section>						
çilingir (locksmith)	1	600	-	-	600	15.0
doğramacı (carpenter)	3	2850	1500	550	950	593.3
dülger (builder)	3	4000	2200	600	1333.3	802.3
kaldırımcı (paver)	1	800	-	-	800	425.0
kuyucu (well digger)	1	700	-	-	700	135.0
mimarbaşı (manager of architect)	1	1500	-	-	1500	5754.0
<Transportation Section>						
deveci, deve kiracısı (camel owner, camel lessor)	9	6050	1450	200	672.2	2115.6
mekkareci (who hires out pack animals and looks after them)	7	4800	1250	0	685.7	465.4
sürücü (drover)	6	2550	850	200	425	76.0
<Service and Commerce Section>						
barutçu (gunpowder maker)	1	550	-	-	550	940.0
berber (barber)	30	18120	2000	0	604	448.8
çarhçı (knife-grinder)	1	600	-	-	600	75.0
çerçi (peddler)	2	650	400	250	325	202.5
dellal, tellal (broker)	4	1550	400	350	387.5	238.1
duhancı (tobacco seller)	4	2650	1800	250	662.5	803.8
eskici (seller of secondhand wares)	9	2725	750	0	302.8	121.4
hamamcı (keeper of a public bath)	4	3365	2300	165	841.3	1530.9
han odabaşı (room manager of inn)	1	300	-	-	300	0.0
hancı (innkeeper)	2	3000	2000	1000	1500	9424.0
hekim, tabib (doctor of medicine)	2	850	450	400	425	195.0
kapıcı (door keeper)	1	400	-	-	400	450.0
kıyıcı (mincer of tobacco)	5	1700	600	0	340	168.4
kömürcü (coal seller)	3	1050	400	300	350	171.7
muvazene (who weighs or measures)	1	350	-	-	350	845.0
natur (attendant in a woman's bath)	4	920	325	45	230	56.9
oduncu (firewood cutter and seller)	2	700	500	200	350	512.5
tablakar (vendor with circular tray on his head)	2	1050	750	300	525	117.5
tüccar (merchant)	8	21050	5000	1500	2631.3	8025.8
tütüncü (tobacconist)	1	1500	-	-	1500	1600.0
yağhaneci (oil mill manager)	1	1500	-	-	1500	830.0
Total	737	568056			770.8	

(5) physical labor

	Num. of households	Income Total	Max.	Min.	Average	Value of property
amele (worker)	2	375	200	175	187.5	467.5
dellak (hamam worker)	8	3160	750	0	395	328.8
hammal (porter)	1	300	-	-	300	20.0
hizmetkar (servant)	26	10500	2000	0	403.8	374.6
ırgad (workman, day-laborer)	147	52910	1250	0	359.9	309.6
Total	184	67245			365.4	

(6) Others

	Num. of households	Income Total	Max.	Min.	Average	Value of property
sail, derviş etc. (mendicants and so on)	11	4450	1300	0	404.5	627.8

3. Landholding Conditions

As mentioned earlier, the personal property recorded in the Temettuat register were divided into the livestock (*hayvanat*) and the real and movable properties (*emlak*). The respective ratio of *hayvanat* to *emlak* of all urban residents in Balıkesir was about 1: 2.8 as shown in Table 6. *Emlak* includes two categories, the land, and properties excluding land (i. e, urban buildings and movable properties). First of all, we will analyze the land held by urban residents in this section.

Landholdings among the Urban Residents

The estimated value of land accounts for 47.6% of the entire value of properties of urban residents. Table 7 shows landholding conditions according to types of land use.

Table 7 suggests that most of the lands held by urban residents were arable fields and vineyards for farming. Land properties inside the city are categorized into the "others" of Table 7, for example, shop lots (*dükkân arsası*), residential lots (*hane arsası*), threshing fields (*harman yeri*), sheep pen fields (*mandıra yeri*), wheel fields (*çarh yeri*), water-mill fields (*asiyab yeri*) and so on. These "others" were not recorded with land dimensions but instead by number of items, except a mill place (*değirmen yeri*: 0.5 *dönüm* /

Table 6: Distribution of Estimated Value of Properties

Types of properties	Total (*kuruş*)	%
Livestock	326151.5	26.2
Lands	591105.7	47.6
Urban buildings and movable properties	326160	26.2
	1243417.2	100.0

Table 7: Landholding of the Urban Residents

	Dimensions (*dönüm*)	Total estimated value (*kuruş*, %)		Average value per *dönüm* (*kuruş*)
Arable field (*tarla*)	25,146.5	448,856.2	75.9%	17.8
Vineyard (*bağ*)	1,315.6	99,478.0	16.8%	75.6
Vegetable garden (*sebze bahçesi*)	233.3	33,507.5	5.7%	143.6
Mulberry garden (*dut bahçesi*)	30.2	2,999.0	0.5%	99.3
Clover garden (*yonca bahçesi*)	15.5	2,335.0	0.4%	150.6
Garden (*bahçe yeri*)	9.5	1,145.0	0.2%	120.5
Pasture (*mera*)	10.0	200.0	0.1%	20.0
Others	—	2,585.0	0.4%	—
Total		591,105.7	100.0%	

50 *kuruş*) and two residential lots (1 *dönüm* / 25 *kuruş* and 1 *dönüm* / 20 *kuruş*). Clearly, however, the sizes of such properties were insignificant and the total estimated value was 2,585 *kuruş*, a mere 0.4% of total estimated land value. In other words, the tradesmen and craftsmen did not at that time own expensive land, such as residential lots or shop lots, on a large scale inside the city.

Let us move on to a discussion of farmlands. Even religious leaders, government officials, tradesmen and craftsmen were often holders of arable fields and vineyards. The urban residents hold 25,146.5 *dönüm* of arable fields, and 1,315.6 *dönüm* of vineyards in all, as shown in Table 7. If we divide them by 1,562, the total number of households of the city, the average size of arable fields and vineyards held by a household reached 16.1 *dönüm* and 0.84 *dönüm* respectively. The products of these two types of farmlands seem to be used for home consumption. The average estimated value of various lands used for farming demonstrates that vegetable and clover fields with high commercial value were about eight times more expensive than arable fields for grain. Owners of the vegetable and clover fields in the city were, in order of total dimensions of land, gardeners (*bahçevan*), herbalists (*attar*), farmers (*rençber*), cloth merchants (*bezzaz*), and goat woolen cloth makers (*muytab*). [17]

Table 7 makes clear that the total size of all vegetable fields was not even one hundredth of all farmlands. For clover fields, the total size was merely 15.5 *dönüm*. These results prove that market-oriented crops were not cultivated on a large scale in these fields of vegetables, mulberry, and so on. On the other hand, according to a record, some urban residents held or owned real estate such as arable fields (*tarla*) or water mills in surrounding villages of Balıkesir like Akçakısrak, Paşaköy, and Karamanköy, or in neighboring *kazas* like Ayazmend, Mandahora and Balya. Therefore, rich tradesmen and craftsmen like herbalist or cloth merchants particularly seem to have made investments in the country region.

Basically, the urban residents under the *timar* system had not held arable fields (*tarla*) in the village area. In fact, however, their holding of arable fields in the village area seems to have increased with the changing times. For example, in Bursa in the seventeenth century, investments in villages by butchers who lived in the city were documented.[18] Moreover, in the eighteenth century, a gradual increase of investments by urban residents in the province of Manisa was also reported.[19] Therefore, the information about urban residents as recorded in the Temettuat register of Balıkesir can be regarded as evidence of investments in villages.

---

[17] According to Yuzo Nagata, in a case of Manisa in the early nineteenth century in *çiftlik* of Hüseyin Ağa, arable fields were estimated to be 12-30 *kuruş* per *dönüm* (Nagata, *Tarihte Ayanlar: Karaosmanoğulları Üzerinde Bir İnceleme*, Ankara, 1997, p. 121). In 1836 and 1839, in other *çiftlik*, arable fields were estimated to be 3 to 4.5 *kuruş* per *dönüm*. Therefore, in the same period, the average estimated amount in Balıkesir was much higher than the cases in 1836 and 1839 mentioned by Nagata. Although there is a difference in time and area, the Balıkesir's average value seems to have been close to that of the Hüseyin Ağa's *çiftlik*.

[18] Haim Gerber, *Economy and Society in an Ottoman City: Bursa, 1600-1700*, Jerusalem, 1988, pp. 88-93.

[19] Nagata, *op. cit.*, pp. 89-93.

Table 8: Arable Fields Held by Farmers among the Urban Residents

	Independent farmer	Tenant farmer	Other land holder
Number of households (*hane*)	133*	63*	1055
Dimensions (*dönüm*)	6125.5	1222.3	17873.8
Estimated value (*kuruş*)	74079.5	14041.5	361355.2
Average piece number per household (piece)	1.6	3.6	
Average dimensions per household (*dönüm*)	46.1	21.8	13.1
Average estimated value per *dönüm* (*kuruş*)	12.1	11.5	20.3

* Excluded in each, one household whose dimensions or estimated value was not written on the register.

Farmers Living in the City Boundary and the Continual Çift-hane System

Now, let us limit the discussion to farmers (*rençber*) engaged in agriculture among the urban residents. Of the total 198 farmer households, 134 were independent farmers living inside the city. A comparison of arable fields held by independent farmers and tenant farmers is shown in Table 8. Clearly, both groups held arable fields, whose value was estimated as 12.1 *kuruş* or 11.5 *kuruş* in average per *dönüm*. These average values are significantly less than those of arable fields held by non-*rençber* urban residents, estimated as 20.3 *kuruş*. Therefore, the non-*rençber* urban residents, such as tradesmen and craftsmen, seem to have held more expensive arable fields than the farmers who lived in the city, in terms of the estimated value of arable fields.

Although we see no notable gap in average estimated values of arable fields per *dönüm* between the independent farmers and the tenant farmers, a large gap does appear as to average number of arable fields as well as in the average dimensions of arable fields per household. The independent farmers' arable fields were relatively large, average size per household being 46.1 *dönüm*. Comparing this with the average size of arable fields owned by the Balıkesir villagers, about 38 *dönüm* (about 3.5 ha),[20] urban independent farmers seem to have held arable fields with average dimensions about 8 *dönüm* wider than those of independent farmers in the villages.

20 Egawa, "Tanzimat Reforms and Provincial Society," p. 16.

Table 9: Scale of Farmers' Farm Management

	Less than 10 *dönüm*		10 *dönüm* -50 *dönüm*		More than 50 *dönüm*		Total	
	hane	%	*hane*	%	*hane*	%	*hane*	%
Independent farmers living in the city	11	8.2%	87	64.9%	36	26.9%	134	100%
Tenant farmers living in the city	37	57.8%	20	31.3%	7	10.9%	64	100%
Urban residents who held arable fields, except farmers	622	59.0%	373	35.4%	60	5.7%	1055	100%
Independent farmers living in the villages	117	10.4%	681	60.6%	326	29.0%	1124	100%
Tenant farmers living in the villages	8	8.5%	64	68.1%	22	23.4%	94	100%

It is difficult to know whether the arable fields were sown (*mezru*) or unsown (*hali*), as this distinction was not consistently made in the documentation. This makes impossible a calculation of the exact ratio between sown and unsown fields. Clearly, however, the value of arable fields was the total of the value of sown and unsown fields.[21] On the other hand, some of the registers prepared by the Balıkesir villages show descriptions of "every other year" (*aşırı*), in which case the ratio between sown and unsown fields was about 1:1.[22] Therefore, the Balıkesir villages could have traditionally practiced double-sowing farming. As Yuzo Nagata indicates, although *hali* fields were unsown, they would not necessarily be neglected because of a shortage of labor forces but, instead, to recover fertility of the soil. That is why the Temettuat register had the total dimension both of sown (*mezru*) and unsown (*hali*) fields as the dimension of arable fields. Thus, the total dimension of arable fields indicates the management scale of farming households.

[21] Unsown lands were called *nadas* in general and *gelembe* in the law. They were owned with land certificates and defined as arable fields resting for one or two years in order to recover fertility of the soil. See Article 11 in the 1858 Land Law (*Düstur*, 1 series vol. 1, 1858-1872, p. 168).

[22] The ratio of 1:1 also agrees with Nagata's opinion. (Nagata, *op. cit.*, pp. 129-30). For more about unsown land, see Tevfik Güran, *19. Yüzyıl Osmanlı Tarımı Üzerine Araştırmalar*, Istanbul, 1998, pp. 88-90.

In general, under the *timar* system, the main labor force was *çift* peasants who cultivated lands estimated at about 60 to 150 *dönüm*, with two head of oxen.[23] Tevfik Güran classified the management scale of farming families by combining "sown" with "unsown" fields in this way: Less than 10 *dönüm* was small, from 10 to 50 *dönüm* was medium, and greater than 50 *dönüm* was large. Güran pointed out that a management scale of farming families in the beginning of the twentieth century was 40 to 80 *dönüm* per household.[24] Furthermore, Güran was interested in how much capital a small-scale farming family needed for basic living expenses in the Ottoman society of the nineteenth century. He looked at the redevelopment cases of four villages in Kastamonu in 1844 and at the settling cases of nine villages in Dobruca. In addition to these cases, he pointed out that thirteen-one families of one village belonging to the *kaza* of Cumapazarı had an average of 2610 *kuruş* per household as property in 1844.[25]

In the *kaza* of Balıkesir, according to that scaling system, 64.9% of the independent farmers in the urban quarters and 60.6% of those in village were of medium management size. The farmers managing medium-size farming therefore predominated in this region. The average management scale of farm families in Balıkesir was 40.1 *dönüm* in the urban area and 38 *dönüm* in the village area. Furthermore, in the Balıkesir urban area, farm families had their properties estimated to 1132 *kuruş*, on average.

Various reasons might explain the reduction of the size of arable fields, such as improvement in agricultural techniques, increasing population size, poverty among the farmers, and so on. Generally, the Balıkesir region in 1840 seems to have been in a transitional condition of reducing dimensions of arable fields from the traditional *çift-hane* system to the average size seen in Anatolia and Rumelia at the beginning of the twentieth century.

No more than ten *çiftlik* (farms) existed in all of the Balıkesir region, with the arable fields (*tarla*) consisting of a total of 154 pieces of land. The average dimension of one piece of land was 37.1 *dönüm* (about 3.4 ha). This

---

23 Nagata, "Turkish Rural Society in the sixteenth century" (in Japanese), *The Toyo Gakuho*, no. 58/3-4, 1977, pp. 55-6; İnalcık, "Köy, Köylü ve İmparatorluk," *V. Milletlerarası Türkiye Sosyal ve İktisat Tarihi Kongresi Tebliğleri*, Ankara, 1990, pp. 4-7.

24 Güran, *op. cit*, pp. 81-2. Güran also pointed out that some families who had been newly settled were given 40 to 100 *dönüm* by government in the nineteenth century.

25 Güran, *op. cit*, pp. 83-84.

is almost the same as the average of 38 *dönüm* (about 3.5 ha) for farmers living in the villages of Balıkesir and owning arable fields. The arable fields of the *çiftlik* also consisted of accumulated small pieces of land on which mostly grain was grown.[26] Thus, commercial crops were not covering the whole large farming area in the *çiftlik*. This corresponds to the suggestion made by Nagata regarding Manisa, which shows that the *çiftlik* was not similar to a plantation and that a continuation of the *çift-hane* system had been kept in the *çiftlik*.[27] The *çiftlik* shown in the Balıkesir Temettuat registers would have consisted of arable fields with small pieces of land and livestock, like the farms of independent farmers. The owners of the ten *çiftlik* were villagers, residents of Istanbul, and descendents of Zağanos Paşa, not always residents of the city of Balıkesir. The largest *çiftlik* was owned by Şerif Ağa, the former *mütesellim*. He was the richest individual in the Balıkesir city and village areas, and had properties estimated to be 121,435 *kuruş*. His properties in *çiftlik* and in the urban area, however, were exempt from taxation. It should be especially noted that nine of the ten *çiftlik* farms were exempted from taxation. This shows that *çiftlik*, as the farm under the taxation system, was given special treatment in the Temettuat tax exemption, though *çiftlik* included a lot of arable fields called *miri* land.

4. Economic Situation

The 1840 Temettuat registers did not have separate information for income

---

26 For example, see a study of the Temettuat registers of three *kazas*: Kaya Bayraktar, *Maliye Nezareti Temettuat Defterlerine Göre 1844 Yılında Çorlu, Silivri ve Ereğli Kazalarının Sosyo-Ekonomik Durumu*, Master thesis of Istanbul University (unpublished), 1996, p. 34. In Edirne Province, it explains, 34 villages had 31 *çiftlik* where independent farmers mainly dealt with grain cultivation. Moreover, another analysis of arable lands, including fallow lands, indicates that peasants held about 60 *dönüm* of arable land on average.

27 Nagata, *Tarihte Ayanlar*, p. 124. Moreover, it also agrees with an indication that in the same period of the eighteenth and nineteenth century, the commercial cultivation in Mosul was not in the form of *çiftlik* (Dine Rizk Khoury, "The Introduction of Commercial Agriculture in the Province of Mosul and its Effects on the Peasantry 1750-1850," Çağlar Keyder & Faruk Tabak eds., *Landholding and Commercial Agriculture in the Middle East*, Albany, 1991, p. 159).

earned from each property. Instead, they show the estimated values, as mentioned above. These could be rather useful for calculating the average value of livestock and each kind of property, to provide an economic index for the Ottoman Empire at that time.

Livestock

The estimated value for livestock seems to have been more stable than that for arable fields, although some complicated cases for calculating figures did arise, such as "mare with foal (*taylı kısrak*) " or "milch cow with calf (*sığır ineği danalı*)." It was not clear how livestock was counted in these cases. Omitting these complications in the calculations, Table 10 consists of records made for a single kind of livestock.

Based on the maximum and minimum values for livestock, 99% of beehives were estimated as 12 *kuruş* per box. The estimated value of a sheep and a goat was almost fixed at 25 and 20 *kuruş*. As camels were used for long-haul transportation, their estimated value was highest.

Here, the average estimated value for livestock was not so different from that for livestock owned by nomads.[28] The estimated value of arable fields was relatively less than that of livestock in 1840. This shows that arable lands (*tarla*) still had a lower commercial value at that time and suggests that many nomads were richer than the urban residents at that time.

Table 10: Number and Estimated Value of Livestock

	Number of livestock	Estimated value of livestock			
		Total (*kuruş*)	Average (*kuruş*)	Max. (*kuruş*)	Min. (*kuruş*)
Cattle (*sığır*)					
milch cow (*sığır ineği*)	187	17935	96.4	200	20
milch cow with calf (*sığır ineği danalı*)	53	4920	92.8	150	50
heifer (*sığır düğesi*)	91	4975	54.7	133.3	25
calf (*sığır danası*)	41	1530	37.3	80	10
ox (*sığır öküzü*)	230	27705	120.5	250	50
bull (*sığır tosunu*)	49	3327.5	67.9	125	7.5
Sub-total	651	60392.5			

[28] ML.VRD.TMT no. 7226.

Buffalo (*camus, manda*)					
buffalo cow (*camus ineği*)	206	44425	215.7	500	80
buffalo milch cow with baby (*camus ineği malağılı*)	39	9100	233.3	390	120
buffalo heifer (*camus düğesi*)	116	13935	120.1	250	30
buffalo calf (*camus danası*)	12	1200	100.0	200	45
buffalo ox (*camus öküzü*)	158	37060	234.6	500	80
buffalo bull (*camus tosunu*)	6	710	118.3	200	60
young buffalo baby (*camus malağı*)	82	7235	88.2	200	10
Sub-total	619	113665			
Horse (*at*)					
mare (*kısrak*)	42	4910	116.9	250	60
mare with foal (*taylı kısrak*)	33	5605	169.9	400	105
mare foal (*tay*)	27	1850	68.5	120	20
colt (*erkek tay*)	3	290	96.7	150	50
packhorse (*bargir*)	308.5	45495	147.5	300	20
Sub-total	413.5	58150			
Camel (*deve*)					
camel (*deve*)	33	12000	*428.6	1350	350
small camel (*şütürek*)	9	2800	*400.0	400	400
young camel (*deve yavrusu*)	2	175	87.5	100	75
Sub-total	44	14975			
Sheep and Goat					
sheep (*ağnam*)	1503	37675	25.1	26.1	25
goat (*keçi*)	73	1470	20.1	30	20
Sub-total	1576	39145			
Donkey					
male donkey (*himar*)	85	3735	43.9	150	20
donkey (*merkeb*)	328	15790.5	48.1	150	10
donkey with foal (*sıpalı merkeb*)	48	2525	52.6	100	15
donkey foal (*merkeb sıpası*)	30	825	27.5	60	5
Sub-total	491	22875.5			
Mule					
mule (*ester*)	2	400	200.0	250	150
mule (*katır*)	1	250	250.0	250	250
mule foal (*katır sıpası*)	7	870	124.3	200	50
Sub-total	10	1520			
Others					
Beehive (*arı kovanı*)	597	7620	12.8	15	12
Others (whose estimated value per animal cannot be calculated)		7808.5			
Total Amount of Estimated Value		326151.5			

Urban buildings and movable properties

What besides land and livestock did they consider as properties? Table 11 shows the answer: licenses (*gedik*), building of shops, ovens, trees, *aba dingi*, wheel of goat woolen cloth maker (*muytab çarhı*), share of mill lots (*asiyab-ı dakik hissesi*), and so on. Among them, the most important properties are buildings, *gedik*, and *aba dingi*.

As for licenses, we can find three categories: for public baths (*hamam*), for tannery (*debbağhane*), and for wheel of goat woolen cloth maker (*muytab çarhı*). The people who worked with them did not always own these items. The three public bath licenses had estimated values of 800, 1000, and 2000 *kuruş* and were all owned by a keeper of a public bath (*hamamcı*). On the other hand, the estimated value of more than ninety percent of the tannery licenses was about 50 *kuruş* per *gedik*. As for the license of wheel of goat woolen goods maker, its estimated value was 25 or 50 *kuruş*. Both estimated values were stable. Therefore, these licenses would have been traded since they were highly valuable or relatively stable properties. Originally, *gedik* were licenses given to the members of the commercial and manufacturing guilds. In the eighteenth century, tradesmen and craftsmen were not able to open their shops for handicraft production without a license.

Licenses of tanners were also cited. The register indicates that the tanners concentrated in quarters along a river because water was needed for their tanning work. Among them, many tanners in the Hacı İsmail and Okçukara Quarters had their licenses. The proportion of the tanners having licenses was lower in the Oruçgazi and Hacı İshak Quarters, compared with the Hacı İsmail and Okçukara Quarters.

Total estimated value of buildings is 229540 *kuruş*. According to Table 12, the building with the highest estimated value was an inn (*han*), called Halil Ağa Hanı. As mentioned above, the city had several inns, but except for Halil Ağa Hanı and Nebioğlu Hanı, the estimated value of inns was not recorded. After inns, the shops with the highest average estimated values were herbalist shops, pottery shops, coffeehouses and grocery, which seemed to get much cash income. The largest number of shops were those of shoemakers, *abacı* shops, and tailor shops. The average estimated value of *abacı* shops was not so high, but the estimated value of the share (*hisse*) of *abacı* shops, not included in Table 12, was 2700 *kuruş*. Adding 2700 to 4970 gives us 7670 *kuruş* as the total estimated value of *abacı* shops.

Table 11: Urban Buildings and Movable Properties

	Number of property	Estimated value Total (*kuruş*)	Average (*kuruş*)	Max. (*kuruş*)	Min. (*kuruş*)
License (*gedik*)					
public bath (*hamam*)	3	3800.0	1266.7	2000	800
tanner factory (*debbağhane*)	221.5	11655.0	52.6	250	25
wool of goat weave (*muytab çarhı*)	11	475.0	43.2	50	25
Buildings					
shops (*dükkan*)		229540.0			
oil mill (*yağhane*)	8.0	11600.0	1450.0	2500	500
Oven (*Fırın*)					
bakery (*simitçi**)	6	4600.0	766.7	1500	300
pie maker (*börekçi*)	5	3250.0	650.0	1000	250
bakery (*ekmekçi*)	0.5	500.0	1000.0	-	-
Tree					
sapling of mulberry (*dut fidanı*)	45	22.5	0.5	0.5	0.5
mulberry (*dut*)	175	350.0	2.0	2	2
olive (*zeytin*)	209	2089.0	10.0	30	5
walnut (*ceviz*)	30.5	352.5	11.6	20	5
The others					
*aba dingi***		400.0			
muytab çarhı	7	375.0	53.6	50	25
share of mill flower (*hisse-i asiyab-ı dakik*)		52600			
others		4551.0			
Total		326160.0			

* Excluded one bakery oven whose estimated value was not recorded and two share of bakery oven, 750 *kuruş*

** *aba dingi* were recorded as follows: one *hisse*, 250 *kuruş*; 2/3 *hisse*, 100 *kuruş;* one, 50 *kuruş*.

Table 12: Number and Estimated Value of Shops

	Number of shops	Estimated value Total (*kuruş*)	Average (*kuruş*)	Max. (*kuruş*)	Min. (*kuruş*)
pabuşçu (shoemaker)	40	17975	449.4	1250	100
terzi (tailor)	28.5	8980	315.1	500	125
abacı (coarse woolen cloth maker)	24.5	4970	202.9	350	120
sarraç (saddler)	17.5	3515	200.9	300	150
bezzaz (cloth merchant)	15	5800	386.7	700	250
sergi (stall for selling)	15	2585	172.3	600	100
nalband (farrier)	14.5	3650	251.7	500	75
attar (herbalist)	14	7755	553.9	1225	115
arpacı (barley seller)	13	3115	239.6	550	100
bahçevan sergisi (gardener's stall for selling)	13	1897.5	146.0	185	100
berber (barber)	13	5015	385.8	1000	150
demirci (blacksmith)	11.5	3225	280.4	425	125
debbağhane (tannery)	11	2370	215.5	316.66	50
muytab (goat woolen cloth maker)	11	1830	166.4	300	100
panayır, pazar (fair, bazaar)	11	10300	936.4	300	100
kahveci (coffee seller)	10.5	4150	395.2	650	150
çizmeci (bootmaker)	10	2000	200.0	200	200
helvacı (sweet maker)	8.5	2755	324.1	500	205
bakkal (grocer)	8	3445	430.6	545	200
doğramacı (carpenter)	6	1900	316.7	500	280
kalaycı (tinsmith)	6	1070	178.3	250	120
boyacı (dyer)	5	1100	220.0	300	200
kuyumcu (goldsmith)	4.5	850	188.9	200	150
basmacı (maker of printed material)	4	950	237.5	250	200
çivici (nail maker)	3	450	150.0	200	100
hallaç (cotton fluffer)	3	570	190.0	250	160
leblebici(seller of roasted chickpeas)	3	575	191.7	250	125
semerci (packsaddle maker)	3	850	283.3	400	200
börekçi (*börek* maker)	2	250	125.0	200	50
çömlekçi karhanesi (pottery workshop)	2	2400	1200	1200	1200
eskici (seller of secondhand wares)	2	225	112.5	125	100
keçeci (felt maker)	2	450	225.0	300	150
sandıkçı (chest maker)	2	750	375.0	400	350
kasap (butcher)	1.5	530	353.3	760	150
bakırcı (coppersmith)	1	200	200.0		
bıçakçı (knifemaker)	1	300	300.0		
çubukçu (pipestem maker)	1	200	200.0		
duhancı (tobacco seller)	1	450	450.0		

ekmekçi (baker)	1	350	350.0
mumcu (candle maker)	1	100	100.0
sirkeci (vinegar maker)	1	150	150.0
süprügeci (broom maker)	1	100	100.0
Halil Ağa Hanı (Halil Ağa inn)	1	10000	10000.0
Nebioğlu Hanı (Nebioğlu inn)	1	4000	4000.0
çömlekçi (potter)	0.5	300	600.0
kal (metal refiner of smelting)	0.5	150	300.0
urgancı (rope maker)	0.5	200	400.0
sub Total	350	124752.5	356.4
Other shops		93777	
Share of shops		11010.5	
Total Amount of Estimated Value		229540.0	

The* aba *Manufacturing in Balıkesir

In this section, we would especially like to consider *aba* manufacturing, which was traditional in Balıkesir.[29]

The origin of *aba* manufacturing in Balıkesir could date back to the sixteenth century. Clearly, *aba* production as a traditional industry in Balıkesir had reached such maturity before the uniform reformation that it was able to deal with the designation for *aba* production and was capable of fulfilling the requirements.[30]

After the abolition of the Janissary in 1826, *aba* textiles for the European-style military uniforms were ordered by the new imperial armed forces. According to the research of Mübahat Kütükoğlu, the *aba* was mainly produced in Bulgarian areas, such as Plovdiv (Filibe), Sliven (İslimye), Kotel

29 İlgürel, "Balıkesir," p. 14. For example, the documents recording the official price of products in Balıkesir in the middle of the seventeenth century has a description of *aba*. Mühabat Kütükoğlu ed., *Osmanlılarda Narh Müessesesi ve 1640 Tarihli Narh Defteri*, Istanbul, 1983, p.38. Kamil Su, "Balıkesirde Eski Tarihlerde Abacılık," *Kaynak*, no. 50, 1937, pp. 33-37.

30 Kamil Su suggests that the Karakeçili nomadic group began to produce *aba* textiles for the army because the traditional clothes woven by them displayed their highly skilled technique in spinning and weaving wool yarns. This most likely led to construction of *aba* factories in Balıkesir, where the Karakeçili nomadic group was employed as the labor force. Su, *Balıkesir ve Civarında Yürük ve Türkmenler*, Istanbul, 1938, p. 69.

(Kazan), and Pazardzhik (Tatarpazarcığı), as well as in Balıkesir.[31] In the later period around 1843, a nomadic group called Kıldonlu was relocated as a labor force for spinning yarn at the Balıkesir's *aba* shops (*abahane*).[32] By 1835, Balıkesir's *aba* production was planned to supply one fourth of the total demand of the Empire. It is also known that in the period between 1848 and 1849 the government planned establishment of an *aba* factory (*aba fabrikası*) in Balıkesir as well as introduction of French-made production equipment.[33]

Regarding this situation in Balıkesir, Kütükoğlu introduced an interesting case in her study.[34] In 1842, Şerif Ağa, *kaymakam* of the *kaza* of Balıkesir, who controlled *aba* production in the city, committed an injustice by trading poor quality *aba* at a high price. The governmental inspectors examined the governor's suspicious pricing of the *aba* products. They ordered the *aba* makers to produce high quality *aba* products at a lower price and dismissed the governor (Şerif Ağa). Following the incident, a major (*binbaşı*) Ahmed Efendi visited Balıkesir for investigation and met Giridi-zade Mehmed Bey, who had been temporarily excluded from governmental affairs and lived in retirement in the countryside. Giridi-zade Mehmed Bey showed Ahmed Efendi a sample that demonstrated the practicality of producing high quality *aba* products at lower costs. Thus, Giridi-zade Mehmed Bey was honoured with an appointment to work as a controller of the *aba* production, and also as governor.

This is the historical evidence introduced by Kütükoğlu. The dishonest governor, Şerif Ağa, is the person recorded on the Temettuat register as the former *mütesellim* having the most property, as mentioned above. Giridi-zade Mehmed Bey, who was reinstated to public position, was also referred to in the earlier section as the contributor of the clock tower. His brothers made their family recognized as having the second highest average amount of properties. Thus, these families were two dominant elements in Balıkesir. They competed with each other for concessions in the *aba*

---

[31] Mübahat Kütükoğlu, "Asakir-i Mansure-i Muhammediyye Kıyafeti ve Malzemesinin Temini Meselesi," *Doğumunun 100. Yılında Atatürk'e Armağan*, Istanbul, 1981, p. 550.

[32] Cevdet–Dahiliye. no. 9122.

[33] Cevdet–İktisat. no. 499. D. Quataert, "The Age of Reforms, 1812-1914," H. Inalcık & D. Quataert (eds.), *An Economic and Social History of the Ottoman Empire 1300-1914*, Cambridge, 1994, p. 899, 932.

[34] Kütükoğlu, *op. cit.*, pp. 552-53.

manufacturing developed by the uniform reformation and for interest in trading the textile. These disputes could reflect the struggle for concessions among local leaders, who were former *ayans*.

Let us go on to learn the actual *aba* production process. Wool was used to produce *aba*. In order to make *aba* softer and better in quality, two kinds of wool were mixed: wool clipped from living sheep in August, and "tanners' wool (*debbağ yünü*)." According to Kütükoğlu, wool clipped from dead livestock was called, "wool of the head of the butchers' guild (*kasabbaşı yünü*)" and wool chemically treated in the tanning shops was called "tanner's wool."[35] This suggests that *aba* was produced not only by the *abacı* (*aba* maker) but also by the butchers and, especially, the tanners.[36] Kütükoğlu's study reports that Balıkesir was the center of *aba* production in Anatolia, and nomads and peasants around the city were also involved in the production, the so-called wave of manufacturing for the need to secure wool.

People related to the *aba* manufacturing were *abacı*, the head of *abacı* guild (*abacıları kethüdası*), tanners, *aba* finishers (*dinkçi*),[37] and butchers. We find 36 *abacı* and one head of an *abacı* guild, 4 *aba* finishers, and 119 tanners in the Temettuat register of Balıkesir. Although *aba* finishers were physical laborers and had small properties, the estimated value of the properties and incomes of *abacı*s were larger than average. We also note that the cash earnings of people connected to *aba* manufacturing seem comparatively higher in value than their properties.

The *aba* finishing machines (*aba dingi*) were recorded as the properties of only four residents in all. But the correlation between estimated value and number is not clear to us from the record (Table 11). On the other hand, in

---

35 Tanners' wool was not from living sheep and was chemically treated. It was simply a kind of wool with slightly more strength than the others, not highly rated in quality. Kütükoğlu, *op. cit.*, pp. 553-54.

36 *Ibid.*, pp. 554-56.

37 *Dinkci* also means rice threshers. However, in hat-making *dink* means finishing instruments used for processing wool for making felt ("Dink," *Meydan Larousse Büyük Ansiklopedisi*). At the end of the eighteenth century, there were a guild named *dinkçi* and finishing instruments called *aba dingi*, mentioned later in this paper. Aydın Ayhan also interpreted *dinkçi* as *aba* finishing instruments (A. Ayhan, "Balıkesir'e Ait Eski Bazı İsimler ve Bilgiler," *Balıkesir Ekspres*, 1998, issued on February 5). Therefore, *dinkçi* should be understood here as owners of the machines called *aba dingi* or actual operators of *aba* finishing instruments.

Taşköy village five kilometers south of Balıkesir, five out of eight households had *aba* finishing machines.[38] This suggests that the *aba* industry had penetrated into the village region as home manufacturing. The estimated value was about 750 *kuruş* per *aba* finishing machine, about equal to two packhorses. During our fieldwork, the people in today's Taşköy village told us that they stopped *aba* production in the 1950s. Two out of nine households in Dağbayındır village were also reported to have the *aba* finishing machine, but its estimated value was not shown in the record.[39] Clearly, the *aba* manufacturing promoted by the government significantly influenced the village region.

The head of the *abacı* guild was called *kehtüda*. He also had a job as *imam* at a mosque in the Mirzabey Quarter. His properties included 21.5 *dönüm* of arable fields, a half *dönüm* of vineyards, and shops. He was financially powerful, with more properties and income than the average. Moreover, he was exempt from taxation because of his *imam* status. From these facts, we can assume that he was an influential Balıkesir local figure, having both an important secular position, and a religious one.

Thus we can find some information about *abacı* and their manufacturing in the Temettuat registers. The *aba* guild organization played the role of producing the product in a quantity assigned to Balıkesir by the central government, while maintaining product quality and controlling the price.

Conclusion

The following are conclusions from our analysis of the local societies of Balıkesir, as based on the Temettuat register.

First, the old center of commercial activities of the city maintained that function, while the administrative function stretched out to the south around the clock tower with the increase in population. The development of *aba* manufacturing increased the need for a labor force, which caused a movement of village population to the urban area. This would have also increased the number of unlicensed tanners, and that led the tanner guild to lose control of their organization.

---

38 ML.VRD.TMT. no. 7227, pp. 134-135

39 ML.VRD.TMT. no. 7227, p. 138.

Second, the landholding situation of the independent farmers was based on the traditional management of small farming and did not allow *çiftlik* to specialize in commercial crops.

Third, the Balıkesir region was selected for *aba* production and thus involved in the central government's policy. In a socio-economic transition, the two most influential families, members of which were former local notables, or *ayan*, built up an economic foundation in the city of Balıkesir and in the villages, competing with each other for concessions in the *aba* manufacturing.

Fourth, not only urban residents carried out *aba* manufacturing. The manufacturing infiltrated into villages and nomad societies, and consequently the villagers and nomads were also involved into the divisions of labor as a labor force for the *aba* production.

The considerations in this paper explain one aspect of transition in Balıkesir society, which was greatly affected by the development of the *aba* industry from the 1820s to the 1840s. The Temettuat register sheds light on these matters, providing specific information about the people who lived there.

Chapter 5

Güzelhisar-ı Aydın: Portrait of a West Anatolian City

Arzu TERZİ

1. Setting the Scene

Aydın is a city of Western Anatolia, situated between the northern edge of the valley of Büyük Menderes and the southern outskirts of the Aydın Mountains, at an altitude of approximately 55-80m above sea level. The city was named Güzel Hisar-ı Aydın on Aydın Güzelhisarı during the time of the Ottomans, but its ancient name is Tralles.

The city was supposedly founded by the Thracian tribe Tral between the tenth and fifteenth centuries B.C., and thereby took this name.[1] Unlike Aydın today, Tralles was not founded on the plain but instead on a square, flat area at an altitude of 160-170m, and its interior castle was built on a fortified hill completely separated from the mountains behind. Because of the fertility of the land, and its location at the crossroads between the Ephesus and Miletus ports and the inner lands, the city became prosperous and rich.[2]

Until the Turks conquered Tralles, within its historical course it was under the hegemony of the Lydians and Persians, and at some time became

---

1 Asaf Gökbel & Himmet Şölen, *Aydın İli Tarihi*, Vol. 1, Aydın, 1936, p. 52.

2 Besim Darkot & Mükrimin Halil Yınanç, "Aydın, " *İslam Ansiklopedisi*, Vol. 2, Istanbul, 1943, p. 61.

the capital of the Pergamum Kingdom. It experienced successive Roman and Byzantine domination. The Turkish rule began in 1282 with Menteşe Bey,[3] and the city was given the name Güzelhisar[4] because it was a fortified city (*hisar*) and beautiful (*güzel*). After the rule of the Menteşe Beyliği, the city had been under the rule of the Aydınoğulları starting in 1307[5] and was annexed to the Ottoman lands in the year 1426 during the reign of Murat II.[6]

The Ottomans joined the Aydınoğulları Beyliği to the Ottoman provincial system as a *sancak* belonging to the Anadolu Province and named Aydın İli or Liva-i Aydın. Within this administrative unit, the center of the *sancak* was Tire, and Güzelhisar was the center of the *kaza* belonging to Tire. The Ottomans gave the town the name Güzelhisar-ı Aydın to differentiate it from Güzelhisar in the north of Menemen.[7]

In the fifteenth century, Güzelhisar, according to the Tapu Tahrir registers, was a small town with seven quarters whose population consisted mostly of Turks. In the first half of the sixteenth century the number of quarters declined to six, and population also decreased. However, the town, beginning to prosper in the second half of the same century, grew to 1000 people.[8] Katip Çelebi, in the mid-seventeenth century, wrote that the town had public baths, streets, vineyards and gardens, as well as eight mosques; that two quarters were located outside the fortress; and that the town was rich with figs.[9]

Evliya Çelebi, coming to town in 1671, wrote that Güzelhisar was composed of 26 quarters and 6770 families.[10] A survey for taxation called

---

3 Paul Wittek, *Menteşe Beyliği*, tr. Orhan Şaik Gökyay, Ankara, 1944, p. 26.

4 Ch. Texier, *Küçük Asya,* Vol. 2, tr. Ali Suad, Istanbul, 1339, p. 112.

5 Himmet Akın, *Aydın Oğulları Tarihi Hakkında Bir Araştırma*, Ankara, 1968, pp. 24-25.

6 Akın, *op. cit.*, p. 84.

7 Tuncer Baykara, *XIX. Yüzyılda Aydın Eyaleti*, unpublished graduation thesis (Department of History, Istanbul University), Istanbul, 1966, p. 4; Feridun Emecen, "Aydın," *İslam Ansiklopesidisi*, Vol.4, Türkiye Diyanet Vakfı: Istanbul, p. 235. A. Gökbel and H. Şölen in their work mentioned above, relying on their observations, remark that the denomination of the city is due to the fact that Aydınoğlu Mehmet Bey added his own name to Güzelhisar when he dominated the city, p. 86.

8 Emecen, "Aydın," p. 235.

9 Katip Çelebi, *Cihannüma*, Wien, Österreichische Nationalbibliothek, Mxt 389, vr. 119b.

10 Evliya Çelebi, *Seyahatnâme*, Vol. 9, Istanbul, 1935, p. 152.

"avarız tahriri" held in 1677 identified 22 quarters, two non-Muslim communities, and a population of more than 5000.[11] Evliya Çelebi writes that the town had 600 shops, 200 tanneries (*tabakhane*), 200 fountains, 40 coffeehouses, 40 primary schools, nine inns, and four public baths. He also frequently mentions the market place called Kurşunlu Bedestanı, saddleries (*saraç*), sellers of round copper trays (*sinici*), coppersmiths, and sweet (*helva*) shops.[12] Although Katip Çelebi notes that the plain of Güzelhisar was sandy and not suitable for agriculture,[13] he also remarks that the land here was fertile and adds that sesame and almonds, cotton and thread made of cotton, *dimi*[14] and its cloth, white bread, melons, watermelons, lemons and oranges were famous. We also learn from the notes of Evliya Çelebi that in the same century much cloth was brought to Güzelhisar from Denizli and other places to be dyed, and a busy market had been there once a week.[15] From what Evliya Çelebi has written, we can determine that Güzelhisar was an important center of settlement that was experiencing continuous development, especially from the second half of the twelfth century, and beginning to expand towards the plain. At the beginning of the nineteenth century, in 1811, Güzelhisar was the center of the *sancak* of Aydın.[16] In 1826, the Anadolu Province was divided into two parts, and the *sancaks* of Hamid, Saruhan, Teke and Sığla came together to form Aydın Province, with Güzelhisar-ı Aydın declared the center of the province.[17] Güzelhisar did not permanently remain the center; from time to time the governors of the province moved the center to Izmir. In 1843, however, during the second period of the governorship of Yakup Paşa, the center was moved to Güzelhisar[18] until 1850. During the time we have studied, therefore, Güzelhisar was a center in which the administration of the province was carried out and the governor of the province resided.

According to the population census (*nüfus tahriri*) of 1845, Güzelhisar (or its later name, Aydın City) had 24 quarters, 21 of which were Muslim and

---

11 Emecen, *op. cit.*

12 Evliya Çelebi, *op. cit.*, pp. 150-59.

13 *Cihânnüma*, vr. 119b.

14 *dimi*: diagonally woven cotton or woolen fabric.

15 Evliya Çelebi, *op. cit.*, p. 158.

16 Baykara, *op.cit.*, p. 4.

17 Ahmed Lûtfi, *Tarih-i Lûtfi*, Vol. 1, Istanbul, 1290, p. 207.

18 *Takrir* dated in 21 Cemaziyelevvel 1259 (20 June, 1843): Cevdet–Dahiliye, no. 7217.

three non-Muslim.[19] The Temettuat registers of the city, the main source of our study, were compiled during the surveys of that same year.

Unfortunately, Temettuat registers for two of the 21 Muslim quarters are not to be found. The remaining 19, however, are available in the Prime Ministry Ottoman Archives of Turkey in Istanbul, as are the registers of the three non-Muslim quarters (Jewish, Greek and Armenian residents). In this study, when presenting the social and economic panorama of the city of Güzelhisar in the nineteenth century, we have depended on the records of these 22 quarters, lacking only the missing books of the other two quarters.

2. The Social Structure of the City

The Quarters and Population of Güzelhisar

Based on information in the available registers, the names and number of householders for each of 22 quarters in 1845 are shown in Table 1.

The two quarters whose registers we do not have are named Cuma and Mahkeme[20] and are estimated to have had comparatively large populations.[21]

As for the non-Muslim quarters in the town, the Greek quarter with 345 households is the most populated, followed by the Jewish quarter with 174 households. The Armenian quarter of Güzelhisar is the least populated with 10 households. In addition, four Armenian households are in the Yarbaşı Quarter.[22] These non-Muslim subjects were registered in their separate quarters, but this is not a clear-cut system in the Ottoman towns, according to the records available in the registers. As seen, a few Armenians dwelled in the Yarbaşı Quarter, and a few Jewish residents were in the Terziler Quarter in Güzelhisar.[23]

---

19 Cevdet–Dahiliye, no. 9031.

20 For the Mahkeme Quarter, see ML. VRD. TMT. no. 1977; for the Cuma Quarter, ML.VRD.TMT. no. 2011.

21 We can estimate the total number for these two quarters as 763 households. See Note 35.

22 ML.VRD.TMT. No. 1996.

23 At the end of the Temettuat register belonging to the Terziler Quarter (ML.VRD.TMT. no. 2006), Jewish residents were said to live in this quarter; however, they were investigated in their own religious community (*millet*). Their records would not be included in this register but, instead, in the

Table 1: Names of Quarters and Number of Households

Quarters	Number of households	ML.VRD.TMT
Ali Baba Sultan (Kubbe-i Ala)	104	no. 1981
Balcılar	75	no. 2012
Cami-i Atik	54	no. 2008
Cemaleddin	49	no. 1989
Çıksorut	383	no. 2019
Debbağlı	243	no. 2037
Hisar	87	no. 2015
Karaca Ahmed	90	no. 1985
Kaynak Baba Sultan	110	no. 2025
Kemer	52	no. 2007
Kozdibi	135	no. 2031
Köprülü	65	no. 2030
Kubbeli Mescid	64	no. 2043
Orta	266	no. 2020
Ramazan Paşa	89	no. 2011
Sarayiçi	57	no. 1977
Terziler	96	no. 2006
Torbacı	76	no. 2023
Yarbaşı (muslim+*rumiyan*)	168+4	no. 1996
Greeks (*rumiyan*)	345	no. 2039
Jews (*yahudi*)	174	no. 2013
Armenians (*ermeni*)	10	no. 2042
Total	2796	

We see that religious institutions, such as mosques, formed the nucleus of the quarters and gave their names to many quarters in Güzelhisar. Among these, the Ali Baba Sultan Quarter borrowed its name from the mosque and madrasah of Alihan Baba Sultan built during the Seljuks period.[24] The Kaynak Baba Sultan Quarter was named after a convent (*zaviye*) called Kaynak, which was founded by the same person.[25] The Ramazan Paşa Quarter borrowed its name from the Ramazan Paşa Mosque built in 1595 by Ramazan Paşa, who was promoted to *başdefterdar* (chief revenue-officer) of the Ottoman Empire. The Cemaleddin Quarter also owes its name to a

register belonging to the Jewish quarter of Güzelhisar.

24 Asaf Gökbel & H. Şölen, *op. cit.*, pp. 98, 116.

25 Tapu Tahrir Defterleri, no. 166, p. 441.

mosque (*mescit*), called Mescid-i Cemal.[26] Similarly, the quarters Cami-i Atik and Kubbeli Mescit seem to have borrowed their names from religious institutions. Both these quarters, being old, are recorded in the above-mentioned *avarız* registers of the seventeenth century.[27] Ever since the city was brought under Ottoman rule, there has been a quarter called Cami.[28] Probably the name of the quarter became Cami-i Atik (old mosque) upon the construction of new mosques. The Orta Quarter is likely to have borrowed its name from an inn and a public bath called Orta Han and Orta Hamam, which were built by Yavlılı Şemşi Paşa.[29]

Some quarters in the city bear the names of individuals. One of these is the Balcılar Quarter, named for a clan that left its residence in the province of İçel and came to Alaiye, and from there scattered towards the province of Aydın.[30] The leader of the clan was Balcı Hasan,[31] and the quarter he and his family dwelled in was named after him in the seventeenth century. Eventually its name became Balcılar. Another quarter bearing the name of an individual is the Karaca Ahmet Quarter. Similarly, the Sarayiçi Quarter was once called by the name of a person, Hasan Efendi,[32] in the seventeenth century. In the nineteenth century, however, its name was changed to Saray (palace) because a municipal department was located there.[33]

Some of the quarters in Güzelhisar took their names from their locations. One of them, the Çıksorut Quarter, took its name from its sloping terrain. *Çıksorut* means to take a breath when coming up a slope. As for the Hisar Quarter, it was known as Hisar Yakası when the city came under Ottoman rule (*hisar yakası* means side of a castle), but later it was called only *hisar* (castle). We can add other quarters to this group: the Kozdibi Quarter (*kozdibi* means a base of walnut tree); the Kemer Quarter, named for

---

26 TD, no. 166, p. 441.

27 Kamil Kepeci–Mevkufat Kalemi, no. 2791, vr. 16b-17a.

28 Tapu Tahrir Defterleri, no. 166, p. 438.

29 Gökbel & Şölen, *op. cit.*, p. 116.

30 *Ibid.*, p. 235.

31 *Ibid.*

32 *Ibid.* In the Yearbook of 1973, the Sarayiçi Quarter was indicated as having another name as the Hasan Efendi Quarter. *Cumhuriyetin 50. Yılında Aydın: 1973 İl Yıllığı*, Izmir, 1973, p. 523.

33 The beginning of the Temettuat register for this quarter says, "*ikametgah-ı hazret-i müşir-i ekremi*," which means the home dwelling of Yakup Paşa, governor of the Aydın Province, is located here.

the Kemer Stream (one of the River Menderes branches, which passes through this quarter); and the Köprülü Quarter, which probably took its name from one of the bridges (*köprü*) in the city, and which has been called by the same name since coming under Ottoman rule.

The Debbağlı, Torbacı and Terziler Quarters were named after occupational groups who were believed to have dwelled there (*debbağ* means tanner; *torbacı*, bag maker; *terzi*, tailor).

Since the mid-nineteenth century, as the city expanded, eventually some quarters have been absorbed into the more developed quarters. They became crowded, and adopted new names due to administrative divisions. Meanwhile, other quarters—Kemer, Köprülü, Ramazan Paşa, Hasan Efendi, Orta and Cuma—have existed with the same names up to the present day. Around the turn of the nineteenth century, the city of Güzelhisar began to be called Aydın, and the name Güzelhisar became limited to only the quarters Hisar, Kaynak Baba Sultan, and Torbacı.

Of the non-Muslim quarters, *rumiyan* (Greeks) and *yahudi* (Jewish residents) were within the boundaries of the today's Zafer Quarter. Currently, however, a non-Muslim population no longer exists in the city. The former location of the Armenian quarter cannot be determined.

As for the population of the city, according to its Temettuat registers of 1845-46, Güzelhisar had 2796 households, of which 2263 were Muslim and the remaining 533 were non-Muslim (Table 1), However, the total number of Muslim households in the city is shown as 3027 in the population census of the same year.[34] Adding the number of non-Muslim households in the Temettuat registers (533 households) to that of the 3027 Muslim households gives a total of 3560 households. Starting from this point, we can estimate that as of the year 1845-46 Güzelhisar had a population of approximately 17,800[35] people. Of this total, 85% were Muslims and 15% were non-Muslims.

---

[34] Cevdet–Dahiliye, no. 9031. The balance of 763 households should be the number of the household of the above-mentioned two quarters, for which Temettuat registers are not known to be available.

[35] In the calculation, the total number of households is multiplied by five. (Refer to Ömer Lütfi Barkan, "Tarihî Demografi Araştırmaları ve Osmanlı Tarihi," *Türkiyat Mecmuası*, Vol. 10, 1951, pp. 1-26).

Table 2: Occupation of Head of Household

Categories of occupations of heads of households	Number	%
Farmers and peasants	198	7.1%
Workers	628	22.5%
Artisans and tradesmen		
a) Master workmen	1150	41.1%
b) Assistant masters and apprentices	463	16.5%
Civil servants	184	6.6%
Those with no occupations	173	6.2%
Total	2796	100.0%

Occupations of Heads of Households

Occupations of heads of households are among the important items of information provided by the Temettuat registers. Looking at the registers of the 22 quarters, we see a variety of occupations, which we have sorted into five categories as shown in Table 2.

(1) Farmers and Peasants

The chart lists 198 heads of households, 7.1% of the total, who are minor producers in agriculture. This category appears in the Temettuat registers, in general, as *rençber* (peasants), *çiftçi* (farmers), *erbâb-ı ziraat* (agriculturists), and *ortakçı* (sharecroppers).[36] Among the 198 numbered above are 110 *erbâb-ı ziraat*, 84 *rençber*, three *çiftçi* and a *ortakçı*. This group of farmers and peasants sow and harvest a certain amount of their own land and produce various products. To get additional earnings, they usually work in the fields of others as sharecroppers or agricultural workers. A few *erbâb-ı ziraat* and *rençber* also deal in trade.

[36] In and around Aydın, the expressions *erbâb-ı ziraat*, *çiftçi*, and *rençber* are used interchangeably and bear the general meaning of farmer. As a matter of fact, *erbâb-ı ziraat* and *çiftçi* are people working in agriculture, whereas *rençber* literally means a hired man, a workman who performs jobs such as digging the ground or carrying stone and soil. The secondary meaning is farmer (*Temel Türkçe Sözlük*, Vol. 2, Istanbul, 1986, p. 1104), and the word is used in this sense in the registers.

(2) Workers

The *işçi* (workers) number 628, or 22.5% of all households. They live in the city and work at various activities, mostly agriculture and stockbreeding. Most of them, 533, are *ırgad* (agricultural workers). Another group is the *hizmetkâr* (servants), with 48 households in the registers. Whether all these people we counted as *hizmetkâr* were servants in households or were agricultural workers hired for designated periods such as one year or six months is not clear.[37] If some heads of households who were recorded as *hizmetkâr* were counted instead as agricultural workers, the rate of 7.1% for them in the chart will increase. In addition to these are 21 *bahçevan* (gardeners) whom we have counted among the working class. A smaller number of workers are in related jobs: five *çoban* (shepherds), a *çukadar* (footman), a *deşteban* (watcher set over sown field), five *hademe* (servants), 10 *hammal* (porters) and four *sığırtmaç* (cattle drivers) — only a few in the total number of workers.

(3) Artisans and Tradesmen

Artisans and tradesmen with occupations in industry and commerce numbered 1613 and thus were the heads of 57.6% of all households. Of these, 1150 were masters, that is, specialists in their jobs. However, the 463 assistant masters (*kalfa*), and apprentices (*çırak*), shown in the registers as belonging to various occupations do not represent an accurate count of everyone working in these occupations. In the registers only heads of households are registered because dividend registrations were done only to determine the tax for each household. Therefore, assistant masters and apprentices who are not heads of households are not shown in them. We could therefore suppose that the number of assistant masters and apprentices given is less than accurate for many occupations. For this reason, we will consider the number of masters as being the number of all those engaged in the occupation.

The needs of the public are met by 147 types of occupations. Manufacturing and sales activities usually go together in these occupations. We can categorize occupations pertaining to craftsmanship and trade into eight groups, as shown in Table 3.

[37] Tevfik Güran considered the *hizmetkâr* to be agricultural workers. "Osmanlı Tarım Ekonomisi 1840-1910," *Türk İktisat Tarihi Yıllığı 1987*, Istanbul, 1987, p. 252.

Table 3: Types of Occupations of Artisans and Tradesmen

(1) Artisans manufacturing and selling clothes

2 *çamaşırcı* (laundry)
12 *fesci* (fez making)
1 *gömlekçi* (shirt making)
12 *haffaf* (cheap shoemaker)
1 *kürküçü* (furriery)
1 *nalçacı* (iron heel making)
8 *pabuş dikiçisi* (slipper sewing)
3 *pabuş tamircisi* (slipper mending)
36 *pabuççu* (shoemaker)
1 *postalcı* (long boots making)
3 *püskülçü* (tassel making)
77 *terzi* (tailor)
3 *ütücü* (iron making)

(2) Artisans producing goods of food and drink

13 *arpacı* (barley seller)
9 *aşçı* (cook)
14 *attar* (herbalist)
15 *bakkal* (grocery)
1 *balıkçı* (fish seller)
3 *çerezci* (hors d'oeuvres seller)
1 *çorbacı* (soup maker)
7 *değirmenci* (miller)
2 *dondurmacı* (ice-cream maker)
19 *ekmekçi* (baker)
18 *helvacı* (sweet maker)
1 *kabakçı* (squash seller)
10 *kasap* (butcher)
5 *katmerci* (flaky pastry maker)
5 *kebabçı* (kebap seller)
4 *kestaneci* (chestnut seller)
3 *kovancı* (hive seller)
41 *leblebici* (chickpea sellers)
4 *limoncu* (lemon seller)
5 *lokmacı* (morsel maker)
39 *manav* (greengrocer)
20 *mısırcı* (corn seller)
8 *salatacı* (salad seller)
2 *soğancı* (onion seller)
5 *şekerci* (sugar seller)
16 *şerbetçi* (sherbet master)
2 *tuzcu* (salt seller)
7 *uncu* (flour seller)
4 *yağcı* (oil seller)

(3) Occupations pertaining to weaving

9 *abacı* (coarse woolen cloth maker)
17 *bezzaz* (textile merchant)
16 *boyacı* (dyer)
11 *çuhacı* (draper manufacturing cloth made from fine wool)
40 *çulha* (weaver)
6 *hallaç* (wool comber)
4 *ibrişim bükücü* (silk thread spinner)
3 *ipek bükücü* (silk spinner)
5 *iplikçi* (thread maker)
21 *kazzaz* (silk manufacturer)
6 *keçeci* (felt maker)
1 *kırmızcı* (seller of *kırmız*, paint acquire from a tiny insect)
14 *muytab* (goat woolen cloth maker)
2 *penbe burucu* (cotton twister)
5 *şeridci* (lace maker)
4 *tehril bükücü* (spinner of *tehril,* silk thread spun thickly)
1 *tülbentçi* (*muslin* seller)
2 *urgancı* (rope maker)

(4) Tradesmen and merchants

38 *çerçi* (peddler of small wares; haberdasher)
23 *eskici* (dealer in second-hand wares)
3 *kömürcü* (coal dealer)
10 *manifaturacı* (draper)
3 *oduncu* (firewood dealer)
2 *oturakçı* (ready-made goods dealer)

4 *panayırcı* (fair business)
13 *pazarcı* (marketer)
1 *satıcı* (seller)
28 *tüccar* (merchant)

(5) Artisans producing and selling miscellaneous goods

2 *bakırcı* (coppersmith)
1 *bardakçı* (mug and glass maker)
3 *bıçakçı* (knife maker)
4 *billurcu* (cut-glass ware maker)
1 *çenberci* (hoop maker)
24 *çengelci* (hook maker)
41 *debbağ* (tanner)
16 *demirci* (blacksmith)
2 *destici* (pitcher maker)
2 *elekçi* (sieve maker)
4 *fenerci* (torch maker)
2 *hasırcı* (mat maker)
12 *kalaycı* (tinsmith)
3 *kalburcu* (sifter)
2 *kaltakçı* (saddletree maker)
3 *kantarcı* (steelyard maker)
3 *kasacı* (safe maker)
3 *kirişçi* (catgut maker)
10 *koltukçu* (armchair maker)
4 *kundakçı* (gunstock maker)
19 *kutucu* (box maker)
6 *kuyumcu* (goldsmith)
2 *mineci* (enameller)
1 *mumcu* (candle maker)
16 *nalbant* (farrier)
2 *saatçi* (watch maker)
16 *sabuncu* (soap maker)
2 *sandıkçı* (chest maker)
12 *sarraç* (saddler)
14 *semerci* (packsaddle makers)
1 *seleci* (wicket basket maker)
1 *sepetçi* (basket maker)
1 *süpürgeci* (broom maker)
6 *tenekeci* (tinsmith)
3 *usturacı* (razor maker)
14 *yorgancı* (quilt maker)
1 *zencirci* (chain maker)

(6) Occupations pertaining to construction

4 *çilingir* (locksmith)
3 *duvarcı* (bricklayer)
5 *dülger* (carpenter)
1 *keresteci* (timber seller)
2 *kiremitçi* (tile seller)
2 *kuyucu* (well digger)
1 *mimar* (architect)
1 *sıvacı* (plasterer)
7 *suyolcu* (responsible for maintaining waterway)
3 *taşçı* (stonemason).
23 *yapıcı* (builder)

(7) Occupations pertaining to transportations

4 *arabacı* (transporter by horsecart)
35 *deveci* (transporter by camel)
1 *eşekçi* (transporter by donkey)
4 *katırcı* (transporter by mules)
14 *kiracı* (an occupation in transport business by animals and carts)

(8) Occupations performing a variety of services

26 *berber* (barber)
1 *cambaz* (horse dealer)
4 *cerrah* (surgeon)
5 *çalgıcı* (musical instrument player)
1 *dana boğazlayıcı* (heifer slaughterer)
29 *dellal* (broker)
29 *duhancı* (tobacco seller)
19 *duhan kıyıcısı* (tobacco cutter)
3 *eski yamacı* (old-clothes mender)
6 *hancı* (inn-keeper)
3 *hamamcı* (keeper of public bath)
24 *kahveci* (coffee seller)
1 *kısrakçı* (mare dealer)
10 *meyhaneci* (tavern keeper)

4	*natır* (attendant in a women's bath)	2	*tahmis döğücü* (grinder of coffee)
4	*seyis* (horse keeper)	3	*tönbekici* (seller of tobacco for water-pipe)
5	*simsar* (broker)		
2	*tahmisci* (roaster of coffee)		

As can be seen in Table 3, in the 22 quarters of Güzelhisar more than 140 occupations in industry and commerce were active, and the people involved made up 57.6% of the total number of households.

The high number of heads of households working in certain branches of the professions shows that these were widespread in the city. Among them, we can list the manufacturing of clothing and shoes (including 212 tailors and 36 shoemakers); weaving and its side branches (including 40 weavers and 21 silk manufacturers, total 167 masters), tannery (including 113 tanners), transportation with animals (59 heads of households), and so forth.

(4) Civil Servants

The fourth occupational classification is civil servants, the people in charge in state departments or institutions. We can study these people in two groups, the first of which is those serving in the religious and educational institutions, a total of 109 people. There are 38 *imams* (prayer leaders) who are the heads of their households. This number is important because it shows the multitude of mosques in and around the city. The number of *müderris* (professors in madrasah) serving education is 18. Other people in charge in the educational and religious fields include a *cabi* (collector of the revenue of a pious foundation), three *haham* (Jewish rabbis), a *hahambaşı* (the chief rabbi), three *hatib* (preachers), four *kayyum* (caretakers of a mosque), six *muallim* (teachers), nine *müezzin* (those calling Muslims to prayer), a *müfti* (registered as the müfti of Algeria), a *mütevelli* (an administrator, especially the trustee of a pious foundation), two sheikhs, 10 *talebe* (students), a *türbedar* (keeper of a tomb) and four ulema.

Those in the second group, who number 75, served in the military, social and administrative fields and include the *müşir* (governor) of the province of Aydın, Yakup Paşa. The number of *muhtar*s who are also the heads of their households and whose sole occupation is headmanship is 10; we have classified those holding another job beside their headmanship in the charts related to the other job. Others are two *menzilci* (post riders)[38], two *sa'is* (foot messengers), a superintendent supervising the censuses, four *mahalle ağası* (notables of a quarter), a *mahalle kahyası* (bailiff), two *karakullukçu* (military officers), 11 *kapualtı askeri* (soldiers in a governmental building), eight *katip* (secretaries), a *muameleci* (money lender), four *muhzır* (officers of a court who summoned persons and produced them in court), a *mukayyid* (registrar), a *pazvandbaşı* (chief of watchmen) and his three assistants, a *sandık emiri* (treasurer), a *sekban* (formerly, keeper of the imperial hounds; a soldier), six *sipahi* (cavalry soldiers), an artillery man, a *yiğitbaşı* (formerly, the man responsible for carrying out the regulations of a guild; or a foreman in the army), four *yazıcı* (scribes, clerks) and eight soldiers of gendarmerie. The number of heads of households residing in the 22 quarters of Güzelhisar and serving in various civil servant jobs is 184, or 6.6% of all households.

(5) Those with No Occupation

In these occupational categories, we have put last the heads of households who do not have specific jobs. In this group, 40 women are heads of their own households, and 21 children are recorded in the registers as orphans. In this category, we can also cite 32 rentiers (those who live on their limited lands just enough to make their sustenance through cultivation with a partner, those who live on the incomes from their immovable properties and are registered in the registers as "those busy with their own sustenance," and those who live on the rents of their immovable properties). Those registered as the old and the poor, people who have no incomes and are not able to work, number 62 and live on the help or grants of other people. Heads of households included in this group are seven beggars, five *meczup* (crazy, insane), a poet and five retired. The total of people with no certain job is 173, which is 6.2% of all households.

---

38 The Ministry of Postal Service was established in 1840, and in 1842 both service from the regular Service Head Office and the charging of directors in Aydın, Isparta, Kütahya and İzmir began. Nesimi Yazıcı, "Tanzimat Döneminde Osmanlı Haberleşme Kurumu," *150. Yılında Tanzimat*, Ankara, 1992, p. 155. However, coming into the year 1847 the Post Head Office in the centre of Aydın still had no director (*Ibid.*, p. 156, 84 n.). In places without such directors, in a sense the *menzilciler* (couriers) substituted for them. p. 171.

In conclusion, with a rough classification we can say that, of the people in the city, two-sevenths live on agriculture or labor and four-sevenths work in industry or deal in trade. Two categories, those in charge and those with no jobs, constitute the remaining one-seventh.

Buildings

In the registers, immovable commercial properties of heads of households are registered with their types, one by one. They are either resided in or used as shops by their owners, or rented to other people for extra income. If immovable property has been rented, then the annual rent is shown as income. The registration of immovable properties in this way is useful for classification of the immovable properties belonging to heads of households according to their types (See Table 4).[39]

When a shop was registered, its purpose—in other words, what kind of profession was to be practiced—was often not clearly stated, and therefore we do not always know what kinds of professions used the shops. The data we have shows that shops were used by 27 tailors, 11 greengrocers, 10 tobacco sellers, nine cloth merchants, nine grocers, eight corn sellers, seven sweet makers, seven herbalists, and five barber shops. In addition to these shops, 14 workshops are listed as rented; the purpose for which workshops were used is not known.

The number of coffeehouses in Güzelhisar, we find, is 31. It is registered that a head of household residing in the Balcılar Quarter owned a coffeehouse with operating license (*gedik*) and also another coffeehouse. A coffeehouse owned by a head of a household dwelling in the Sarayiçi Quarter was originally the property of a pious foundation. For other coffeehouses, the registers offer no record as to what type of ownership the owners had. Of the total 31 coffeehouses, their owners reside in two and the remaining 29 are let for rent.

Heads of households living in the city owned 13 inns. Their owners resided in four of them, and the rest were rented. Güzelhisar also has 25 halting places and 20 households let on hire by their owners. Of the three

[39] The count for real estate does not show the exact number of immovable properties in the city, because properties owned by those who lived outside the city limits or in another city were not registered. Besides that, ownership of a property could be divided into lots, which makes knowing the exact number of immovable properties difficult.

Table 4: Types of Buildings

Types of buildings	Number
Shop (*dükkan*)	347
Flour mill (*değirmen*)	3
Inn (*han*)	13
House (*hane*)	20
Coffeehouse (*kahvehane*)	31
Workshop (*kârhane*)	14
Store (*mağaza*)	5
Halting place (*menzil*)	25
Tavern (*meyhane*)	3
Soap manufactory (*sabunhane*)	8
Rental room (*oda*)	21
Jewish residence (*yahudihane*)	1
Oil mill (*yağhane*)	6
Total	497

halting places registered in Sarayiçi Quarter, two are recorded in registers as halting places resided in by the tenants doing transport business. The remaining 18 are recorded in registers just as property halting places. How many are residences for couriers to halt, and how many are halting places for passengers or individual residences, is not shown. Güzelhisar also has three watermills, two being rented.

The Jewish residence (*yahudihane*) is listed as having 13 rooms.

Besides the rooms of inns and *yahudihane*, there were 21 individual rental rooms (*oda*) in the city. It is not known how these rooms (*oda*) were used, but among them were the rooms registered in the Ramazan Paşa Quarter and listed as for attendants in the convent of Mevlevi dervishes in the Ramazan Paşa Quarter.

Of six oil mills owned by heads of households, two are resided in by two heads of households whose occupations are sweet making and sesame oil making. In addition, two are rented, and it is not known by whom they were run. Of the eight soup factories, one is resided in by its owner but is not in use, another three have been out of use for three years, the owners reside in two, and two others are rented.

The division of immovable properties according to the quarters enables

Table 5: Amount of Land Owned by Urban Residents

Types of land	Size (in *dönüm*)
Field (*tarla*)	9,179.5
Vineyard (*bağ*)	4,154.0
Garden (*bahçe*)	1,097.0
Others	85.0
Total	14,515.5

us to have an opinion about the economic condition of the residents living in these quarters. The people of some quarters have more immovable properties, which shows that wealthy people live in certain quarters. On the other hand, none of the people living in the Kaynak Baba Sultan Quarter have any immovable properties at all. And among the people living in the Ali Baba Sultan, Hisar, Karaca Ahmet and Torbacı quarters, only a few heads of households have their own immovable properties. These quarters are considered poor. Besides, people living in the Cami-i Atik, Ramazan Paşa, Sarayiçi, Terziler and Yarbaşı quarters have comparatively far more immovable properties, and this allows us to assume that the people of these quarters have better living conditions.

3. Agriculture and Stockbreeding

The Amount and Division of the Land and its Use

The data recorded in the Temettuat registers enable us to determine the size and type of land owned by the heads of households living in the 22 quarters of Güzelhisar. The land reserved for agriculture and owned by heads of households living in the city can be classified as Table 5

14,515.5 *dönüm* of land are used as fields, vineyards and gardens. Of this land, 63.2% is used as fields and 36.8% as vineyards and gardens. Of the rest, 44 *dönüm* are uncultivated vineyards and gardens; 38 *dönüm* of the land around the houses are cultivated for fruit and vegetables. The land for olives (shown in the registers as number of trees, not *dönüm*) is not included in the figures above. Heads of households own 14,315 olive trees.

Table 6: Landholding by Types of Occupations

Size of land	Farmers and peasants		Artisans and tradesmen		Workers		Civil servants		Those with no occupations		Total	
dönüm	*hane*	*dönüm*	*hene*	*dönüm*	*hane*	*dönüm*	*hane*	*dönüm*	*hane*	*dönüm*	*hane*	*dönüm*
0	23	0	1180	0	384	0	107	0	127	0	1821	0
1-10	32	229.5	285	1428	190	999	32	207	33	150	572	3013.5
11-20	56	874	81	1243	42	617	20	294.5	6	84	205	3112.5
21-30	32	817.5	24	627	9	222	11	264	2	51	78	1981.5
31-40	18	626.5	22	775	1	35	4	155	3	108	48	1699.5
41-50	17	786	9	409	1	44	4	189	1	48	32	1476
51-60	7	398	5	266	1	55	4	216	0	0	17	935
61-100	7	532	6	471.5	0	0	2	152	1	99	16	1254.5
over 100	6	911	1	132	0	0	0	0	0	0	7	1043
	198	5174.5	1613	5351.5	628	1972	184	1477.5	173	540	2796	14515.5

The figures above give the amount of land used for agriculture. Lands shown in the registers as *gayrı mezru* (uncultivated) were those left uncultivated during the years when Temettuat registrations were held; they total 1249 *dönüm*. Most of those *gayrı mezru* fields are likely to be fallow lands. In addition, heads of households own 121 *dönüm* of pasture. Most heads of households living in the city (2796, or 65%) do not have any land. Most of those who do own land have between one and ten *dönüm*.

Looking at how land ownership is divided in terms of the occupations by which heads of households earn their sustenance (Table 6), we determined that landowners work at all kinds of occupations. Of the heads of households living in Güzelhisar, the group holding the highest proportion of the city's land is the artisans and tradesmen, who hold 37% of all land in the city. Either the owners or their close relatives cultivate most of this land. We can see that some people still practice agriculture alongside their main jobs even though the level of development of urbanization is considerable. However, it is noteworthy that 73 % of the artisans and tradesmen have no land at all. Almost as high a proportion of city land, 35.5%, belongs to those engaged in agriculture; 88.4% of them have their own lands and practice agriculture.

In contrast to these groups, 38.9% of the working class own 13.6% of all city land. Of the government workers, 41.9% own 10.2% of all city land. Last come those without any particular job; 26.6% of them have a certain amount of land, 3.7% of all city land.

We found very few large-scale landowners in the city.

The Crops Produced

Certain crops produced in Güzelhisar are fruits and vegetables, or grains. The total revenue from crops produced in Güzelhisar in 1844 is calculated to be 604,274 *kuruş*.[40]

---

[40] Thanks to the records in the Temettuat registers about the tithe, we are able to acquire information about the products grown in the city. A portion of the tithe was collected *in kind*, and the rest was *in cash*. So, it is possible to calculate the amount of the products whose tithe was paid in kind. For some kinds of farm products like grape and cotton, however, the amount of the product is shown as the amount of its cultivated land, *dönüm*; therefore, we are unable to determine the amounts of these products in measure. For this reason, by multiplying 10 by the tithe collected from the products whose title was paid *in cash*, we tried to get an idea of the amount of the year 1844

Table 7: Crop Production

Kinds of crops	Revenue (in *kuruş*)	%
grapes	185,290	30.7
industrial herbs (mostly, cotton)	176,448	29.2
grains	89,229	14.8
olives	51,524	8.5
figs	44,970	7.4
crops from vegetable gardens	56,813	9.4
Total	604,274	100.0

The crops most commonly produced in Güzelhisar are grapes (30.7%) and the industrial plants (29.2%) such as cotton, sesame, silk and tobacco. Among these cotton is most important, with 27% of the whole production. As the cereal crop, barley, wheat, millet, broadbean, oats and rye are cultivated. The percentage of olive and olive oil production to total products is 8.5%. In our opinion, this is not the average figure for oil, for olive is a crop that yields more in one year and less or no products in another year.[41] Looking at the Temettuat registers for the products of the previous year, we can see that in 1844 many olive trees yielded no crop. Therefore, that year's productivity is at a low level, but in the following year it will increase. Among the major crops produced, figs, 7.4% of all products, follow olives. From the fruits and vegetables, two kinds of tithe were collected. One was collected from early fruits and vegetables called *gögeri,*[42] which shows us that in this region raising early fruit and vegetables is practiced. The other kind of tithe is collected from fruits and vegetables raised in their normal course of time; while in some areas raising early fruits and vegetables is practiced, in other areas both types are seen. The annual revenue from fruits and vegetables, whose kinds we are unable to determine, is 56,813 *kuruş*. Of this amount, 4,087 *kuruş* is from fruits grown in gardens, 6,275 *kuruş* from the vegetable gardens, and 46,451 *kuruş* from the fruits and vegetables raised early. The total percentage relative to all products is 9.4%.

An overall evaluation is that, of all the crops raised in Güzelhisar,

produce.

41 Abdurrahman Vefik, *Tekâlif Kavâidi*, Vol. 2, Istanbul, 1330, p. 298.

42 *Ibid.*, p. 278

four-sevenths are from vineyards, gardens and vegetable gardens; two-sevenths are from industrial plants; and one-seventh are from grains.

Stockbreeding

As seen everywhere in Anatolia, some heads of households in Güzelhisar raise animals in order both to utilize their products and powers and to use them in the transport business. Furthermore, agriculture is practiced widely in the city. Of the 22 quarters recorded in the Temettuat registers, the heads of households in 19 quarters have various animals due to the reasons cited above. The people living in Sarayiçi, and the Jewish and Armenian populations, have no animals at all according to the register.

The various kinds of cattle in Güzelhisar, used for their power in tilling the fields and in the transport business, as well as for their milk and other products, include 95 milch buffaloes, seven buffalo heifers, 11 cart buffaloes, 190 milch cows, two cow heifers, three cattle calves, six cattle cows, 31 cattle oxen, 40 mares, 31 female buffaloes, 18 male buffaloes, 83 oxen and three young horses. While the number of milch cows, buffaloes and mares is shown in the registers, the amount of annual products from them and the annual income they bring to their owners is not shown in every Temettuat register. Sometimes, even in the book of the same quarter, some are recorded and others not. We are unable to determine whether this is out of negligence or due to a specific reason.[43] Therefore it is not possible to determine precisely how much annual income milch animals brought to their owners.[44] The three colts we cited above among the cattle belong to the head of a household residing in the Ramazan Paşa Quarter.

As shown in the section on occupations, the transport business holds an important place in the city. Therefore some of the cattle in Güzelhisar are used in such occupations as camel driving (*deveci*), as well as keeping livery horses (*kiracı*), horse-cart driving (*arabacı*) and mule driving (*katırcı*). The transport business uses 109 baggage horses, 108 camels and three mules. The 86 donkeys in the city were presumably also used in this business.

---

43 As noted in Chapter 1 of this volume, how the income from animals should be registered in the surveys was under dispute.

44 The annual total income from the records is 880 *kuruş* from the milch buffalo, 140 *kuruş* from the milch cow and 40 *kuruş* from the milch mare. But we don't include them in the calculation of income of their owners.

Table 8: Apiculture in Güzelhisar

Quarters	Number of beehives	Annual income (*kuruş*)
Çıksorut	102	2650
Karaca Ahmed	10	90
Kemer	5	200
Kubbeli Mescid	4	25
Orta	34	380
Torbacı	4	20
Total	159	3365

The sheep and goats in the city include 25 milch goats, 10 young goats, 731 milch sheep, and 50 male sheep. The products from milch goats and sheep are properly recorded in the registers. According to these records, the annual income from milch goats is 75 *kuruş* and from milch sheep, 3,540 *kuruş*.

Apiculture is also practiced in Güzelhisar on a small scale. The division of the number of the beehives and the annual income from them, as of the year 1844 and by quarters, is shown in Table 8 below.

In view of the above data, we can say that stockbreeding is not a common source of livelihood in Güzelhisar. The landowners living in the city kept some animals just to cultivate their lands, or used animals mostly in the transport business. The annual income from animals is registered as 8,040 *kuruş*, only 0.3% of the entire annual revenue of the city; of this, 4,675 *kuruş* is from cattle, and goats and sheep; the rest, 3,365 kuruş, is from apiculture. This amount could reasonably be considered unreliable, however, because not all income from cattle was included.

4. Economic Condition

Sources of Income and Distribution of Income in the City

From data recorded in the Temettuat registers, it is possible to determine six different sources of income by which heads of households living in the city sustained themselves. (See Table 9.)

Table 9: Amount of Income by Sources of Income (in *kuruş*)

Sources of income	Farmers and peasants	Workers	Artisans and tradesmen	Civil servants	Those with no occupations	Total	
1. Agriculture							
a. Agriculture	127668	19239.5	83936	22450	3605	256898.5	9.6%
b. Horticulture and viniculture	82266	47015	121719.5	21444	12402	284846.5	10.6%
c. Stockbreeding	2810	1970	2650	60	550	8040.0	0.3%
2. Share cropping							
a. Agriculture	17987.5	1677.5	32265	4233.5	1603	57766.5	2.2%
b. Horticulture and viniculture	3349	870	3828.5	1110	2093.5	11251.0	0.4%
3. Trade and craftsmanship	8995	0	1447332.5	16400	0	1472727.5	55.2%
4. Workmanship	16250	338661.5	0	0	0	354911.5	13.3%
5. Salaries	0	0	0	82441	2000	84441.0	3.2%
6. Rental income							
a. Building rents	4123	3323.5	78622	22534.5	18323	126926.0	4.8%
b. Land rents	425	1470	2450	950	6315	11610.0	0.4%
Total	263873.5	414227	1772803.5	171623	46891.5	2669418.5	100.0%

Table 10: Ratio of Income by Sources of Income

	Farmers and peasants	Workers	Artisans and tradesmen	Civil servants	Those with no occupations	Total
	%	%	%	%	%	%
1. Agriculture	80.6	16.5	11.8	25.6	35.3	20.5
2. Share cropping	8.1	0.5	2.0	3.1	7.9	2.6
3. Trades and craftsmanship	3.4	0	81.6	9.6	0	55.2
4. Workmanship	6.2	81.8	0	0	0	13.3
5. Salaries	0	0	0	48	4.3	3.2
6. Rental income	1.7	1.2	4.6	13.7	52.5	5.2
	100.0	100.0	100.0	100.0	100.0	100.0

One of these is agriculture, which we can classify into two divisions, agricultural production and viniculture and horticulture. Some heads of households practice agricultural production, growing various kinds of grains, pulses and industrial plants. The annual income from this agriculture is 256,898.5 *kuruş*, 9.6% of the total annual income of the city. The other branch of agriculture is horticulture and viniculture, in which mostly grapes, olives and figs (in general, the products of vineyards, gardens and vegetable gardens) are produced, another 10.7% of the total income. Sericulture, not important as a source of income, is also included in this total. Horticulture and viniculture require more labor than field production and therefore are more common in and around the towns, where populations are bigger; the garden and vineyard products are for market.[45] Finally, as noted above, stockbreeding, with 0.3% of all income, does not hold an important place in the economy of the city.

Another source of income for people living in Güzelhisar is collective agriculture, called *ortakçılık* or "sharecropping,"[46] in which income is shared between two partners, one the landowner and the other cultivating the land. The tithe tax is deducted from the income total. Sharecropping makes up 2.6% of total income;[47] this includes 2.2% from agricultural production collectively practiced, a total of 57,766.5 *kuruş*, and 0.4% from viniculture and horticulture, a total of 11,251 *kuruş*.

Craftsmanship and trade is an important category of income, with a total annual income of 1,472,727.5 *kuruş*. Of the total income in the city, 55.2% is from craftsmanship and trade.

Another source of income for heads of households is workmanship. The annual income earned by workers in Güzelhisar is 354,911.5 *kuruş*. The percentage in the total revenue for workmanship is 13.3%.

We have already pointed out the existence of people who are serving in various fields, and the places they are employed. So, the salaries received by the people who are in charge in the city constitute another source of income. These salaries, totaling 84,441 *kuruş*, make up 3.2% of the income.

Among the sources of income of the heads of households, rental income from immovable properties comes last. A certain amount of the

---

45 *Ibid.*, p. 239

46 İrade Mesâil-i Mühimme, no. 65, lef 7.

47 Because sharecropping is a kind of income for the landowner obtained from the agricultural sector, we report it as a different source of income.

rental income is received from the buildings, such as shops, coffeehouses, home dwellings, halting places, inns, baths, and so forth, owned by the public. Building rents, totaling 126,926 *kuruş*, make up 4.7% of total income. Rents received from letting the land out to someone else total 11,610 *kuruş*; the percentage is 0.4% with respect to total income.

In general, the most significant source of income by which people in Güzelhisar sustain themselves is craftsmanship and trade. For craftsmanship and trade to account for 55.2% of total income is normal for a city like Güzelhisar, which was a provincial center in those days. The many service jobs as well as vocational groups are typical of city life. In addition, however, income received from cultivation, collective cultivation and stockbreeding is second, accounting for approximately 23.2%. Such a percentage with respect to total income suggests that townspeople still cling to country lifestyles.

If we look at the distribution of sources of incomes received by heads of households dealing with these different occupations, the annual gross income of the heads of households living in 22 quarters of Güzelhisar could be set at a total of 2,669,418.5 *kuruş*.[48] (See Table 10.)

The heads of households who lived in Güzelhisar and had certain occupations, that is, farmers and peasants, workers, and artisan and tradesmen, earned more than 80% of their annual income from their primary jobs. Peasants obtained their additional income from sharecropping, commerce, workmanship, and rental incomes. Workers, artisans and tradesmen obtained their additional income from agriculture, stockbreeding, share cropping, and rental incomes. The income earned by civil servants in return for the services they executed, considered "salary," constituted only 50% of their total income. The other half came from sources such as agriculture, sharecropping, commerce and rents. Those with no professions but having the financial resources to sustain themselves received their incomes from sources such as agriculture, sharecropping, salary and rent.

The income data provided by the Temettuat registers could include some concealing of individual incomes, but we can confirm the general tendency by examining the tables.

Taxation

It is possible to identify three types of tax collected from heads of households

[48] All incomes in the Temettuat registers are gross income.

Table 11: Tax Distribution by Quarters

Quarter	Tax (in *kuruş*)
Ali Baba Sultan	15,970
Balcılar	12,668
Cami-i Atik	7,600
Cemaleddin	5,744
Çıksorut	60,921
Debbağlı	33,753
Hisar	9,825
Kaynak Baba Sultan	6,670
Karaca Ahmed	13,560
Kemer	6,210
Kozdibi	22,591
Köprülü	10,401
Kubbeli Mescit	8,545
Orta	33,352
Ramazan Paşa	15,707
Sarayiçi	9,328
Terziler	12,815
Torbacı	5,127
Yarbaşı	21,401
Armenians (*ermeni*)	2,051
Greeks (*rumiyan*)	58,768.5
Jewish (*yahudi*)	15,357
Total	388,364.5

in Güzelhisar in light of the data in the Temettuat registers. The first of these is *vergi-i mahsusa*, that is, special tax. Temettuat registers kept in 1845-46 were intended to fix the annual tax paid to the state by people living in a village or a quarter. Complaints arose, however, about unfair distribution of the tax collected from the quarter communities. When the Temettuat registers were prepared, to protect against injustice in the distribution of the taxes each and every household was allotted a section in which the annual dividend of the household was indicated. On the upper right corner, the amount of tax paid by the head of the household in question was to be written. In this way, any injustice between income and tax paid could be determined.

Indeed, an investigation identified some injustices in the taxes households paid. It is possible to see these unfair tax distributions here and there in the Temettuat registers. Sometimes different amounts of taxes were collected from two persons whose annual incomes were the same, and sometimes one person with a high income would pay a low tax whereas another with less income paid half of that income in tax. From the records in the Temettuat registers, we can determine the total annual tax collected from the 22 quarters of Güzelhisar in 1844, and the distribution of this collection according to the quarters as shown in Table 11.

The table shows that, of the total tax of 388,364.5 *kuruş* collected from people living in Güzelhisar, the Muslim population paid 312,188 *kuruş* and the non-Muslim population paid 76,176.5 *kuruş*. The Muslim population paid 80% of the whole and the non-Muslim population, 20%.

Viewing the distribution of the tax according to quarters, the Çıksorut Quarter, the most populated quarter of the city with 383 households, pays 60,921 *kuruş*, 15.6% of the total. The Greek quarter, with 345 households, pays 58,768.5 *kuruş*, 15.1% of the total. Also, some people in the city are tax-exempt. Those male and female heads of the households who are unable to work and live on the support of others were of this group. We also find that orphan children who were heads of households were exempted whereas some of the other children pay tax.[49] Teachers, newcomers in the quarters, handicapped people, insane people, and beggars were also tax-exempt. *Imams*, *muhtars*, the notables, madrasah professors, ulemas, *müezzins*, students and certain people in religious and administrative positions (for example, pulpit orators) are sometimes tax-free.[50]

The second type of tax is the tithe.[51] In Güzelhisar, tithe was collected from the heads of the quarters in two ways, tithe in kind and tithe in cash. Tithe from grains was generally to be paid in kind. Besides grains, tithe from olive oil, sesame and the rarely produced chestnuts were collected in kind.

---

49 İrade Mesâil-i Mühimme, no. 65.

50 The intermittent collection of taxes from this group cannot be determined exactly. Even though at first glance we get the impression of collection of taxes from these persons if they have a secondary source of income, with close inspection we realize this is not true. Despite the extra income, we encounter expressions in the records such as "no tax demanded because they serve as the *imam* of the quarter," or "they are savants."

51 Tithe is a kind of tax collected in different quantities from the produce of the land; after Tanzimat, a certificate was promulgated stating that tithe would generally be collected for all produce on the basis of 1/10. A. Vefik, *op. cit.*, p. 241.

Table 12: Title Taxation

Tithe	*akçe*	%
In kind	13606.6	22.4%
In cash	47141.8	77.6%
Total	60748.4	100.0%

Of several kinds of the tithe in cash, that from grapes is the highest, followed by *gögeri*, tithe collected from cotton, fig, early fruits and vegetables, and *bahçe ve bostan öşürleri* (garden and vegetable garden tithes) collected from olives and various fruits and vegetables. The tithe collected from pastures, and the honey and hive tithes, are of this kind of tithe collected in cash. Tobacco production in Güzelhisar is fairly low despite the high number of tobacco producers, and the tithe taken from tobacco is a mere five *kuruş*. Presumably, tobacco is brought to Güzelhisar from outside to be marketed and sold. Based on this information, the amount of the tithe collected in 1844 in Güzelhisar is shown in Table 12.

Another kind of tax, paid by the heads of non-Muslim households, was *cizye*. In Güzelhisar, the Greek and Jewish quarters had 495 households, who were required by the government to pay *cizye* tax.[52] Although we know of 14 Armenians in the city, no *cizye* records appear in the Temettuat registers for them. Because of this, we could not include the Armenians in Table 13, which shows households classified into three groups according to their tax. [53]

As shown in the table, of 345 heads of Greek households, the *cizye* tax was imposed on 336, of whom 226 (67%) were classified as "medium." In addition, two children in the position of heads of household and four old men were exempted from the *cizye* tax. A Greek who engaged in *çalgıcılık* (musician) was exempted from both *cizye* and *vergi-i mahsusa*, although a Greek merchant and a Greek tobacco seller (*duhancı*), who had an Imperial

[52] In the sections of the Temettuat registers allotted to each household belonging to these quarters, the class of head of the household is recorded as *alâ*, *evsat* and *ednâ* with abridged symbols. Owing to these symbols, we can determine the amount of tax to be paid by non-Muslim heads of households by the time the records were kept. Furthermore, we are able to determine which class they were in and the amount of the tax they would pay.

[53] ML.VRD.TMT. no. 2042; no. 1996.

decree issued by the Sultan, were exempted from *cizye* but had *vergi-i mahsusa* imposed on them.

In Güzelhisar, *cizye* tax was imposed on 168 Jews. Of these, 10 were not heads of households,[54] and their economic conditions were recorded in the register as "poor." Of the remaining 158, most of the Jewish heads of households were considered "poor" according to the classification of wealth. Because we know 174 Jewish heads of households lived in the city, we can assume that 16 of them were exempt from tax. One of these was the chief *haham*, who had the Sultanic decree. The other two *haham* did not have the Sultanic decree; however, they were also exempted from *cizye* tax. A Jewish heifer slaughterer and two primary school teachers did not pay any *cizye*, and six handicapped people, three old men, and an insane person were also exempted.

In 1834 (1250H), the classification of *cizye* was somewhat changed. People whose economic condition was "good" were to pay 60 *kuruş*; "medium," 30 *kuruş*; and "poor," 15 *kuruş*.[55] This criterion continued until the *cizye* tax was abolished in 1856. If we use these amounts, in the year 1845-46, Greek and Jewish heads of households paid their *cizye* tax to the government as shown in Table 14.

The total of the annual *cizye* tax paid by the Greek and Jewish heads of households living in the city is 12,675 *kuruş*. Of the total *cizye* tax, 75% is paid by Greek, and 25% by Jewish, heads of households. The proportion of *cizye* tax paid by the Jewish population was lower than that of the Greek population because far more Jewish heads of households were listed as having low incomes ("poor").

We have mentioned above three kinds of taxes and their amounts collected from people living in Güzelhisar, as of the year 1844. These taxes, and the total income of the Muslim and non-Muslim population, were as shown in table 15.

The percentage of taxes the Muslim population paid is 17.8% of annual

54 In the Temettuat register belonging to the Jewish Quarter, these 10 persons were determined to have some income, although slight, and they did not pay *vergi-i mahsusa*. We had the impression that they lived with relatives in the same house or in the rooms of *yahudihane* as bachelors because they are relatives of the person who lives in the house cited prior to theirs (ML.VRD.TMT. no. 2013).

55 Süleyman Sudi, *Defter-i Muktesid*, Vol. 1, Istanbul, 1307H, p. 126.

Table 13: Number of Households for Each *Cizye* Category

Non-Muslim Communities	*alâ* (good)	*evsat* (medium)	*ednâ* (poor)
Greeks	24	226	86
Jewish	4	31	133
Total number of households	28	258	219

Table 14 : Amount of *Cizye* Paid by Non-Muslim Population

Non-Muslim Communities	*alâ* (good)	*evsat* (medium)	*ednâ* (poor)	Total
Greeks	1440	6780	1290	9510
Jewish	240	930	1995	3165
Total Amount of *Cizye*	1680	7710	3285	12675

gross income; this can be divided into 2.8% for tithe and 15% for *vergi-i mahsusa.* The percentage paid by the non-Muslim populations is 15.4% of their annual gross income of 58,1945.5 *kuruş*. Of this total amount, 13% is *vergi-i mahsusa*, 2.2% is the *cizye* tax, and 0.2% is the tithe tax. As seen, the tax burden of the Muslim population in relation to income is slightly more than that of the non-Muslim population.

Neither the tax amounts paid by residents of the two Muslim quarters for which we have no Temettuat registers, nor the *cizye* tax of Armenian heads of households, are included in the totals. Nonetheless, these figures cast light on the total tax burden in the city.

Table 15: Total Tax Revenue

	Total	Muslim	non-Muslim
Income	2,669,418.5	2,087,471	581,945.5
vergi-i mahsusa	388,364.5	312,188.0	76,176.5
tithe	60,748.4	59,547.9	1200.5
cizye	12,675.0		12,675.0
Total	461,787.9	371,735.9	90,052.0

Conclusion

In the mid-nineteenth century in Güzelhisar, a city that was a provincial center, various jobs were carried out to meet the requirements of the public. In these jobs, production and sales activities were usually executed side by side. Some branches in the city, especially weaving and tannery, developed specializations. Tailoring and dealing in footwear, which we can consider the extensions of weaving and tannery in industry, were among the outstanding professions. Also, even though people lived in the city, they maintained their agricultural activities. One out of three heads of households had their own land, and a large part of this land was sown. Although viniculture and horticulture were emphasized, agricultural plants were also produced. The abundance of the production of vineyard-garden products and industrial plants contributed to the increase of commercial activities in this city located on the route to Izmir. As a consequence, all these factors contributed to the revival of social and economical activities and elevated the level of welfare.

Chapter 6

Erzurum: A Border City of East Anatolia

Haydar ÇORUH

1. Setting the Scene

The city of Erzurum, on the down slopes of Mount Palandöken, lies over an inclined territory at an altitude of from 1850 to 1900 meters. The Romans probably built the castle of the city during the years 415-422 AD in defense against Persian attacks directed at Anatolia. The city, called Karin by the Armenians, was later named Theodosiopolis after the Byzantine Emperor Theodosios. In 653, during the time of the Caliph Uthman, his army conquered the city, and it is cited as Kalikala or Kali in the Islamic Source readings.

Dominated by Turks after the Battle of Malazgird, Erzurum has undergone various conquests throughout history. Ruled by the Mongols in the year 1242, by Eretnaoğulları in 1360, and by the Karakoyunlu Beyliği in 1387, it was likely conquered by the Ottoman Empire in 1518-1519.[1] Under Ottoman domination, Erzurum remained a strategically important city because of its location on the Iranian border. The Russians occupied it on July 8, 1829. This last occupation forced some residents to move to other

1 Cevdet Küçük, "Erzurum," *İslam Ansiklopesidisi*, Vol.11, Türkiye Diyanet Vakfı: Istanbul, 1995, p. 322.

regions. Fatih Efendi, an official in the army who fought in the Russian-Ottoman War, described the Castle of Erzurum as a fortified place and added that houses, shops and inns surrounded it.[2]

Starting in the 1840s, however, applications of Tanzimat began a new era for the city.[3] Before analyzing the Temettuat registers of Erzurum, which were the fruits of Tanzimat, we should first examine the city's demographics during its history.

The population of Erzurum, a frontier town, has always fluctuated, for a variety of reasons. The frequent invasions played an important part in these fluctuations. Indeed, the city had its first census and a land survey in 1523 soon after its subjugation by the Ottomans. According to this survey, Erzurum, with its 12 quarters, was tied to the *kaza* of Şogayn (Aşkale) in the *sancak* of Bayburt. The center of the *kaza* was later moved to Erzurum. A Tapu Tahrir register from the same period states that "the city is so dilapidated that it would not be taken into account with respect to *timar*," which suggests that population was low at that time.[4] The next survey was held in the year 1540[5] and reported that 21 households lived in the 27 quarters of the city,[6] including five households each in the Bab-ı Kan and Bab-ı Tebriz Quarters, four households each in the Mescid-i Mirza Mehmed[7] and Kırkçeşme Quarters, and three households in the Cami-i Kebir Quarter.[8] No one lived in the remaining 22 quarters. After the city came under Ottoman rule, the stability that prevailed led people to return. At this time,

2 Mehmed Arif, "Rusya ile 1244 ve 1245 Senelerinde Vuku Bulan Harbe Dair Bir Vesika," *Tarih-i Osmani Encümeni Mecmuası*, no. 14, 1328-1330, pp. 882-904. My thanks to Prof. Dr. Kemal Beydilli for this information.

3 Tanzimat reform was launched in Erzurum in 1845. Cevdet–Maliye, no. 8570. See Chapter 1 of this volume, p. 20.

4 Tapu Tahrir Defterleri, no. 387, p. 867.

5 Ö. Lütfi Barkan, indicating the survey dated in 946H (1540), states that some of the Eastern provinces were in ruins and scarcely populated. For instance the city of Erzurum, with the exception of a few *zaviye* sheikhs and *sipahizade* (cavalry soldiers), was entirely unsettled. Ömer Lütfi Barkan, "Tarihî Demografi Araştırmaları ve Osmanlı Tarihi," *Türkiyat Mecmuası*, Vol. 10, 1951, p. 18.

6 Neşe Erim, "Trade, Traders and the State in Eighteenth-Century Erzurum," *New Perspectives on Turkey*, no. 5-6, 1991, p. 127.

7 Archive records indicate that this quarter existed with the same name in the year 1892 (Y.A.RES. dos. 62/11).

8 Tapu Tahrir Defterleri, no. 205, pp. 15-16.

the Armenians who lived in the villages also began to settle in the city.

In the first half of the sixteenth century, the population of Erzurum was about 2000 civilians, plus the soldiers and their families who lived in the castle. Towards the last quarter of that century, the population of the city was approximately 2620, of whom 1475 were Muslims and 1145 were non-Muslims.[9] Almost all of this population, it is understood, was subject to taxation. When military and civilian officials were included, the city's population was estimated at between five and six thousand persons.[10]

The seventeenth century was a new period of public improvements and population growth for Erzurum. Evliya Çelebi, who came to town in the first half of that century, stated that the population comprised 1700 households.[11] Tournefort, who visited the region in the first quarter of the eighteenth century, reported the population to be at least 25,000. According to him, 18,000 were Turks; 7000-8000, Armenians; and 500, Greeks.

The development and expansion of Erzurum as one of the most important centers of trade in Anatolia has continued into this century as well. However, the population, which was 200,000 at the beginning of the nineteenth century, decreased to 130,000 by about 1826; an important factor in this decrease was the departure of soldiers after abolition of the Janissary organization. Nonetheless, available documents show a continued increase in population under the Ottoman domination throughout history.

The Russian occupation in 1828-29 could be expected to cause a population change. After this occupation, however, Erzurum was excluded from an 1831 census of the Ottoman provinces, thus preventing any population estimate. This census was finally applied to the province of Erzurum in 1836, but the registers have not yet been found. In a document dated 16 August 1842, however, we find that 15 of the 18 quarters in the city were vacant.[12] Three years later, in 1845, the Temettuat survey was attempted in the Ottoman provinces. The application in Erzurum does not

---

9 For the population and composition of the city of Erzurum in the sixteenth century, refer to Dündar Aydın, "Erzurum Şehri'nin Osmanlı Fethini Müteakip İmârı, İskânı ve İlk Sâkinleri," *Atatürk Üniversitesi Edebiyat Fakültesi Dergisi*, no. 1, 1970, pp. 110-14.

10 Küçük, "Erzurum," p. 326. As for the population statistics, see Cem Behar, "The Ottoman Empire and the Population of Turkey 1500-1927,"*Devlet İstatistik Enstitüsü Tarihi İstatistikler Serisi*, Vol. 2, Ankara, 1996, p. 8.

11 Evliya Çelebi, *Seyahatname*, Vol. 2, Istanbul, 1314, p. 209.

12 Cevdet–Dahiliye, no. 12901.

seem to have been easy,[13] as some incidents against the Tanzimat reform were taking place, especially in the eastern regions of Anatolia.[14]

2. The Quarters and the Population

The Temettuat registers of Erzurum confirm the existence of 45 quarters in the city of Erzurum.[15] On the other hand, a census register dated 1847 reports 53 quarters in the city. The registers that might include information on the remaining eight quarters appear to have been lost.

With 262 Muslim households, the Hasan Basri Quarter was the most populated in the city. The Ali Paşa Quarter also had a large population, half of which was Armenian. Of the other quarters, seven had populations of 120 to 200 households each. In many of these larger quarters, Muslims and non-Muslims lived side by side. For example, Armenians were two-thirds of the Emin Kurbu Quarter population, one-third of the Yeğen Ağa Quarter, and one-half of the Mumcu-i Süflâ and Mumcu-i Ulyâ Quarters. The city also had 61 Catholic households, all in the Erzurum Quarter. The registers do not indicate ethnicity for these Catholics,[16] but the names of heads of households show them to be Armenians.[17] Including the Erzurum Quarter, twelve quarters were of medium size, with populations of between 50 and

---

13 İrade Mesâil-i Mühimme, no. 102, lef 5; for more detailed information with respect to the applications of Tanzimat and the reactions against them refer to Musa Çadırcı, *Tanzimat Döneminde Anadolu Kentleri'nin Sosyal ve Ekonomik Yapıları*, Ankara 1991, pp. 192-97.

14 Note the information in a petition written 12 June 1845 (7 Receb 1261). To summarize: in addition to four battalions of soldiers sent to the region, two more battalions were sent to the city of Erzurum to suppress the conspiracy that arose in and around Van and Muş. (Cevdet–Dahiliye, no. 14948). ML.VRD.TMT, no. 6868, p. 15.

15 Temettuat registers used in this study are: ML.VRD.TMT from no. 6850 to no. 6897.

16 In the documents the minorities are stated as *millet*.

17 For more detailed information with respect to the Catholicization of Armenians refer to Cevdet Küçük, "Osmanlılarda Millet Sistemi ve Tanzimat," *Tanzimat'tan Cumhuriyet'e Türkiye Ansiklopedisi*, Vol. 4, Istanbul, 1985, pp. 1012-13. For a recent study on this matter refer to Kemal Beydilli, *Recognition of the Armenian Catholic Community and the Church in the Reign of Mahmut II (1830)*, Harvard University, 1995.

Table 1: Number of Households of Each Quarter

Quarter	Total	Muslim	Armenian	Catholic	*Rum*
Abdurrahman Ağa	27	27			
Ali Paşa	227	111	116		
Bakırcı	29	29			
Boyahane	9	9			
Cağferiye	81	81			
Cami-i Kebir	81	81			
Cedid	122	96	26		
Çırçır	71	61	10		
Çortanoğlu	15	15			
Çukur	10	10			
Derviş Ağa	45	45			
Emin Kurbu	192	49	14		
Erzurum	109	48		61	
Feyziye	24	24			
Gez	101	101			
Habib Efendi-i Süflâ	68	68			
Habib Efendi-i Ulyâ	65	65			
Hacı Cum'a	40	40			
Hanım Hamamı	20	20			
Hasan Basri	262	262			
Kâbe Mescidi	13	13			
Kadana	82	82			
Kasım Paşa (Merkez)	39	39			
Kal'a Derunu	7		7		
Kan Yolu Ali Paşa	19				19
Kavak	21	21			
Kırmacı	19	19			
Köse Ömer Ağa	25	25			
Lala Mustafa Paşa	36	36			
Mumcu-i Süflâ	156	85	71		
Mumcu-i Ulyâ	121	62	59		
Murad Paşa	134	134			
Müderris Efendi	117	117			
Namervanlı Cami-i Şerif	30	30			
Sivasî	5	5			
Sultan Melik	129	129			
Şeyh Emir	37	37			
Şeyhler	36	36			
Topçu Oğlu	106	99	7		
Üveys Efendi	88	88			
Vanî Efendi	110	110			
Yeğen Ağa	155	101	54		
Yoncalık-ı Süflâ	69	69			
Zağracı Ali Ağa	38	38			
Total	3190	2617	493	61	19

120 households. Except for the Erzurum Quarter, other quarters of medium size had mostly Muslim populations. The least-populated quarter was the Sivasi Quarter with five households.

According to the Temettuat registers, the 3190 households in the city included 2617 that were Muslim; 493, Armenian; 61, Catholic; and 19, Orthodox Greek (*rum*). Of the 3190, only three heads of households appeared to be women whose husbands died leaving little children. A *sabi* (male child) was also the head of a household; he had probably lost both parents. To summarize the population of the city, we estimated the number of persons in a household as five, thus estimating the entire population of the city of Erzurum to be close to 16,000 in the first half of the nineteenth century. When we obtain the Temettuat registers of the eight missing quarters, we expect this figure to exceed 17,000.

Although the Temettuat registers give detailed information concerning the urban population, whether all people in the city were registered is open to question, for two reasons. First and most important is a wish to evade heavy taxation. Second and less likely is delay by the clerks who carried out the Temettuat surveys, who were unable to arrive at some households before March 1846.

According to the French itinerant Vital Cuinet, who came to Erzurum in the last quarter of the nineteenth century, the Muslim population of the city was 26,564. The *reaya* (non-Muslim tax-paying subjects) included 9422 Gregorian Armenians, 717 Catholic Armenians, 296 Protestant Armenians, 484 Orthodox Greeks, 6 Jewish and 1417 other minorities including Iranian and Europeans, for a city total of 38,906.[18]

Taxpayers were registered quarter by quarter for the Temettuat registers. However, the separate registers for Muslims and non-Muslims living in the same quarter deserve attention. Catholic Armenians living in the Erzurum Quarter and the Armenians in the Yeğen Ağa Quarter and the Kal'a Derunu, even though living alongside Muslims in the same quarters, were registered

[18] Vital Cuinet, *La Turquie d'Asie*, Vol. 1. Paris 1891, p. 137. Cuinet did not mention any sources with respect to the table that supplies these figures. Refer to Adnan Mahiroğulları, "Fransız Seyyahı Vital Cuinet'nin Notlarıyla 100 Yıl Önce Erzurum," *Tarih ve Medeniyet*, no. 25, 1996, pp. 57-61.

in separate registers.[19] Greeks who lived in the Kanyolu Ali Paşa Quarter were also registered in a separate register.[20]

3. Occupations

Occupations of registered heads of households were classified as shown in Table 2.

Table 2: Occupations of heads of households

		Number of households	%
(1)	Those who dealt with agriculture and stock-breeding	66	2.1%
(2)	Builders and physical laborers	462	14.5%
(3)	Craftsmen and tradesmen	1819	57.0%
(4)	Civil servants and other occupations		15.3%
	Military and administrative occupations	221	
	Occupations related to religious, educational and social services	268	
(5)	Those with no jobs	354	11.1%
	Total	3190	100%

Agriculture and Stockbreeding

Taxpayers working only with agriculture and stockbreeding made up 2.1% of the city's population. This occupation, with 66 households, included the *çiftçi* (farmer), *ziraatçi* (agriculturist), *ortakçı* (sharecropper), *otçu* (grass cutter), *rençber* (day laborer), and *çiftlik ağası* (farm owner). Few non-Muslims were engaged in agriculture and stockbreeding, except for two Catholic heads of households who were dealing with stockbreeding.

Those who dealt with stockbreeding in Erzurum were called *cambaz*

---

19 With respect to the archives documents, it is understood that special announcements were made to prevent the registration of Muslims and non-Muslims in the same register (A. MKT. UM, dos. 86/38, 24 November 1851, official report (*mazbata*) written to the governors of Adana and Maraş).

20 ML.VRD.TMT, no. 6868, p. 15.

(animal dealer) and *çoban* (shepherd).[21] These included 26 heads of households, classified as *koyun cambazı* (sheep dealer), *koyun çobanı* (shepherd), *mal cambazı* (cattle dealer), *taycı* (colt dealer), *ayıcı* (bear trainer), *celeb çobanı* (shepherd to the cattle), *himar cambazı* (donkey dealer), *sığır cambazı* (cattle dealer), and *esb cambazı* (horse dealer). One head of household in this group was *baytar* (veterinarian), which suggests that the city of Erzurum, a center of stockbreeding, had only one veterinarian. This might explain why the epidemic diseases that emerged in and around Erzurum caused the loss of many human and animal lives.[22]

Only a few urban residents in Erzurum, then, engaged in agricultural activities as their principal occupation. This suggests that full-time farmers lived solely in the villages and *mezraa*s (arable fields) outside the city. Or people who engaged in agriculture were not likely to be recorded as urban residents of Erzurum, whether they lived in urban quarters or not.

Builders and Physical Laborers

Those who worked in construction and in occupations requiring physical strength totaled 462 heads of households, 14.5% of all heads of households.

This group included 85 constructors, which we enumerate as *alçıcı* (plasterer), *çilingir* (locksmith), *çıkrıkçı* (lathe operator), *çivici* (nailer), *duvarcı* (bricklayer), *dülger* (carpenter), *hızarcı* (pit sawyer), *keresteci* (timber merchant), *kerpiççi* (maker of sundried bricks), *kireççi* (lime seller), *kazıcı* (engraver), *mıhçı* (nailer), *suyolcu* (man responsible for the maintenance of water conduits),[23] *tahtacı* (sawyer), *neccar* (carpenter), *nakkaş* (decorator) and *purutluk* (stone mason). Although such workers were primarily non-Muslim, some Muslims did work in such occupations.

Some of the laborers using physical power chose stockbreeding as a calling. With 377 heads of households, they constitute 11.8% of the working

21 Tevfik Güran defines the *çoban*s as temporary agricultural workers receiving wages and working in vineyards and gardens. (Refer to "XIX. Yüzyıl Ortalarında Ödemiş Kasabası'nın Sosyo Ekonomik Özellikleri," *İstanbul Üniversitesi İktisat Fakültesi Mecmuası*, Vol.41, no. 1-4 (*Ord. Prof. Ömer Lütfi Barkan'a Armağan Özel Sayısı*), 1985, p. 303.

22 Cevdet–Maliye, no. 22496; a decree dated in Şaban, 1258.

23 With respect to *su-yolculuk* (maintenance of the water conduits) in the Ottoman State refer to Abdullah Martal, "Osmanlı İmparatorluğu'nda Su Yolculuk," *Belleten*, no. 161, 1977, pp. 1585-652.

population of the city. Some of them were registered as *çoban* and *cambaz,*[24] but they should not be confused with those so described in the previous section. Instead, physical laborers of *çoban* and *cambaz* would receive wages for their services, as they did not own any animals or property. The *temettuat* (income) of specialists in this occupation with the status of laborer should have been reckoned according to the amount of wages received. As already mentioned, the non-Muslims were not involved in agriculture and stockbreeding in Erzurum and therefore had little interest in groups such as the wage earners of *çoban* or *cambaz*.

The same group also had three other occupational categories: *hamal* (porter), *hizmetkar* (servant),[25] and *ırgad* (day laborer). People in these occupations were mostly Muslims. Of the 35 day laborers, however, 11 heads of households lived in the Armenian quarters.

Craftsmanship and Commerce

Urban craftsmen and tradesmen organized in the *esnaf* (guilds) numbered 1,819 heads of households, 57.0% of all such. Excluding occupations such as serving in the army and combining those with similar names into craftsman groups, we can identify 250 occupations pertaining to craftsmanship and commerce in the city. Major occupational groups are classified below:

(1) Weaving

With 171 heads of households, the craftsmen dealing with weaving constituted 5.4% of the heads of households. *Çulfalık* (from *cülehâlık*; business of a weaver) were numerous in this group.

---

[24] *Cambaz* were responsible for looking after the horses of the vizier and the other notables in the army and working in the stables and field services. They were probably doing the same kind of job as the *sefer voynukları* (non-Muslims serving as horse grooms in the Ottoman army). Midhat Sertoğlu, *Osmanlı Tarih Lügatı*, Istanbul, 1985, pp. 60-61.

[25] *Hizmetkar* were presumably agricultural workers. With respect to this matter refer to Tevfik Güran, "Osmanlı Tarım Ekonomisi 1840-1910," *Türk İktisat Tarihi Yıllığı 1987*, Istanbul, 1987, p. 252. Nevertheless, Ali İhsan Bağış indicates that some of the *hizmetkar* were also serving the non-Muslim tradesmen. *Osmanlı Ticareti'nde Gayri Müslimler, Kapitülasyonlar, Beratlı Tüccarlar, Avrupa ve Hayriyye Tüccarları, 1750-1839*, Ankara, 1983, pp. 65-66.

Boyacı (dyer) was registered as *boyakçı* by the clerks who performed the survey, due to either a regional variation or a survey error. Among the other important craftsman groups are *abacı* (coarse woolen cloth maker), *bükücü* (twister), *hallaççı* (cotton or wool comber), *hasırcı* (mat maker), *kazzaz* (silk manufacturer), *keçeci* (felt maker), *muytab* (goat woolen cloth maker), *penbeci* (cotton dealer), and *tiftikçi* (mohair dealer). We are able to define *muytab* as the craftsman who produced material out of hair (also called *mutaf* or *mutafçı* by the public). We have used the word "maker" above, but the translation can also be "seller." The information does not reveal whether the region had a native weaving industry or not, although the abundance of looms in Erzurum is well known.[26] We cannot tell from the registers whether the native weaving industry in Erzurum served domestic or international demand.

(2) Production of Garments

Those in the business of ready-made cloth, with 165 households, made up approximately 5.1% of the heads of households. They included the *bezzaz* (cloth seller), *terzi* (tailor), *yemenici* (seller of coloured cotton handkerchief), *peştemalcı* (seller of large bath towels), *ihramcı* (seller of *ihram*, a seamless garment worn by pilgrims in Mecca), *şalcı* (seller of shawls), *şilteci* (seller of thin mattresses), *gaytancı* (maker of woolen braid lace), *hayyat* (tailor), *yorgancı* (quilt maker), and *tikeciler* (patch maker).

(3) Production of Leather Goods

As the city still maintained its importance in stockbreeding, craftsmen producing and selling leather goods occupied a considerable place. With 337 households, they constituted 10.6% of the heads of households. Most of them were *dikici* (sewers) and *debbağ* (tanners). Tanners had changed the raw leather into *sahtiyan* (Morocco leather), *meşin* (leather in general, roan), or *kösele* (stout leather) and dyed these according to market demand. After that they sold their goods to craftsmen in the leather business. Tanners in the city had plenty of assistants, including *kalfa* (assistant master), *çırak* (apprentice), *şakird* (inexperienced apprentice), *perdahçı* (polisher, burnisher), and *kethüda* (steward). We know that tanners were working in five tanneries, in the quarters of Boyahane, Kumludere, Tebrizkapısı, Kebir

---

26 Şevket Pamuk, *Osmanlı Ekonomisinde Bağımlılık ve Büyüme (1820-1913)*, Istanbul, 1994, p. 129.

Gürcükapısı and Sagîr Gürcükapısi.[27] *Kethüda*, who seemed to belong to the tanners in the documents, was probably one of those in charge, as head of the administrative committee formed during the first stages of the craftsman organizations.[28]

Among the related occupations were such craftsmen as *sarraç* (saddler), *haffaf* (shoemaker), *mestçi* (maker of light thin-soled boots worn indoors or inside shoes), *çarıkçı* (maker of sandals), *kürkçü* (furrier), *çizmeci* (boots maker), *papuççu* (shoemaker), *kayışçı* (belt maker), *na'linci* (clog maker), *meşinci* (roan seller), *göncü* (saddler, leather worker), *na'alçacı* (maker of the iron tip on a boot), and so forth.

(4) Metal Workers

Another craftsman group, fewer in number but significant as to what they did, produced the raw material for the craftsmen who produced and sold metal commodities. This group had 118 households, and of these the craftsmen who processed and sold raw material included *bakırcı* (coppersmith), *demirci* (blacksmith), *nalbant* (farrier), *tenekeci* (tinsmith) and *dökümcü* (founder, metal worker). Other craftsmen were *barutçu* (gunpowder maker) who produced material for the war industry; *çinici* (tile maker), who produced decorative items; *kavcı* (punk seller); and *kömürcü* (coal dealer), who produced flammable substances. We can also cite *palancı*, who produced harnessing equipment for the animals; *rişmeci*, who produced the bit (of a bridle) out of chain for horses; and the *mukavvacı*, who produced paper.

(5) Production of Implements and Tools

With 151 households, the group producing implements and tools constituted 4.7% of the heads of households. They manufactured practical tools and home utensils. *Baltacı* (ax maker) is important in this group. Among the craftsmen who produce and sell cutting tools are *bıçakçı* (knife maker), *kılıççı* (sword maker), *usturacı* (razor maker), and *çakıcı* (pocketknife maker). Those who sharpened these tools were called *bileyci* (knife grinder). In addition, this group includes *kibritçi* and *tüfenkçi*, who deal with the production of flammable and burning substances; *kuyumcu* (jeweler), who produced and sold ornamental items; *lüleci* (pipe bowl maker), who

27 ML. CRD, no. 1146, p. 3.

28 Mehmet Genç, "Osmanlı Esnafı ve Devletle İlişkileri," in *Ahilik ve Esnaf 1*, Esnaf ve Sanatkarlar Dernekleri Yayınları, Istanbul, 1986, p. 116.

processed the *lületaşı* (meerschaum); *saatçi* (clockmaker) and *yüzükçü* (ring maker); *çömlekçi* (pottery maker), who produced items to hold food and drink; *fıçıcı* (barrel maker); *kazancı* (cauldron maker); *kırbacı* (water skin maker); *sandıkçı* (chest maker); *koltukçı* (chair maker); *şişeci* (bottle maker) and *zenbilci* (rush basket maker); *kepçeci* (hardware maker); *kantarcı* (steelyard maker); *mumcu* (candle maker), who produced and sold illuminating substances; *kaltakçı* (maker of the lower parts of a saddle); *kundakçı*, who produced the wooden parts of the guns; *oturakçı*, who presumably produced seats or chamber pots for little children and the old or infirm; *raftar*, who we believe produced and sold cupboards to keep objects; and *sabuncu*, who produced and sold soaps.

(6) Production of Victuals

Those who produce and sell foodstuffs make up another craftsman organization that facilitates social life and accelerates trade. With 374 households, they constitute 11.8% of the heads of households in Erzurum. Craftsmen producing foodstuffs present a great variety, including the *alaftar*, who produce and sell varieties of provisions; *uncu* (or *dakik-füruş*; seller of flour); *kahve bayii* (coffee dealer); and *yemişçi* (seller of fresh fruit).

Among those who process provisions for use are *asiyabcı* (miller), *kahve döğücü* (coffee pounder), *ekmekçi* (bread seller), *fırıncı* (baker), *uncu* (seller of flour), and *attar* (herbalist). Among those who sold readymade foodstuffs were the *bakkal* (grocer), *buzcu* (ice transporter), *limoncu* (lemon seller), *manav* (greengrocer), *sergici* (keeper of a stall for the sale of goods), and *şerbetçi* (seller of sweet drinks). Others are *çeyrekçi* (seller of meat products);[29] *kasap* (butcher); *kebapçı* (seller of roasted meat); *çubukçu*, who produced the pipes good for smoking tobacco in the palaces and mansions; *duhancı* (producer and seller of varieties of tobacco); and finally the various craftsmen performing jobs such as *enfiyeci* (snuff seller); *aşçı* (cook); *ayrancı* (maker or seller of a drink made from yogurt); *kahveci* (coffee dealer, owner of coffeehouse); *sucu* (water-carrier, a seller of potable water), and *sebzevatçı* (seller of vegetables). Occupations such as *bakkal* (grocer),

---

[29] *Çeyrekçi* is the name given to the foot butchers selling meat in the markets. It is a deteriorated form of the word *çeyrek*, which means 1/4 in the Persian language. This name was given due to the fact that they usually sold 1/4 of the sheep. (M. Zeki Pakalın, *Osmanlı Tarih Deyimleri ve Terimleri Sözlüğü*, Vol. 1, Istanbul, 1993, p. 361)

duhancı, and *alaftar* made up a substantial proportion of the population. These occupations were well distributed between Muslims and non-Muslims in proportion to the number of each in the population. It is noteworthy, however, that in Erzurum those who produced bread (*ekmekçi*), the basic food of the populace, were always non-Muslims.

(7) Transportation and Communication

Those who dealt with transportation and communication were vital to the continuity of commercial life and made up a considerable proportion of the working population. Not surprisingly, this city had a multitude of transporters, situated as it was at the meeting point of the Eastern and Western trade routes. With 117 households, craftsmen dealing with transportation constitute 3.7% of the heads of households. This group was composed of *deveci* (camel driver); *himarcı* (donkey driver); *herbendeci* (muleteer); as well as *katırcı* (muleteer), who dealt with the care, breeding, rent and sale of animals used in transportation; *kervancı*, who dealt with organization of the transportation; and *kiracı*, who transported commercial commodities (the experts of the craftsmen who worked as a guide for the caravans). Of the craftsmen cited above, a few did the same job but had different job titles.

(8) Tradesmen

The various types of tradesmen important to commercial life totaled 231 persons, 7.2% of the heads of households. Many of these tradesmen were *çerçiler*. Peddlers, selling all kinds of small items and exchanging commodities, could be encountered in almost every quarter. A second group was the tradesmen, who were cited in registers as "*ticaretle uğraşmakta olan*" (people engaged in trade) or "*tacir*" (tradesman) in general. Two European merchants were in this group, one a privileged (*beratlü*) merchant recognized by the Ottoman government. *Eskici* was the name given to tradesmen who bought and sold all kinds of worn-out items. Other tradesmen specialized as merchants for particular animals, for example, *Koyun tüccarı* (sheep), *koyuncu* (sheep), *celepçi* (cattle), and *sağmalcı* (milch-giving animals). Other tradesmen included *tavukçu*, who dealt with buying and selling animals; *zahire-fürus*, who dealt with the trade of wheat and cereal grains; *çiçekçi* (florist); *gülcü* (rose dealer); and *tohumcu* (seed dealer), who dealt with horticulture; *hatab-füruş* or *oduncu*, who sold firewood; *hurdacı* (scrap dealer), who sold worn out but usable items of all kinds; *hırdavatçı* (hardware seller); *köşeci,* who changed money or carried out small transactions with his drawer in the streets or at the corners of shops; *köhneci* (dealer in secondhand or antiquated wares); *sermaye tüccarı* (capital merchant), who we believe received or paid out interest in return for money; and *samancı* (fodder dealer), who sold animal food. This great variety of occupations constituted the commercial potential of the city.

(9) Others

Erzurum, a frontier town that had experienced outward migrations, has also attracted population from other regions of the country as one of the prominent trade and business centers of the nineteenth century. *Müste'cir* (tenants) who came to the city from other regions constituted 58 of the heads of households. Most were Muslims, living in the Hasan Bahri and Müderris Efendi Quarters and engaged in various occupations. Also, for 97 assistant masters, apprentices and workers no occupational specialties were mentioned in the registers.

Civil Servants and Miscellaneous Occupations

(1) Military and Administrative Occupations

Those charged with military or administrative duty occupied a considerable place, being 221 in number and 6.9% of the heads of households. Among these were 42 soldiers in charge in the Asâkir-i Nizamiye Army, including *beybaşı, binbaşı* (major), *teğmen* (lieutenant), *onbaşı* (corporal), *çavuş* (sergeant), *bölge emini* (custodian), *müdür* (director), *mülazım* (lieutenant), *tabur katibi* (battalion clerk), *topçu yüzbaşı* (gunner captain), *tüfenk-endaz* (musketeer), and so forth. In addition, there were 32 higher army officers. Also in military service were *sancaktar* (standard bearer), *sipahi* (cavalry soldier), *timarlı* (one who has a fief), *kolağası* (adjutant major), *topçu* (gunner), *tüfenkçi başı* (head of the guard).

Those charged with the security of the city include *rahtar*s (served at the Customs and important passages), *zaptiye* (gendarmerie), *süvari zaptiyesi* (cavalry gendarmerie), *bostancılar* (worked as wardens in the vineyards and gardens), *kavvas* (doorkeeper of a big establishment), *korucu* (guard, watchman), and *cizye kolcusu* (watchman for the *cizye* taxation, responsible for protection of the tax collectors). The *muhzır* and *muhzırbaşı,* who guarded state officials of higher ranks, were also among those in charge.

Administrators included in the provincial organization after Tanzimat were *kaza müdürü* (*kaza* chief), *nüfus nazırı* (superintendent of population survey, answerable for the organization and execution of the census), *su nazırı* (superintendent of the distribution of water, responsible for the distribution of water), *muhtar* (headman of quarter), and *müfettiş* (inspector). *Tahmis mültezimi*s were responsible for collecting taxes for coffee and similar items. *İhtisapçı*s and *ihtisap memuru*s were responsible for the control of prices and the maintenance of security of commercial districts. Their activities indicate the liveliness of the city's commercial life.

Some high officials had titles in the central government, for example, *dergah-ı ali kapıcıbaşısı* (head of the palace doorkeepers), *hacegan-ı divan-ı hümayun* (the department chief of the Imperial chancery), *enderun ağası* (eunuch of the Sultan's palace), and *kapıcı* (doorkeepers in the Sultan's court).[30] The existence of *şehbenderlik* in Erzurum, changed into the mission of consulate in the nineteenth century, and the fact that it represented the Shah of Iran was an indication of the city's strategic position.

As other administrative officials, we can cite *tatar* (courier, especially a state courier, who worked as a messenger or postman), *gümrükçü* (customs official in charge at the Customs), *naib* (substitute judge), *mahkeme başkatibi* (head of the clerks in a court), and *yazıcı* and *katip* (clerks).

(2) Occupations Related to Religious, Educational and Social Services

We include 268 heads of household in this category, of whom 103 heads of households were in religious and educational positions. This rather small number seems to indicate that Erzurum did not have as many religious and educational institutions, compared with their population.

The most important occupation was *imam* (prayer leader) of a mosque, because each one was both the religious and the secular leader of the quarter where the mosque was located.[31] *Müezzinbaşı* (head of the *müezzin*s), and *müezzin* (one who calls Muslims to prayer) also worked in mosques. The

---

30 *Kapıcılık* (doorguard) was a term used at one time for those in charge in the palace but later given to those permanently in charge in the provinces. This occupation survived until 1908. (İ. H. Uzunçarşılı, *Osmanlı Devleti'nin Saray Teşkilâtı*, Ankara, 1988, pp. 396-407).

31 For more detailed information refer to Ziya Kazıcı, "Osmanlılar'da Mahalle İmamlarının Bazı Görevleri," *İslam Medeniyeti Mecmuası*, Vol. 5, no. 3, Istanbul, 1982, pp. 29-35.

müderris (madrasah professor)[32] was fundamental to education in the city, as was the *mektep hocası* (teacher), whose presence suggested the existence of institutions supplying Western-style education. We can also list people who were engaged in religious or educational occupation, such as *ders-i am* (teacher), *emin-i fetva* (custodian of fatwa, an opinion on legal matters), *erbab-ı kitap* (expert on books), *fakih* (expert on the canon law of Islam), *hattat* (calligrapher), *hafiz* (one who knows the whole Quran by heart), *keşiş* (monk), *müftü* (official expounder of the Islamic Law), *muallim-i sıbyan* (male teacher of small children), *muallime-i sıbyan* (female teacher of small children), and the students.

We also include the following occupations related to urban social services in this category: *tellal* (town crier), *arzuhalci* (writer of petitions), *ayak tellali* (wandering town crier), *cami-i kitabet hizmetkarı* (mosque attendant), *ferraş* (cleaner of mosques), *kilise hizmetkarı* (verger of a church), watchman in and around the city (*bağbekçisi, bağçeci, gececi, solak* etc.), *paspan* or *pazvant* (quarter watchman), garbage collectors (*çöpçü, mezbe temizleyici* or *zibilci*), musicians (*davulcu, çalgıcı, kaval çalgıçısı, zurnacı* and *sazendar*), dervish, *saka* (water carrier), *sandık emini* (treasurer), and so forth. The number of heads of household engaged in these social services is 163.

Those with No Jobs

Our final information about the composition of occupations relates to heads of households who have no jobs. People who seem not to belong to any particular occupation are 354 households making up 11.09% of the households. They are also almost entirely Muslim; in the non-Muslim quarters, relatively fewer heads of households had no jobs. Only eight non-Muslim households lived on donations.

The jobless were of two groups. First, 137 households were completely jobless and sustained themselves on the donations of others, or as official beneficiaries of religious foundations. They included the aged, sheikhs, dervishes, widows, children registered as *sabi* (infant, male child), beggars,

32 According to a decree promulgated on 25 June 1840, *müderris* (professors) who were formerly subject to taxation would no longer be taxed provided they were sustaining themselves on the donations of the others. (Cevdet–Maliye, no. 23670).

fakir (poor man), *mecnun* (the insane), *yetim* (orphan), and others. As for the beneficiaries of religious foundations, they included students in the madrasah, *evkaf mütevellisi* (trustee of a foundation), *fakih* (expert on the canon law of Islam), *mevali-i kiram* (chief judges), *nakşibendi tarikatı hülefası* (deans of the Nakşibendi sect), and others.

The remaining 217 households were those with no jobs but holding considerable real estate. Rather wealthy people had property inherited from their forefathers.

4. Movable and Immovable Properties

The Erzurum Temettuat registers show that urban residents owned considerable urban real estate, agricultural land in the city, and livestock.

Urban Real Estate

In its building types, Erzurum was not much different from the other Ottoman cities. Table 3 lists these types for the 493 buildings registered as properties of urban residents of Erzurum.

Table 3: Buildings

Type of buildings	Number
shop (*dükkan*)	265
house (*hane, ev*)	78
rental lodging (*kirahane etc.*)	49
flour mill (*asiyab*)	22
coffeehouse (*kahvehane*)	16
halting place (*menzil*)	11
inn (*han*)	10
tannery (*debbağhane*)	7
vakıf property	9
rental room (*oda*)	5
bakery (*fırın*)	4
public bath (*hamam*)	3
stable (*ahır*)	3
workshop (*kerhane*)	2
others	9
Total	493

The number of shops (*dükkan*), expected to be high, was actually low during this period; nonetheless, they were approximately 53.8% of the 493 city buildings.[33] Some shops were shared by several persons. Of the shops in the city, nine qualified as *kepenk*, which means large pull-down shutter.

From the registers, we can get some information about shops and other buildings donated to pious foundations: Shops in the Gülahmed Quarter were donated as properties of the pious foundation to maintain a public fountain in the Kavak Quarter. Four shops belonged to the pious foundation of Şeyhler Camii. On behalf of heads of households in the Yoncalık-ı Süflâ Quarter, 14 shops belonging to the pious foundation of Kundakçı Camii were registered. A shop in the Erzurum Quarter belonged to the foundation of Misafir Camii. Beside these shops included in the "shop" category of Table 3, nine other *vakıf* properties, of which the types of buildings are not known, are found in the registers.

*Han*s (inns) in the city were usually in the Muslim quarters. The city had ten inns, of which four had no shares and five had half shares.[34] Two of the four inns in the Şeyhler Quarter had half shares. One of the inns owned by a resident of the city was situated in the Ali Paşa Quarter, with its predominantly non-Muslim population. Two other inns belonged to the pious foundations of Şeyhler Camii and Murad Paşa Camii. Pervizoğlu Hanı, located in the city of Erzurum but not cited in the Temettuat registers, was one of the most important activities in the commercial life in the city. It was probably in ruins when the Temettuat surveys were being made. Later, Iranian tradesmen repaired this inn.

As is shown above, ownership of inns was generally in the form of shares. The heads of households who lived in the Caferiye Quarter had nine pieces of shares of Gazzaz-zade Hanı; eight were half shares, and the other was a full share. One share of Gazzaz-zade Hanı belonged to a person who lived in the Boyahane Quarter. Those who lived in the Çukur Quarter had one half share of Gazaz-zade Han and an uncertain real estate share of the pious foundation of Kızılbey. Heads of households who lived in the Hasan Bahri Quarter, we found, had two half shares of the inn of Sinanoğlu and those in the Kadana Quarter had one. Those who lived in the Namervanlı Camii Quarter had one share of inns of Zorlu-zade and Mazlum Ağa.

---

33 In the sixteenth century, Erzurum had 277 shops. For the number of these and other buildings refer to Dündar Aydın, *op. cit.*, pp. 107-8.

34 The number of inns mentioned is indicated as 17. (ML. CRD, no. 1146, p. 4)

The 22 flour mills owned by urban residents were recorded as "*asiyab*."[35] Most were located in the villages surrounding Erzurum. Only three of them belonged to Armenians. Three mills were devoted to mosques, two to the Şeyhler Camii and one to the Murad Paşa Camii. All four *fırın* (bakeries) in the city belonged to Muslims.[36] Two of these bakeries were with half shares, one in the Ali Paşa Quarter with its medium population and the other in the Topçuoğlu Quarter.

The dwellings (*hane*) in which the taxpayers lived were registered as totaling 78. One such house was reported to be an "*ev*." On the other hand, five houses in the Şeyhler Quarter were devoted to the pious foundation of the Murat Paşa Quarter. We do not have any documents with information about the other houses.

Of the seven *debbağhane* (tanneries) in the city, six were in the Yeğen Ağa Quarter, and one tannery share was registered in the Kasım Paşa Quarter.[37] These tanneries belonged to Muslims.

*Hamam*s (baths) were among the indispensable factors of social life; we can identify only three of them, all belonging to pious foundations and located in the Şeyhler Quarter.[38] A share of the Gedik Hamamı was also registered, on behalf of the pious foundation of the Murad Paşa Camii. The person who managed it was living in the Erzurum Quarter.

The city had 16 *kahvehane*s (coffeehouses), one of which was registered on behalf of the owners, who lived in the Kadana Quarter; this coffeehouse was in Gülahmed Çarşısı. It is also known that a coffeehouse with half share in Erzincankapısı was registered on behalf of residents of the Vani Efendi Quarter. These coffeehouses were located in Muslim quarters and also run by Muslims.

---

35 In 1881, the city had 36 mills (*Salname-i Vilayet-i Erzurum*, Year 1299, p. 157).

36 The 1847 census recorded 28 mills in the city, located in quarters such as Mahallebaşı, Tebrizkapısı, Gülbaşı, Sarayönü, Arapkirler, Erzincankapısı, Nazikçarşısı, Gülahmed, Hasan Basri and Mumcu-i Süflâ (ML. CRD, no. 1146, p. 2).

37 According to the census of the year 1847, however, they were located in the quarters of Boyahane, Kumludere, Tebriz Kapısı, Kebir Gürcükapısı and Sagîr Gürcükapısı, as mentioned above.

38 In the year 1881, there were 17 baths in the city. *Salname-i Vilayet-i Erzurum*, p. 154.

Two *kârhane* (workshops), qualified as *kerhane* (in the colloquial language), were located in the Mumcu-i Süflâ Quarter in which the Armenian community lived. The number of these may possibly be greater, but the registers have no further information. Oddly enough, there was no information regarding the existence of *meyhane* buildings (taverns). This being the case, we are able to assume that the term *karhane* was used instead of the term *meyhane* in the Temettuat survey in Erzurum.[39] In this case, the use of the term might be due to the clerks.

Of the 49 real estate properties owned for rental, nine belonged to Armenians, and three of the nine were recorded as *kirahane* (rental lodging). The clerks should have used the term *menzil*, meaning the place where a family lives (a dwelling). Eleven buildings qualified as *menzil*. With the exception of two *menzils* belonging to Muslims and qualified as foundations, non-Muslims owned them. Three were *icarede*, that is, let out for rent.

Odalar (rooms), presumably used as small-business locations, totaled five, all belonging to Muslims. One was found to be a *dikici odası* (sewer's room). Another belonged to a household living in the quarter of Hanım Hamamı Mescidi, located in the marketplace (*çarşı*) of Arapkirli. Two others were registered on behalf of the residents of the Vani Efendi Quarter and were somewhere around Gürcükapısı.

We can also list one *kiremidhane* (tile factory) recorded in the Erzurdum Quarter and belonging to Armenians who were Catholicized, as well as two *mereks*, one *maranhane*, and one *güm* (or *kem*) in which fodder, hay and similar animal food was kept. It was stated that although the owner of the *güm* lived in the city, the building itself was in the *kaza* of Tercan. One *sabunhane* (soap manufactory) in the marketplace of Artuk was registered in the Ali Paşa Quarter, and a *muytaphane* (workshop for hair rope maker) in the Topçuoğlu Quarter.

Agriculture Land in the City

Only a few agricultural lands are registered on behalf of urban residents. These lands were classified in two ways. The first classification, based on area, used the units of measure "*kıt'a*" and "*dönüm,*" and the second, based on the weight of the produce from the fields, used "*samar*" and "*kot.*" The

---

[39] In the year 1881, there were 16 *meyhane* (taverns) in the city (*Salname-i Vilayet-i Erzurum*, Year 1299, p. 154).

clerks applied these terms at the scene of the survey, thus making it difficult for us to calculate the total amount of agricultural land by types of land use. But, having accepted these units as basic, we found 84 *kot*,[40] 251.5 *samar*, 192.5 *kıt'a*, and 886.5 *dönüm* of land in the city. The lands in question can be classified as *mezru tarla* (cultivated field), *gayrımezru tarla* (uncultivated field), *bostan* (vegetable garden), *çayır* (pasture), *çehrilik*, *bağ* (garden), and *yoncalık* (field in which weeds of good quality are grown).

Cultivated lands available for agriculture were composed of 189 *samar*, 84 *kot*, 50 *kıt'a* and 145 *dönüm*. These lands comprised 74.1% of the land as *samar*, 100% as *kot*, 26.0% as *kıt'a*, and 16.4% as *dönüm*. For uncultivated lands, the produce was not mentioned in the registers, but the number and measures of units given were probably followed. They were composed of 62.5 *samar* and 278 *dönüm*; they comprised 24.9% of the lands as *samar* and 31.4% as *dönüm*.

The fields spread throughout the city, with no indication of the kind of agriculture applied therein, were 46 *kıt'a* and 43.5 *dönüm*; those designated as *kıt'a* constituted 23.9% of the whole *kıt'a* land, and those indicated as *dönüm* made up 4.9% of that land.

Bostan (vegetable gardens) were another type of land. With 17.5 *kıt'a* and 10 *dönüm*, their ratio of the total land was 9.1% as *kıt'a*, 1.1% as *dönüm*. *Çayır* (pastures) were fields in which grass was grown to be cut and animals grazed. With 76 *kıt'a*, they were 39.5% of the total land as *kıt'a*.

The fields called "*yoncalık*," rarely found in the city, were in the Erzurum Quarter; with two *kıt'a* and six *dönüm*, they constituted 1.03% of the total land as *kıt'a*, 0.68% of it as *dönüm*.

The Erzurum Quarter had 241 *dönüm* of *bağ* for vegetable gardens (6 *dönüm* of them not available for agriculture); this was 27.2% of the whole *dönüm* land. Nevertheless, the Temettuat registers give no information about

---

40 A document belonging to the *ta'şirat* (pertaining to tithing) in the city of Erzurum in the year 1846 states that four *kot*s were one *kile* (A. MKT. UM, no. 99/42). Also, in the second of two *vakfiye* (deed of a trust of a pious foundation) belonging to the Kağızmanlızadeler, published by Kırzıoğlu, four *kot*s of wheat is stated to be equal to 96.5 kg. Consequently, we can estimate 1 kot as 24.1 kg. Refer to M. Fahrettin Kırzıoğlu, "1753 ve 1846 Yıllarında Erzurum Çarşıları ile Esnafını tanıtan Kağızmanlızadelerin İki Vakfiyesi," *Atatürk Üniversitesi Edebiyat Fakültesi Araştırmaları Dergisi*, no. 7, 1976, p. 63. As for *samar*, it is known one *samar* equaled to 386 kg in the *kaza* of Tercan in the Erzurum Province.

the products grown in the fields. *Çehrilik* fields (whose function we still do not understand) with 106 *dönüm* constituted 12.0% of the total *dönüm* land.

All landowners were Muslims, and non-Muslims had no land except the households they lived in.[41] The people who owned cultivated land in the city numbered 572. The remaining 2618 consist of people without their own land and those owning only very little land, not enough for farming. These were 82% of 3190 households.

As a matter of fact, it is understood that the land suitable for large-scale production within the city of Erzurum was owned only by heads of households living in the Erzurum Quarter. The rest of the land had a disintegrated configuration that would not allow sufficient production. In the Erzurum Quarter, 25 heads of households owned land scaled between one and 10 *dönüm*, 10 heads owned 11 to 50 *dönüm*, and two heads owned more than 50 *dönüm*, for a total of 451 *dönüm*.

It is possible that a great variety of produce was grown in the city of Erzurum, including wheat, barley, millet, chickpea, rye, potato, walnut, apple, pear, cherry, morello, mulberry, quince, melon, water melon, almond, hazel-nut, broad bean, bean, olive, *duhan* (tobacco), and *çerviş* (inferior cooking fat).[42] From our studies in the Temettuat registers, however, we are sure of only two such products, wheat and barley.

Stockbreeding

Erzurum was until recently one of the leading centers for stockbreeding.[43] These registers, however, record rather few livestock, 3661. In 1845, cows (*inek*) constituted the bulk of the livestock, numbering about 1500 in 42 quarters of the city. Livestock such as sheep and goats were also numerous, 1256 and 72 respectively. On the other hand, there were only 152 buffalo (*câmûs*). Some animals were used for transportation, most often the donkey. The young, sterile, and male of each kind of animal were recorded using

---

41 Haydar Çoruh, *Temettüat Defterlerine göre Erzurum Şehri*, Master thesis of Istanbul University (unpublished), 1997, p. 83.

42 *Salname-i Vilayet-i Erzurum*, Year 1288, p. 154.

43 Ramazan Özey, "Fırat-Karasu Kaynakları Çevresindeki Kırsal Yerleşmelerin Başlıca Sosyo Ekonomik Sorunları ve Çözüm Yolları/Erzurum Merkez İlçesi ve Çevresi,"*Atatürk Üniv. Fen-Edebiyat Fakültesi Edebiyat Bilimleri Araştırmaları Dergisi*, no. 18, 1990, pp. 213-14.

peculiar names in the registers. They were not included in the number of cows, buffaloes, and sheep, mentioned above.

The total of 3661 animals included those used in transportation or valued as expensive in the markets, for example, black cattle cow, goat, sheep, buffalo, *moziga* (known as *mozik* in the city and a kind of cow yielding very little milk, bred for its meat and found in the Eastern Black Sea Region), Angora goat, horse, calf (not weaned), camel (female camel), *camus ineği* (water buffalo cow) used in traction, female heifer, female young of water buffalo, sterile cow, sterile mare, sterile water buffalo, sterile donkey, heifer, horse, donkey, hair-goat, sterile cow, mare, lamb, kid, ox, colt, *tosun* (young bull), and male donkey.[44]

The distribution of animals by community was 191 of the 3661 animals to Armenians, 33 to Catholics, and the remainder to Muslims.

The above data seem to indicate that stockbreeding did not occupy an important place in the city. The sheep and similar animals, which supposedly constituted a considerable number in the city, were actually fewer than one would expect. We can estimate that approximately one of every two households owned one sheep. Cows, intended as a significant commercial export commodity, were the same. For the entire city, two households would average hardly one cow.

The number of beasts of burden reared to maintain the commercial liveliness of the city was also lower than one would expect. Donkeys, primarily, carried out transportation. The number of camels was only 13. To find only 13 horses as saddle beasts in a city of 3190 households is also amazing. The city of Erzurum should have had many more horses, as it not only had commercial importance but also an important strategic military position.

---

44 In the Temettuat registers, 3,661 livestock were listed. On the other hand, a source belonging to the year 1871 cites 30,100 oxen, 5,944 water buffaloes, 3,195 *moziks*, 26,800 cows, 10,422 mares, 4,387 colts, and so forth in the *kaza* of Erzurum. (Refer to *Salname-i Vilayet-i Erzurum*, Year 1299, p. 156.)

5. Economic Conditions

Distribution of Income

The total income of the city of Erzurum registered in 1845 was recorded as 866,739.5 *kuruş*. Before we continue presenting distribution of revenue with respect to the sources of income, we will first look at the general income level by population distribution. Table 4 shows percentages for the Muslim and non-Muslim population for incomes at various levels, from no income at all to more than 701 *kuruş*.

Table 4: Income Distribution

Amount of income (in *kuruş*)	Total	Muslim	non-Muslim
(no income at all)	8.9	8.4	0.5
1 to 100	18.4	16.6	1.8
101 to 200	36.3	29.1	7.2
201 to 300	16.5	11.7	4.8
301 to 400	8.0	1.7	--
401 to 500	3.8	3.2	0.6
501 to 600	2.2	2.2	--
601 to 700	1.5	1.2	0.3
more than 701	4.4	3.4	1.0
Total	100.0%	82.1%	17.9%

Distribution of Income according to the Sources of Revenue

As shown in Table 5, the sources of income of the urban residents of Erzurum included agriculture, stockbreeding, craftsmanship and trade, rental income, salaries, and other less significant sources.

People were able to earn 562,575.5 *kuruş* in various kinds of craftsmanship and trade, which was 64.9% of annual income in the city.

Agricultural income, another slice of the income total, was 52,045.5 *kuruş*, 6.0% of annual income. The income derived from arable fields (*tarla*) was approximately 3.4% of total income; from the vineyards and gardens (*bağ ve bağçe*), 0.5%; and from agricultural activities performed "*ortak*"

Table 5: Income According to the Sources of Revenue

Types of income	*kuruş*	%
Agriculture	52,045.5	6.0
Stockbreeding	77,058.0	8.9
Craftsmanship and trade	562,576.5	64.9
Rental revenue	60,555.5	7.0
Salary	69,365.0	8.0
Other	45,139.0	5.2
Total	866,739.5	100.0

(shared), 0.9%. Stockbreeding was 8.9% of annual total income, at 77,058 *kuruş*.

Rental income came from real estate such as shops, *hane* (houses), *asiyab* (mill), bakeries, and so forth. At 60,555.5 *kuruş*, this revenue made up 7.0% of the total income. Of that amount and percentage, 85.7% was from urban buildings like shops and houses and an additional 14.3% was from land rent.

Salaries from occupations were 69365.0 *kuruş* and constituted 8.0% of total revenue. The revenue identified as *zuhurat*, for which we have no clear definition with respect to register content, totals 45,139 *kuruş* and was 5.2% of annual income.

Distribution of the Sources of Income with Respect to Occupational Groups

The population of the city divides into five distinct groups with respect to the occupational types presented in an earlier section of this paper. The income of each group is as below.

Whereas the craftsmen and tradesmen, builders, and workers were deriving more than 80% of their annual income from their own work (namely, craftsmanship, tradesmanship or wages for labor), both those listed as dealing with agriculture and stockbreeding and the civil servants in charge in Erzurum were deriving more of their income from second and third sources such as rent, agricultural activities, or trade.

The income of the 66 households who dealt with agriculture and stockbreeding was 26,632.5 *kuruş*; 9.0% of this was agricultural revenue and

Table 6: Types of Occupation and Their Income

Types of occupation	Number	Total incomes (*kuruş*)	(%)
Those who deal with agriculture and stockbreeding	66	26632.5	3.1%
Builders and physical laborers	462	94587	10.9%
Craftsmen and tradesmen	1819	438663.5	50.7%
Civil servants and other occupations, military and administrative occupations	221	126370	14.6%
Occupations related to religious, educational, and social services	268	52784	6.1%
Those with no occupation	354	126803	14.6%
Total	3190	865840	100%

16.1% was from stockbreeding. But the most important source of income for this group was from craftsmanship and tradesmanship, which constituted 69.9% of their annual income. Because the city land was in small patches and was insufficient, those who constitute this group had to work in those aspects of craftsmanship and tradesmanship related to agriculture and stockbreeding as well as in agriculture itself. Additional income came from the rental income of land and other miscellaneous revenue

Other occupational groups worked in education, religion and miscellaneous similar occupations. These groups have approximately 268 households, with an annual income of 52,784 *kuruş*. The income they earned from craftsmanship and trade constituted 28.9% of their annual income. In addition, they had agriculture and stockbreeding income as well (5.4%). Also, miscellaneous income, a great amount with 12,924 *kuruş*, made up 24.5% of their income. Total salary from the state was 12,943.5 *kuruş*, and their share was 24.5%. *İmam* and *müderris* received most of these salaries. A large proportion of the income of the experts of this occupation was rental income: 11.4% of the rental income (6,054 *kuruş*).

Those who worked in the military and administrative fields had 221 households, and their annual income was 126.370 *kuruş*, of which 4.5% was derived from agricultural income, 4.0% from arable field agriculture, and 5.1% from stockbreeding. The occupations of craftsmanship and tradesmanship participated in by state employees also working in the military and administrative fields occurred during the eighteenth and nineteenth centuries. For military and administrative personnel, the annual ratio of income received by those who dealt in trade was approximately 40.5%; they also got a ratio of 3.5% from miscellaneous other opportunities. The income obtained by the members of this occupation from their salaries in return for their duties was less than the income they received from craftsmanship and trade; it constituted 30.5% of their annual income, with rental income, another source of income, constituting 15.9% annually.

The total of those with no jobs and no particular occupation, recorded only by their names in the registers, totaled 354 households; the total annual income obtained by this group, however, reached 126,803 *kuruş*, 14.6% of all income. This category not only includes completely jobless people but also those such as sheik, dervish, *sabi* (infant, male child), women, those who sustain themselves on the donations of others, and people who had some kind of real estate for rent. Their most important sources of income were stockbreeding and agriculture. Also, even though heads of households in this category do not have an occupation, they did have income derived from craftsmanship and tradesmanship one way or another. The most important source of income of those with no jobs, however, was rental income.

As a result, we could visualize the social and economic life of the urban residents of Erzurum as multifarious and complicated. In addition to the information above, workers and constructors obtained extra income from agriculture, stockbreeding, and rents; craftsmen d and tradesmen obtained most of their income from rents and *zuhurat*. The income of those who worked for the state remained even less than what they derived from craftsmanship and tradesmanship. The income of those with no jobs, derived primarily from stockbreeding and rental income, constituted a substantial amount.

Distribution of the Income per Household

The 3190 households in the city generated 866,739.5 *kuruş* of income, which averages 271.7 *kuruş* per household. The several quarters, however, show considerable variation (Table 7). The average was 405 *kuruş* in the Abdurrahman Ağa Quarter, which had only Muslim residents, whereas in the Ali Paşa Quarter, where Muslims and non-Muslims lived side by side, the average annual income of Muslim residents was 268.6 *kuruş* and that of non-Muslims was 339.1 *kuruş*. In other quarters, the annual ratios were as

Table 7: Distribution of the Income per Household

Quarter	Number of household	Total income	Average (in *kuruş*)
Abdurrahman Ağa (Muslim)	27	10957	405.8
Ali Paşa (Armenian)	116	39332	339.1
Ali Paşa (Muslim)	111	29812	268.6
Bakırcı (Muslim)	29	6445	222.2
Boyahane (Muslim)	9	8210	912.2
Caferiye (Muslim)	81	31838	393.1
Cami-i Kebir (Muslim)	81	9117	112.6
Cedid (Armenian)	26	7440	286.2
Cedid (Muslim)	96	24354	253.7
Çırçır (Armenian)	10	2400	240.0
Çırçır (Muslim)	61	12187	199.8
Çortanoğlu (Muslim)	15	2690	179.3
Çukur (Muslim)	10	12022	1202.2
Derviş Ağa (Muslim)	45	12945	287.7
Emin Kurbu (Muslim)	49	18840	376.8
Emin Kurbu (Armenian)	142	37414	263.5
Erzurum (Muslim)	48	12306	256.4
Erzurum (Catholic Armenian)	61	11554	189.4
Feyziye (Muslim)	24	4873	203.0
Gez (Muslim)	101	26849	265.8
Habib Efendi-i Süflâ (Muslim)	68	10773	158.4
Habib Efendi-i Ulyâ (Muslim)	65	11007.5	169.3
Hacı Cuma (Muslim)	40	7637	190.9
Hanım Hamamı Mesc.+ Sivasi	20+5	12054	482.2
Hasan Basri (Muslim)	262	43618.5	166.5
Kâbe Mescidi (Muslim)	13	3170	243.8
Kadana (Muslim)	82	23832	290.6
Kal'a Derunu (Armenian)	7	1700	242.9
Kanyolu Ali Paşa (*rum*)	19	2680	141.1
Kasım Paşa (Muslim)	39	9265	237.6
Kavak (Muslim)	21	4600	219.0
Kırmacı (Muslim)	19	4870	256.3
Köse Ömer Ağa (Muslim)	25	8702	348.1
Lala Mustafa Paşa (Muslim)	36	9457	262.7
Müderris Efendi (Muslim)	117	19796.5	169.2
Mumcu-i Süflâ (Armenian)	71	17193	242.2
Mumcu-i Süflâ (Muslim)	85	16310	191.9
Mumcu-i Ulyâ (Muslim)	62	35890	578.9
Mumcu-i Ulyâ (Armenian)	59	12660	214.6
Murad Paşa (Muslim)	134	32830	245.0
Namervanlı Cami-i şerif (Muslim)	30	13840	461.3
Sultan Melik (Muslim)	129	20840	161.6

Şeyh Emir (Muslim)	37	6623	179.0
Şeyhler (Muslim)	36	32527	903.5
Topçuoğlu (Muslim)	99	33617	339.6
Topçuoğlu (Armenian)	7	6150	878.6
Üveys Efendi (Muslim)	88	20183	229.4
Vani Efendi (Muslim)	110	32150	292.3
Yeğen Ağa (Armenian)	54	12575	232.9
Yeğen Ağa (Muslim)	101	28560	282.8
Yoncalık-ı Süflâ (Muslim)	69	40184	582.4
Zağracı Ali Ağa (Muslim)	38	9860	259.5
Total	3190	866739.5	271.7

high as 800-1000 *kuruş*: some examples of averages are 912.2 *kuruş* per household in the Boyahane Quarter, 1,070 *kuruş* in the Sivasi Quarter, and 878.6 *kuruş* for each of the seven Armenian households of the Topçuoğlu Quarter.

Non-Muslims in the other quarters averaged from 100 to 300 *kuruş* annual income, and the Muslim households varied between 200 and 500 *kuruş*. The average income of a Muslim was 281.4 *kuruş* and that of a non-Muslim was 227.8 *kuruş*.

Urban Notables and People with High Income

In all of Erzurum, only 59 persons—from miscellaneous occupations and each with an income of over 1000 *kuruş*—received 20.1% of all the income of the city.

The data show that state officials in charge in the administration or province had the highest incomes. Among them, living in the Mumcu-i Ulyâ Quarter, was a certain Cennet-zade Abdullah Efendi, who was one of the notables of Erzurum and qualified as "Cehennem-zadeler"[45] in a report prepared by a state official. Having served the state in many admirable deeds, he later turned out to be a swindler involved in robberies and usurpation. In the Temettuat register, his annual income was recorded as 21,555 *kuruş*, of which 5000 *kuruş* was a one-fifth dividend of *zeamet* (salary) income supplied in return for the pension of his son, Ziya Efendi, who was a *müderris* (professor). Using the available documents, we can determine that

[45] *Cennet* means heaven, and *cehennem* means hell, in Turkish.

this family had established a close relationship with the state. They even sent valuable products such as olive oil to Istanbul from time to time.[46] According to the note cited in the registration of income and property of Abdullah Ağa in the Temettuat register, it is understood that he had fields and animals in the neighboring villages of Erzurum such as Özbek, Söğütlü, Ürünlü, Sitavuk, Hınıs, and Gez, as well as in Peteriç village in the *kaza* of Tercan; he also had sheep in the Gümler village.

Hacı Abdurrahman Efendi-zade Ibrahim Efendi, the *müderris,* was another of those earning a good income. He lived in the Yoncalık-ı Süflâ Quarter and had 20,000 *kuruş* of income. He received nearly 17,000 *kuruş* of it from *zuhurat* and *akçe murabahası* (silver usury). Kadı-zade Müftü Edhem Efendi, who lived in the Şeyhler Quarter, possessed fields in Özni village besides the property he had in the city, and his total income was 12,562 *kuruş*. (See Appendix IV). Part of his income was 1000 *kuruş* received monthly from the Erzurum Commodity Customs (*Erzurum emtia gümürüğü*).

Among the heads of households with high income, we find the *katip*s (clerks), who presumably dealt with the surveys, and the *şehbender* (consul, in a foreign country) charged with the mission of commercial envoys according to the Treaty of Erzurum signed between Iran and the Ottoman State.[47] The income of the *şehbender* was recorded as 5000 *kuruş*. The income of someone who works as a *müderris* in the madrasahs was 1000 *kuruş*. However, Dursun Efendi, whom we identified as one of these *müderrrise*s, received a considerable amount of his income, 350 *kuruş*, from the Erzurum Commodity Customs monthly. As for the Temettuat records of Ahmed Ağa, who was the trustee of the pious foundation of Kağızmanlı and came from one of Erzurum's well-known families, he had no property on his own behalf but had been handling the restoration and maintenance of immovable property belonging to a woman known as Hatuni Kadın. This property consisted of 29 shops, including 18 shops in good condition and 11 shops in ruins.

Among those having 2000-3000 *kuruş* of income were the *arabacı* (cart driver), *terzi* (tailor), *kundakçı* (gunstock maker), and some of the

---

46 A. AMD, dos. 95/19, 5 Cemaziye'l-evvel 1270H.

47 With respect to the "*şehbender*" (the position of a consul in a foreign country) refer to Bruce Masters, "The Treaties of Erzurum (1823 and 1848) and the Changing Status of Iranians in the Ottoman Empire," *Iranian Studies*, 24/1-4, 1991, p. 13.

non-Muslim tradesmen. Among those having 1000-2000 *kuruş* of income were *celepçi* (cattle merchant), *tüccar* (merchant), *nüfus katibi* (clerk who performed the population survey), two *kavvas* (doorkeepers of a big establishment) who worked as guards, one *hamamcı* (keeper of public bath), sheep merchant, *cambaz* (horse dealer), *süvari zaptiyesi* (cavalry gendarmerie), *zaptiye memuru* (gendarmerie official), *katip* (clerk), *naib* (substitute judge), *oturakçı* producer of chamber pots, *kal'a topçusu* (gunner), *ketan tüccarı* (linen merchant), and *sermaye tüccarı* (capital merchant.)

The most prominent of those we have cited are those whose annual income is high, This information sheds light on the kinds of occupations that are most profitable, as well as on the social conditions of the period and the ratio of this income to its distribution among the communities.

The Types and Amount of the Tax

Erzurum Temettuat registers provide only limited information concerning the tax revenue from Erzurum.

(1) *Vergi-i Mahsusa*

Vergi-i mahsusa (special tax) of 1844, previous year of the Temettuat survey, was recorded in the Temettuat registers for only a few quarters of the city. Therefore, the total amount of *vergi-i mahsusa* was also very small, 23,829 *kuruş*. The tax payments, of Muslim households especially, were hardly noticeable. It appears that the lack of city taxes for most households in Erzurum in the year 1844 was due to certain factors not clearly stated in the registers.

A review of the register for the Kâbe Mescidi Quarter reveals that the taxation the quarter was subject to was not fixed. The beginning of the register explained this as follows: "The tax of the above-mentioned quarter is not registered because the year before they did not have any tax debt."[48] We were able to find an entry explaining this arrangement in an Ottoman archival document[49] that showed the tax debts of 1844 for Muslims in the city of Erzurum as determined in 1843. The entry said the total tax to be collected from Muslims would be 295,000 *kuruş*, 219,080 *kuruş* of which would be from those who had paid annually and 75,920 *kuruş* from those

[48] ML.VRD.TMT, no. 6878, p. 1.

[49] Kamil Kepeci–Varidat Muhasebesi, no. 5938, p. 1.

who had never paid until 1843. The amount of tax to be paid by Muslims was also divided into two categories; that is, 98,737 *kuruş* would be paid in *ruz-ı Hızır* (the spring), and 105,310 *kuruş* in *ruz-ı Kasım* (the autumn). We have no information available as to distribution of taxes to the quarters in the document. But this arrangement might well have caused serious confusion. We can suppose that the reason why the tax of most Muslim households was not recorded in the register was related to these somehow obscure tax arrangements in 1843.

The registers show that only 4565 *kuruş*, out of 23,829 *kuruş* of tax (19.2%) in ten quarters, belonged to Muslims and the rest, 80.8%, to non-Muslims.

Another point that attracts our attention with respect to taxation is its conspicuous injustice. Whereas 140 *kuruş* of tax was collected from a *penbeci* (cotton dealer) whose income was 700 *kuruş*, 52 *kuruş* of tax was collected from a *enfiyeci* (dealer of snuff) with the same amount of income. An Armenian monk who lived in the Kan Yolu Ali Paşa Quarter had to pay 10 *kuruş* in tax, yet a monk living in the Emin Kurbu Quarter was tax-exempt even though he had 70 *kuruş* of annual income. Also, the amount of tax to be collected from 46 households in the Emin Kurbu Quarter was not specified. They should have been tax-exempt like those who live in other quarters. Of the taxes to be paid by Catholics who lived in Erzurum, a tradesman with 1000 *kuruş* of annual income had to pay 200 *kuruş*, yet the taxes to be paid by the rest of tradesmen varied between five and 60 *kuruş*. The amount to be collected from the Armenians varied between 17 and 420 *kuruş*. Finally, for 31 households taxes were not determined.

(2) Tithe

Tithe was a kind of tax collected with respect to products from the land on a set ratio. In Erzurum, only two kinds of products were subject to tithe in 1844, that is, tithe obtained from 54 *kot* of wheat and 106.5 *kot* of barley in kind, and 718 *kuruş* in cash.

With respect to tithe, eight *kot* of wheat was allotted to the Çırçır Quarter; its market price was 40 *kuruş*. From the same quarter 13 *kot* of barley was derived with a market price of 26 *kuruş*. Tithe derived from products grown in the Erzurum Quarter was not in kind but in cash, amounting to 508 *kuruş*. In addition, 200 *kuruş* was collected as *aşar ve koyun rüsumu* (tithe and sheep tax). Tithe collected from the Gez Quarter was 8.5 *kot* of wheat, whose market price was 122.5 *kuruş*; the amount of barley was 16.5 *kot*, with a market price of 36 *kuruş*. The tithe belonging to the Habib Efendi-i Ulyâ Quarter was 14.5 *kot* of wheat, with a market price of 71.5 *kuruş*. Barley from the same quarter was 42.5 *kot*, with a market price of 109.5 *kuruş*. Barley from the Murad Paşa Quarter was eight *kot* with a market price of 17.5 *kuruş*. The Müderris Efendi Quarter provided 15 *kot* of wheat and 15.5 *kot* of barley. The market price of wheat was 75 *kuruş* and that of barley was 35 *kuruş*. Five *kıyye* (*okka*, about 1300 grams) of wheat tithe that cost 10 *kuruş* was collected in kind from the Namervanlı Quarter. Wheat tithe that was collected from the Topçuoğlu Quarter was three *kot*, with a market price of 15 *kuruş*; tithe collected as barley was three *kot*, with a market price of 6.5 *kuruş*. In the Topçuoğlu Quarter, eight *kot* of barley was collected at a market price of 18 *kuruş*.

The price of product varies from quarter to quarter. On average, wheat cost 6.2 *kuruş* per one *kot*. The market price of barley per one *kot* is 2.3 *kuruş*.

(3) *Cizye*

By a decree promulgated in 1833-1834, the revenue derived from the *cizye* collection of the city of Erzurum was allocated to the salaries, monthly allowance, and commutation of rations of the sixteenth infantry regiment of the new army corps of Mahmud II, named *asâkir-i mansûre-i Muhammediye* and deployed in Erzurum. The total sum of *cizye* belonging to these years was 59,960 *kuruş*.

In the Erzurum Temettuat registers are 128 heads of households whose economic condition was "*alâ* (good);" 382, "*evsat* (medium);" and 51, "*edna* (low)." A *cizye* survey applied in Erzurum in 1842 decided that a non-Muslim of the *alâ* category of the *cizye* should pay 60 *kuruş*; the *evsat*, 30 *kuruş*; and the *edna*, 15 *kuruş*.[50] Considering that this ratio was current in the year 1844, we can determine that the *cizye* amount paid by non-Muslim subject in Erzurum in 1844 reached 7,680 *kuruş* from *alâ*, 11,460 *kuruş* from *evsat*, and 765 *kuruş* from *edna*, for a total of 19,905 *kuruş*.

50 With respect to this document, 427 *alâ*, 2991 *evsat*, and 671 *edna* taxpayers were obliged to pay *cizye*. In return for the *cizye* revenues in adjudication in the same year, 554 *alâ*, 3566 *evsat*, and 1288 *edna* taxpayers were identified (ML. VRD. CMH. no. 136).

Table 8: Annual Incomes of Quarters in Erzurum According to the Source of Revenue

Quarters	Number of households	Total	Agriculture	Stock-breeding	Commerce-Craftsmanship	Rent	Salary	Other
Abdurrahman Ağa (muslim)	27	10957	190	479	4045	1103	5140	
Ali Paşa (Armenians)	116	39332		2272	36960	100		
Ali Paşa (muslim)	111	29812	670	3108	22034	2280		1720
Bakırcı (muslim)	29	6445		300	5095	250	800	
Boyahane (muslim)	9	8210		300	1350	560	6000	
Caferiye (muslim)	81	31838	2236.5	2653	18897	2601.5	4650	800
Cami-i Kebir (muslim)	81	9117		1202	7350	485		80
Cedid (Armenians)	26	7440			7320	120		
Cedid (muslim)	96	24354		2558	21010	406		380
Çırçır (Armenians)	10	2400			2400			
Çırçır (muslim)	61	12187	756	1948	9013	370		100
Çortanoğlu (muslim)	15	2690		240	2450			
Çukur (muslim)	10	12022	1550	252		2120	7900	200
Derviş Ağa (muslim)	45	12945		300	9645		3000	
Emin Kurbu (muslim)	49	18840	550	2285	12460	2075	180	1290
Emin Kurbu (Armenians)	143	37414		834	35720	400		460
Erzurum (muslim)	48	12306	7858	2197	480	1070	701	
Erzurum (Catholic)	61	11554		940	1804	8810		
Feyziye (muslim)	24	4873	30	558	3150	610	410	115
Gez (muslim)	101	26849	9418	4546	11740	185	960	
Habib Efendi-i Süflâ (muslim)	68	10773	300	2065	6219	1280	395	514
Habib Efendi-i Ulyâ (muslim)	65	11007.5	2750.5	654	3775	1370	2258	200
Hacı Cuma (muslim)	40	7637		1088	6549			
Hanım Hamamı Mesc+ Sivasi	20+5	12054	130	866	8250	288	280	2240
Hasan Basri (muslim)	262	43618.5	3609.5	4132	33645	1276	60	896

Kâbe Mescidi (muslim)	13	3170		300	2870			
Kadana (muslim)	82	23832	60	2592	15390	2250	3540	
Kal'a Derunu (Armenians)	7	1700			1600	100		
Kanyolu Ali Paşa (rum)	19	2680			2680			
Kasım Paşa (muslim)	39	9265		1480	5925	550	1010	300
Kavak (muslim)	21	4600		1744	2516	240	100	
Kırmacı (muslim)	19	4870		1670	3200			
Köse Ömer Ağa (muslim)	25	8702	170	1026	7246	110		150
Lala Mustafa Paşa (muslim)	36	9457	400	1017	5300	850	370	1520
Mumcu-i Süflâ (Armenians)	71	17193		846	15757	590		
Mumcu-i Süflâ (muslim)	85	16310	460	1320	13470	200	30	830
Mumcu-i Ulyâ (muslim)	62	35890	6125	1836	19240	7105		1584
Mumcu-i Ulyâ (Armenians)	59	12660			11720	940		
Murad Paşa (muslim)	134	32830	1724	3318	23056	530	2640	1562
Müderris Efendi (muslim)	117	19796.5	1389.5	2166	16146	95		
Namervanlı Cami-i Şerif (muslim)	30	13840	260	1516	4770	2694	4200	400
Sultan Melik (muslim)	129	20840	657	1972	16541	890	80	700
Şeyh Emir (muslim)	37	6623		1136	4109	650	628	100
Şeyhler (muslim)	36	32527	4785	3107	5458	3637	14040	1500
Topçuoğlu (muslim)	99	33617	2100	4356	23411	1200		2550
Topçuoğlu (Armenians)	7	6150		30	5920	200		
Üveys Efendi (muslim)	88	20183	55	2492	14416	2250	150	820
Vani Efendi (muslim)	110	32150	2827.5	3308	16258.5	4965	663	4128
Yeğen Ağa (Armenians)	54	12575		120	12305	150		
Yeğen Ağa (muslim)	101	28560	2512	1920	19388	1580	2450	710
Yoncalık-ı Süflâ (muslim)	69	40184	1590	1199	11805	470	5830	19290
Zağracı Ali Ağa (muslim)	38	9860	564	810	7036	550	900	
Total	3190	866739.5	55727.5	77058	558894.5	60555.5	69365	45139

Of the non-Muslim population, 15 households did not pay any tax. The amount of tax paid by non-Muslims might increase, if we could include information from the eight quarters whose Temettuat registers are missing.

Conclusion

The Russians occupied Erzurum, a border city, after the 1828-29 Ottoman-Russian War. Some parts of the city wall collapsed. Most of the population, starting with the Armenians, was forced to migrate to Iran and Russia. Some of the Muslims (Turkish people, and others) who felt unsafe because of the Russians escaped to the safer parts of Anatolia. The number of families forced to migrate from Erzurum to Iran was estimated to be more than 40,000. The Ottoman Empire spent considerable effort on Iran and Russia, and some of the migrants managed to return. Since the Russian occupation, however, Erzurum has never returned to its prosperous days. Both the Muslim and non-Muslim (Armenians and Orthodox Greeks) population in the region decreased considerably. The villages surrounding Erzurum became deserted.

Temettuat registers give information about a period approximately 15 years after this occupation. But, probably because of the unstable conditions, the survey could not cover all the population of Erzurum. The city at that time had 53 quarters, but only 45 quarters had Temettuat registers. The total number of households recorded in the registers was 3190. Of this population, 493 households were Armenian, 19 were Orthodox Greek (*rum*), and 61 were Catholic. Most non-Muslims were engaged in commerce or craftsmanship. Muslims, with 2617 households, were craftsmen, tradesmen, soldiers, or farmers. Interestingly, some non-Muslims, normally exempt from military duty, worked in military positions. Commerce was concentrated in the city center.

The total income earned throughout the city was about 866,739.5 *kuruş*. Distribution of this income can be seen in Table 8.

The amount of tax that could be collected by the State was problematic. At that time, taxes such as *vergi-i mahsusa*, tithe, and *cizye* existed, but they only added up to a total of 45,080.5 *kuruş*. (This consisted of 23,829 *kuruş* of *vergi-i mahsusa*, 19,905 *kuruş* of *cizye*, and 1346.5 *kuruş* of tithe.) If 295,000 *kuruş*, which was assigned to the Muslim population in the previous year, were added to 45,080.5 *kuruş*, the total amount of tax would have reached 340,080.5 *kuruş*, and thus the average amount of *vergi-i mahsusa* per household (both Muslims and non-Muslims) would have been approximately 100 *kuruş*. However, the numbers for the tax collected from Erzurum do not reflect the reality, and the conducting of an improper and incomplete survey for income and tax was certainly one cause of this problem.

The standard of living in Erzurum in 1845 was surprisingly low, considering to the number of religious and social institutions. Despite the city's favorable location where eastern and western commerce roads intersect, the loss of population during the three-month Russian occupation in the first quarter of the nineteenth century has been an important factor preventing prosperous conditions for Erzurum. A comparison with other Ottoman cities is revealing: Income per household in the poorest quarter of Erzurum was 94.5 *kuruş*, and in the richest quarter it was 1,202 *kuruş*. On the other hand, in the same year in Bilecik the lowest quarter average income was 744.1 *kuruş*, and the highest was about 2,206 *kuruş*. For an average of all quarters, the income level was 271.7 *kuruş* in Erzurum, 1189.7 *kuruş* in Bilecik, and 958 *kuruş* in Güzelhisar-ı Aydin. In spite of this negative outlook based on the Temettuat registers, however, Erzurum survived the occupation, remaining as an East Anatolian commerce center with 250 active professions.

Conclusion

The Ottoman Temettuat Registers: Significant Results from a Failed Venture

HAYASHI Kayoko

The Ottoman Empire conducted its Temettuat survey in the 1840s. If the survey's initial purpose of investigating the income and property of all the empire's taxpayers is used as the standard, the survey ended in failure, both because survey results were not collected throughout the entire empire and because even in the submitted registers some contents were incomplete.

As explained in Chapter 1 of this volume, the primary reason for this failure was the implementation process. Although the purpose of the survey was clearly to investigate the individual ability to pay taxes, the administration of the Ottoman Empire did not sufficiently examine the nature of the implementation methods or the data to be obtained. In other words, they began the survey as if they had been rushed into it, without providing solutions to various complicated issues of ownership and income such as the definition of income, the shared ownership of immovable property, how to register the income earned in areas not subjected to the survey, and what should be considered necessary expenses, all of which were issues that should have been expected to arise. Also, the survey from its beginning did not indicate any policy as to how the survey results would reflect future taxation.

For this reason, it is understandable that a number of people refused to cooperate or comply with the survey, fearing that the results would cause a tax increase. Despite the empire's authority over its people, the administration could not prevent this passive resistance of non-cooperation. As a result, the initial goal of an exhaustive survey did not materialize, and many registers were not sent to the capital until the deadline, March 1846. Since survey results could not be tabulated, the administration would eventually have to give up its goal of tax reform based on the survey. In that respect, it is no exaggeration to say that the Temettuat survey ended in total failure.[1]

From this failure, the Ottoman administration learned the difficulty of determining the income figure of its entire population. Thus, after the survey, the administration continued using the more certain, although unfair, method of allocating tax figures to the units of quarters and villages. This made it more difficult to collect taxes in a fair manner from urban people — the merchants, craftsmen, salaried workers such as government officials, and especially the provincial notables, who had far more complicated income sources and more exemption privileges than other people. The result was frustration for the tax-collecting administration as well as the ordinary taxpayers.

On the other hand, the great number of registers in existence today demonstrates that the Ottoman Empire had enough authority to conduct such a grand experiment. The empire already had a history of conducting a population census, tracing back to the reign of Mahmud II, as well as the centralized power to plan a nationwide survey of individual property and income. The pilot property survey, which would later lead to the Temettuat

1 To judge whether or not the Temettuat survey ended in failure, we must consider its real purpose, going behind the official statement that it was intended to realize fair taxation. In the early Tanzimat period, the urban and rural taxpayers typically paid three kinds of tax: *vergi-i mahsusa*, tithe, and if non-Muslims, *cizye* tax. Of these, the *vergi-i mahsusa* was newly established, unifying some kinds of rubric taxes, after the declaration of Tanzimat reform. At first it was allotted to a community in a lump sun. In the course of the Temettuat survey, investigating the amount of *vergi-i mahsusa* paid by each individual must have been regarded as one of the major tasks of the survey. Until the survey, in rural societies the government did not know who had the privilege of tax exemption, or the exact amounts of tax paid by individuals. Although the purpose of the survey was not clearly expressed, it could be considered the abolition of tax exemption and the individualization of the *vergi-i mahsusa*. For *vergi-i mahsusa* information, refer to Tevfik Güran, *19. Yüzyıl Osmanlı Tarımı*, Istanbul, 1998, p. 199.

survey, was conducted in 1834-35. This was followed by the 1840 local survey on property and income. The 1845 survey differed greatly, however, in its scale and commitment. In a short period of time, necessary public offices (*imar meclisi*) were set up in various regions of "*dâhil-i dâire-i Tanzîmât,*" the decree of survey and its sample sheets were dispatched calling for a simultaneous survey. Even though a considerable portion of the results was not sent to the capital, the survey must have been conducted in one way or another in the targeted area. Considering the political, social and economic conditions of the Ottoman Empire at that time, its ability to conduct such a simultaneous large-scale survey should be highly regarded, despite the lack of adequate preparation.

According to the Prime Ministry Ottoman Archives catalogue, the Temettuat register was submitted from 543 *kaza*s, making minutely detailed materials currently available. Though the registers could include inaccurate information comparison of various registers will help to clarify the problems and inadequacies, now hiding in the existing registers.

Characteristics of the Five Locations

This volume focuses on five cities. Although their experiences were different, the information was similarly organized as to (1) the structure of the city and its quarters, (2) variation in the occupations of urban residents, (3) movable property, immovable property, and livestock owned as property, (4) income, and (5) tax allocation.

Table 1 shows the basic information from the registers, by city.

Attention should be paid once again to the point that the registers used in this volume all belonged to urban quarters, even though most existing registers were compiled using the village as unit (thus, the former targeted urban residents, the latter rural ones). Local administration in the Ottoman Empire can be understood as a double-circle structure, consisting of urban quarters as the center of *kaza* plus their administratively connected villages. The five papers have focused on the inner circle, that is, the quarters of the cities.

The register of the urban quarters varies widely and is far more complex than that of the rural area. It is therefore still risky to rely totally on figures using the "mean value" given in Table 1,, summarizing the

Table 1a: Summary Statistics of Five Cities

	Samokov	Tatarpazarcığı	Balıkesir	Güzelhisar-ı Aydın	Erzurum
POPULATION					
Number of recorded quarters	18	18	20	22	45
Number of recorded households	1,534	—	—	2,796	3,190
Muslim households	605	1,102	1,562	2,263	2,617
Non-muslim households	841	—	—	533	573
Estimated population	8,000	8,000	10,000	17,800	17,000
POPULATION BY OCCUPATION (%)					
Religious and administrative sector	7.9	—	11.5	6.6	15.3
Agriculture sector	3.0	—	14.9	7.1	2.1
Craftsman/tradesman/laborer	74.4	—	72.8	80.1	71.5
Others including jobless	14.7	—	0.8	6.2	11.1
INCOME BY OCCUPATION (%)					
Religious and administrative sector	21.0	—	4.2	—	20.7
Agriculture sector	1.1	—	20.5	—	3.1
Craftsman/tradesman/laborer	74.9	—	74.8	—	61.6
Others including jobless	3.0	—	0.5	—	14.6
INCOME (*kuruş*)					
Total income of recorded households	738,131	798,599	849,411	2,669,419	866,739.5
Average income per household	432.2	452	553.8	954	271.7

Table 1b: Summary Statistics of Five Cities

	Samokov	Tatarpazarcığı	Balıkesir	Güzelhisar-ı Aydın	Erzurum
INCOME DISTRIBUTION BY SOURCE OF INCOME (%)					
Income from agricultural activities	—	—	—	23.1	6.4
Income from stockbreeding					8.9
Income from trade and craftsmanship	—	—	—	68.5	64.5
Income from rent	—	—	—	5.2	7.0
Income from salary	—	—	—	3.2	8.0
Income from other source	—	—	—	—	5.2
TAX (*kuruş*)					
Vergi-i mahsusa	58,177.4	38,142	184,382.5	388,364.5	23,829
Tithe	—	—	—	60748.5	718
Cizye	35,475	—	—	12675.0	19905
Other tax	155,420	—	—	—	—
Proportion of *vergi-i mahsusa* to total income	Muslim 4.8% Non-Muslim 15.8%	Muslim 4.8% —	Muslim 21.7% —	Muslim 15.0% Non-Muslim 13.1%	2.8%(?)
PROPERTIES					
Number of recorded shops	374	734	350	347	265
People owning land inside or outside the city (household)	413	—	1251	975	572
Proportion to the total number of households	27.2%	—	80.1%	34.9%	17.9%
Number of recorded cattle, buffalo and sheep	1268	2169	2846	1333	3661
Number of animal per household	0.8	2.0	1.8	0.5	1.2

characteristics of five cities. For example, a small number of wealthy people lived in each city. If their income or tax amount was included in a total figure, the mean value might not reflect reality. In addition, as one can deduce from the difficulties of compiling the register, infinite possibilities existed for fallacy or tax evasion in a registry based on a self-assessed tax return; actual conditions in each city cannot be judged from numerical values alone. In that sense, we have no choice but to read between the lines of the register while trying to match the relevant material at hand.

The characteristics of the five cities, as clarified by the Temettuat registers, can be summarized, as follows:

Samokov

The Samokov register reflects the social and economic situation of an Ottoman Balkan city and its Muslim Turkish, Christian Bulgarian, Jewish, and Romany population, estimated as approximately 8000 persons and consisting of 1534 households and 174 temporary residents (*perakende*). Muslims make up 39.5%; Christians, 54.8%; Jewish, 2.9%; and Romany, 2.8% of the city's population.

The most interesting information the Temettuat register provides is the relationship among residents belonging to different religions. In Samokov, both Muslim and non-Muslim residents were engaged in the same occupation in one-fifth of the manufacturing sectors. As for other sectors, fluctuation in the ratio of Muslim and non-Muslim residents is observed, except for the administrative and military sectors, predominantly Muslim. Urban residents also appear to be economically homogeneous, as there is no significant difference in income between Muslim and non-Muslim craftsmen or tradesmen.

The tax burden shows a significant difference between Muslims and non-Muslims, since the ratio in *vergi-i mahsusa* of Muslim residents is on average 4.8%, whereas that of non-Muslims is 15.7%. Furthermore, considering also the *cizye* obligation of non-Muslims, the ratio of tax to income would be excessive for non-Muslims as calculated. If the entire tax of the city is taken into account, however, Samokov had a few prominent rich people, and most of the tax was dependent on them. A few Muslims of high income, such as *ashab-ı fabrika*, paid 62.4% of the total tax, that is, 155,420 *kuruş*, as rubric tax, *rüsumat-ı saire*.

The source of income of these rich people was the iron industry. Nine industrialists in that industry, *ashab-ı fabrika*, were registered. They also had other sources of income, such as their own farmland in surrounding villages, and accordingly were the richest class of the city. Muslim industrialists monopolized the traditional iron industry, controlled exclusively by the government.

The *aba* (coarse woolen cloth) manufacturing industry was also characteristic of Samokov. Through *aba* industry, making home manufacturing developed, in which family members like brothers and relatives worked together. The ratio of *aba* workers is high among Bulgarian Christians. How they were organized into larger management can be observed, and it could be said that the shift to a capitalist economy had already begun in such sectors as this. In fact, 22% of the Samokov residents were wage laborers or worked as auxiliaries. Thus, we see a situation unlike that of urban societies consisting of homogeneous master craftsmen.

Tatarpazarcığı

In Tatarpazarcığı, located today in Bulgaria, the ratio of *vergi-i mahsusa* paid by Muslim residents to the total tax paid in the previous year, is 4.8%, the same low ratio as that of Samokov Muslim population. The amount is 38,142 *kuruş*.

Like Samokov, Tatarpazarcığı had a few Muslims with high incomes. The economic foundation was rice agriculture on the banks of the River Meriç. Only 20 Muslim landowners earned 463,618 *kuruş*, which was 60% of the total income (798,599 *kuruş*) of the Muslims of the city. Although these 20 landowners drew income from non-agricultural sectors, their main income depended on rice plantations, using their agricultural workers or sharecroppers. It is probable that the most profitable economic basis of leading Muslim urban residents was the stable income from agriculture.

The number of water buffaloes owned by Muslims was noticeable, since the rice fields of the Muslims were also suitable for breeding buffaloes. Not only Tatarpazarcığı's Temettuat register but also those of other cities describe the kinds and numbers of livestock owned by residents in detail. Based on this, it would be reasonable to consider that livestock is the private property that the executors of the Temettuat survey could identify most easily. In Tatarpazarcığı, it was widely observed that not only the rich landowners but also ordinary Muslim townspeople owned land in villages around the city and were engaged in stockbreeding. This shows that the city was functioning as the center of agriculture. Although most of the city's residents were engaged in manufacturing and commerce, they also drew a certain amount of income from agriculture and stockbreeding.

Up to this moment, information concerning non-Muslim population residents in Tatarpazarcığı has not been put to use. Accordingly, our knowledge is limited to the total income, the total tax amount, and the number of real estate properties attributed to Muslim residents. Yet, 70 types of businesses and 734 stores tell of the lively commercial activity in the city.

Balıkesir

The analysis of Balıkesir is based on the register made in 1840. As is mentioned above, the 1840 survey was on the same track as the survey of property started before it and, accordingly, is clearly distinguished from the Temettuat survey carried out in 1845, which aimed at income. Clearly, however, the experimental survey in 1840 led to the comprehensive survey in 1845. In this sense, detailed study of information obtained from the 1840 register would be quite helpful in comprehending the direction of taxation reform.

The Balıkesir register of 1840, like the registers of 1845, records the makeup of urban quarters along with the category of occupation, the amount of tax in the preceding year attributing, and estimated income of each household. Furthermore, the distinctive feature of the 1840 register lies in the description of the personal appearance of the head of each household and the record of his property's estimated value. Chapter 5 in this volume analyzes how residents amassed property, classifying property evaluated in the 1840 register into livestock, land and others (including movable properties other than livestock and immovable properties other than land.)

Balıkesir is distinguished from the other cities in that we find descriptions in various parts of its register concerning the *aba* industry introduced to the Balıkesir region along with the modernization policy. *Aba* manufacturers were numerous and richer than the other urban residents. It is conceivable that the influence of *aba* industry spread from Balıkesir as a center out to the surrounding area, as the owners of *aba dingi*, the finishing machine of *aba* producing, were also found in villages around Balıkesir. It may be ascribed to the formation of such industry that the register records the traces of workers' migration from villages to the city.

Temettuat registers are certainly difficult to use for studying aspects of historical change because they have no comparable register compiled in the adjacent periods. Only detailed analyses of them may clarify such a process of social change as is found in the introduction of *aba* industry.

Another characteristic of Balıkesir is a large urban population of farmers engaged in traditional agriculture. Although not all of them are exclusively engaged in agriculture, 1253 households, corresponding to 80% of the total urban population, own farmland (usually called *tarla* or *bağ*). A common characteristic of Anatolian cities is a large urban population of farmers that makes the boundary between cities and villages imprecise.

Güzelhisar-ı Aydın

The imprecision of boundaries between cities and villages is also found in Güzelhisar, where 7.1% of the urban residents are engaged in agriculture. Many tradesmen, craftsmen, workers, civil servants and salaried employees also draw part of their income from agriculture. One-third of the urban residents owns farmland of medium or small size. The ratio of agricultural income to the total income of the city reaches 20%. In Güzelhisar various farm products are raised; a concentration on grain is not the case. Grapes and cotton, the principal products of Güzelhisar, are produced in large quantities. From this description, it seems possible that small-scale agricultural production was being made for the consumer market. The existence of seasonal workers in agriculture is expected from the fact that *işçi* and *hizmetkar*, most of which were supposed to be engaged in agriculture, make up 22.5% of the total population of workers.

Neither prominent landlords nor influential figures appear, however, in the register of Güzelhisar. The residents show no significant disparity of income. Their average income, 954 *kuruş*, is relatively high compared to the other cities. The ratio of *vergi-i mahsusa* to income is 15.0% and 13.1% for Muslim and non-Muslim residents respectively. If we add the amount of *cizye* tax to *vergi-i mahsusa*, the ratio of tax to income for non-Muslim residents becomes 15.3%. This shows that both Muslim and non-Muslim residents had the same tax burden.

On the other hand, 57.6% of the urban residents in Güzelhisar are tradesmen and craftsmen. The 147 types of business attributed to guilds (*esnaf*) demonstrate the liveliness of the city's economic activities.

It is worth noting that non-Muslim residents were classified according to their own religious communities as a whole, not counted in the quarters where they were living, in the Güzelhisar registers. This may be only for convenience, however, in the process of the survey. Such classification should not be interpreted as the reflection of their separated spatial distribution, since Temettuat registers are in any case compiled essentially on the basis of religious communities.

Erzurum

Erzurum is the largest of the five cities this volume deals with. Its Temettuat register contains the records of 3190 households and reflects the city's situation in the process of its recovery from the turmoil caused by the Russian occupation.

Some confusion can be found in the Temettuat registers, however. The total amount of *vergi-i mahsusa* is 23,829 *kuruş*, which is quite small, corresponding only to 2.8% of the total income. The amount attributed to Muslim residents is particularly small, no more than 4,565 *kuruş*. These numbers are difficult to interpret as reflecting a normal taxation. According to Çoruh, another contemporary source suggests that the amount of tax assigned to Muslim residents was originally 295,000 *kuruş*. It can thus be presumed that few Muslim residents paid tax in the year before the Temettuat survey was carried out because of the confusion caused by opposition to the large amount of *vergi-i mahsusa*.

The income is considerably less than that of other cities. The average income of a household is 271 *kuruş*, equivalent to one-half or even one-third of that of Balıkesir or Güzelhisar. Of course, we should be careful in interpreting such numbers. Yet, no significant difference appears between either the incomes of different urban quarters or between Muslim and non-Muslim residents. From this, it can be inferred that Erzurum as a whole was under a difficult situation. According to the Temettuat register, the total income of residents in Muslim quarters is 735,514.5 *kuruş*. If this is correct, 295,000 *kuruş*, the amount of the *vergi-i mahsusa* assigned by the government to Erzurum in the preceding year, corresponds to 40% of the total income, which would be easily expected to cause turmoil.

The beginning of Tanzimat reform had actually been declared to Erzurum and Diyarbakır in March 1845. This caused the revolts of local notables in the rural area of Eastern Anatolia, as is well known.[2] Under these unstable conditions, it is rather an unexpected development that the Temettuat survey was carried out in the urban region of Erzurum and the registers were actually sent to Istanbul, even though after the deadline. It was reported to the Porte through the Temettuat registers that most of Muslim residents of Erzurum had not paid any tax in the preceding year of the survey.

The accuracy of the information of the Erzurum register, delayed as it was in being submitted to the government, will have to be discussed later. Yet, in spite of such defective factors, the Temettuat register of Erzurum shows us aspects of life in a major city in Eastern Anatolia.

As soon as we look at the register, a few wealthy people attract our attention. So-called *ayans*, local notables, are identified to a certain extent by the government through the Temettuat register. For example, the income of Cennetzade Ahmed Efendi, named as one of the richest people in the register, reaches 21,555 *kuruş*. Out of this, 5,000 *kuruş* is given as a salary by the government to his son, whose title is *müderris*, teacher at a madrasah. As in this case, most people drawing a large income have a high salary from the government. It is confirmed in Erzurum, as well as in other cities under the Ottoman Empire, that influential people in a local community make a fortune by getting governmental posts.

Concerning the role of Erzurum as a center of surrounding villages, the Temettuat register gives us the following information: First, people who could be defined as farmers are few. They form only 2.1% of the total population. Income from agriculture is also small, 6.4% of total income. Few urban residents own their farmland. This is against our expectation since Erzurum has a vast agricultural hinterland. It could be supposed that rural property owned by the urban population in Erzurum was not recorded in the urban registers. On the other hand, however, 377 heads of household are thought to be mainly wage workers of stock breeding. The 3,661 heads of livestock owned by urban residents make clear that Erzurum has a close relationship with surrounding agricultural lands.

---

2 Musa Çadırcı, *Tanzimat Döneminde Anadolu Kentleri'nin Sosyal ve Ekonomik Yapıları*, Ankara, 1991, pp. 192-97.

Urban Societies Observed from Temettuat Registers

Temettuat registers compiled in the middle of the nineteenth century, a period of change, are the source of valuable information for comprehending how the traditional society and modernization intersected each other in cities. In particular, they present information concerning city quarters (*mahalle*), microcosms functioning as units of the urban residents' everyday life. Although the five studies included in the present volume focus their attention on presenting the whole picture of a city, studies using Temettuat registers can also specifically inform us how city quarters are formed and organized. A city quarter, a collective unit of households, was traditionally represented (if a Muslim settlement) by a mosque at the center of the quarter and by the *imam*. During the reign of Mahmud II, however, a new system of *muhtar* was introduced and, accordingly, the position of city quarters was being changed. This can be summarized as the change from a set of loosely-connected households to an administrative unit. How were city quarters in the process of change reflected in Temettuat registers?

An Example: the Ortacami Quarter in Tatarpazarcığı

For example, in what follows, the Ortacami Quarter in Tatarpazarcığı is described based on the description in the Temettuat register (see Appendix I). The city quarter consists of 21 households, which are also units of taxation. The occupation of the head of household varies considerably. Among them a wool comber occupied the post of *muhtar* and, accordingly, had the privilege of being exempt from taxation. Yet, his annual income reached no higher than 180 *kuruş*, and he had no other property. This shows that a rather lowly person in a city quarter could be chosen for the post of *muhtar*.[3]

In the same quarter were two households with no occupation and no property. It is not known how they could make a living. There were also two brothers with the title of *seyyid*. They were living on the rent from their immovable and were registered as two separate households for taxation purposes. In short, of 21 households, four had no listed occupation. In

[3] As for the *muhtar* system, refer to Musa Çadırcı, "Türkiye'de Muhtarlık Teşkilâtının Kurulması üzerine," *Belleten*, no. 135, 1970.

addition, two households were treated differently because they were *ulemas*: that is, an *imam* and a student of learning, having tax exemption privileges.

The remaining 15 heads of households were a wool comber, a candle maker, a saddler, a tanner, a servant, a coffee seller, two transporters, a hair rope maker, three shoemakers, a wool merchant, a grocery, and a hardware dealer. They can be classified as tradesmen or craftsmen keeping stores in the market place. Their incomes earned by doing commerce in the market place do not differ from person to person, although three of them manage a farm. A hardware dealer, whose income reaches 1,605 *kuruş*, has farmland, raises 15 head of livestock there, and employs two Christian sharecroppers. A shoemaker also has farmland, raises 13 head of livestock, and employs four share croppers (three Christians and one Muslim). He earns only 660 *kuruş* from his commerce. A grocer called Emin Ağa draws the highest income in this quarter, 3,455 *kuruş*, from immovable in the city and from his grocery. He has 29 head of livestock and employs two Christian sharecroppers. In the case of the Ortacami Quarter, since income from farming is not recorded in the register, we do not know the scale of their farming and their income from it. Yet, we know that the income of each of the eight sharecroppers working on their farms exceeds 600 *kuruş*. Also, four other households own livestock kept on farms. All these facts show the close relationship between Muslims in Tatarpazarcığı and farming.

In the register, not only livestock but also commercial estates are listed as the property of urban residents. However, aspects of their ownership are quite complex. Commercial estates are classified into four types: those owned by a head of household and used by the same person, those owned by a head of household and rented to someone else, those rented from someone else and used by a head of household, and those rented from someone else and subleased by a head of household. It is presumed that a person regards even a commercial estate owned by someone else as his own property, because such commercial estates are traded along with license titles or long-term lease contracts on themselves and accordingly regarded as a kind of property.

Many renters of shops are pious foundations. It is conceivable that various people and organizations participate in the city's immovable market. Commercial estates possessed by the residents in the Ortacami Quarter are as follows:

(1) Two shops are owned by heads of household and used by the same people;
(2) Sixteen shops, one storehouse, a quarter share of a bakery, two one-third shares of a tobacco shop and two houses for rent are owned by heads of household and rented to other people;
(3) Eleven shops and one soap factory are rented from other people and used by heads of household (among these are six possessed by pious foundations);
(4) Five shops and one room are subleased by heads of household and owned by pious foundations.

Temettuat registers thus give us information concerning the properties and incomes of the members of the Ortacami Quarter. It is true that Temettuat registers are quite effective in reconstructing a relatively small city quarter such as Ortacami Quarter. But the kind of information they provide is not sufficient for the reconstruction of a city quarter. For example, they do not record houses as property. Floating capital in probable loans is not covered by the survey. Social relations among the members of a quarter, such as those between Muslim landowners and Christian sharecroppers, are little known. There is very little description concerning women. Only two women with independent properties and incomes are found in the register of the Ortacami Quarter in Tatarpazarcığı.

It should be noted here that the record of the register is not guaranteed to be exhaustive. In the case of the Ortacami Quarter, we cannot know whether the register lists all members of the quarter or not. A city quarter is a space in which people of varied religious and ethnic backgrounds may (or may not) be residing. The quarter appears in the Temettuat registers, however, as an administrative unit defined according to the religion of the resident. It is probable that Muslim and non-Muslim residents lived side by side, yet their records were different and were entered in different registers. Whether the Ortacami Quarter had any Christian or Jewish population could not therefore be known. Thus, when we use Temettuat registers, we should carefully avoid confusing city quarters as administrative units in Temettuat registers with city quarters as geographical units.

Wealthy Urban Residents and Local Notables

A grocer called Emin Ağa, the wealthiest person in the Ortacami Quarter, is one of the landowners doing small-scale business. In the four cities other than Güzelhisar, a few residents with high incomes, like Emin Ağa, attract our attention. The properties and incomes of such wealthy residents are important characteristics of these cities. Although hidden in various ways, they are reflected in the Temettuat registers. Industrialists of the iron industry in Samokov, landowners in Tatarpazarcığı, and local notables in Balıkesir and Erzurum should be the objects of Temettuat studies. They monopolize highly productive sectors as their sources of income in each city. They also have connections to the central government by obtaining governmental posts and getting salaries from the tax revenue. They have thus been amassing their fortune. In many cases, the study of their economic basis is indispensable to the study of the modernization of the Ottoman Empire.

Such local notables as these stood most firmly against the Temettuat surveys. The success of the survey in each region was dependent on whether or not their property and income could be identified and recorded in the register, since they controlled principal sources of income and their incomes were quite large. If they were not recorded, Temettuat registers would produce only insufficient information about a region.

As far as the cities dealt with in this volume are concerned, the distribution of income among city residents is uneven. Such an economic situation can be interpreted as the lack of a middle class. That might account for the top-down industrialization in the Balkans and Anatolia in the second half of the nineteenth century.

Varieties of Occupations of Urban Residents

The other rich information Temettuat registers provide is about the variety in traditional occupations, classified into many smaller categories by tradesmen and craftsmen. Such variety in occupation is generally seen in the cities under the Ottoman rule, from Eastern Anatolia to the Balkans. Tradesmen and craftsmen conducted business by borrowing and renting similar small shops with very narrow frontage, and thus they formed the market place. It is not too much to say that a common variation in occupation and the common scenery of markets formed by tradesmen and craftsmen are what make cities under Ottoman rule "Ottoman cities." The variety of occupations found in the five cities is shown in Appendix II.

Setback of Temettuat Survey and its Legacy

Although the Temettuat registers were compiled, including a variety of information concerning local societies, as shown in the previous chapters, the Temettuat survey itself ended in failure. The radical tax reform, once planned for after the survey, was given up; as for the *vergi-i mahsusa*, the former taxation procedures, assigning tax in a lump sum to quarters and villages, were enforced again. The results of the Temettuat survey concerning personal incomes and properties were so vague that the Ottoman government could not introduce a new tax system immediately on the basis of the survey results. Therefore the tax system of the Ottoman Empire remained unfair and inefficient.

But the survey was not totally meaningless for the Ottoman government. The survey left not only a great amount of registers, but also both a direct and an indirect effect on the Ottoman government and its societies.

First of all, the bureaucrats of the central government had not been accurately aware of regional differences and deviation of tax burdens until the Temettuat survey registers were accumulated. One of the results of the Temettuat survey was that the government revised the ratio of the tax burden assigned to each *sancak* based on information obtained by means of Temettuat registers. For the reformist bureaucrats of the central government, the Temettuat survey brought many controversial points of taxation to light. In this sense, we can regard the Temettuat survey as the starting point of substantial reform based on statistical information, something that had been urged by the local delegation, summoned to Istanbul in February 1845, that complained unanimously about the unfairness of the tax system.

Imbalances in the tax burden were conspicuous in the five cities this volume dealt with. In Samokov and Tatarpazarcığı, the tax ratio for Muslim residents was 4.8%, extremely low. Compared to them, the tax burdens of non-Muslims of Samokov and both Muslim and non-Muslim residents of Güzelhisar were relatively heavy. The ratio of tax to their income was around 15 % in these two cities. On the other hand, in Erzurum, taxation could not be carried out in a stable way.

The inconsistency or unfairness of the tax burden could also be observed in the assignment of the *vergi-i mahsusa* to each household in a quarter after the government assigned them in a lump sum to each community. An outsider could never understand the local rules of tax assignment. We can suppose that the customs inherited for generations or practice of mutual aid could be the factors that affected the amount of tax for each household. Also, numerous wealthy local notables had been exempted from taxation, with the excuse of their administrative or religious positions.

To understand these realities of local societies should have been important for the central bureaucrats, even though the solution could not be introduced immediately. If we consider the matter within the long and difficult history of reform of the Ottoman tax system, it was one very important stage of transformation from the lump sum taxation system for each community unit to individual taxation according to ability. The objective was not achieved in 1846, but the major stream of transformation would be pursued in the second half of the nineteenth century.[4]

The second legacy of the Temettuat survey was its effect on the organization of local officials. During the Temettuat survey, local officials at the end of the governing hierarchy, that is, the *kaza* chief (*kaza müdürü*), members of the *kaza* council, and *muhtar*s, played an important role.

The *muhtars* were introduced in the reign of Mahmud II and had already been responsible for the security of villages and quarters. But with the beginning of Tanzimat, their responsibility had been extended. On the other hand, the *kaza* chief and his council, called *kaza meclisi* or *küçük meclis,* were newly established in the year 1842, after the *muhassıl* system was abolished and *kaza* was replaced as an administrative unit.[5] Local representatives, chosen from the Muslim and, also, from the non-Muslim population, attended the council. *Muhtar*s of each of the quarters and villages began to work under the supervision of the *kaza* council from 1842.

---

4 It is not clearly known when the system of allocating taxation to quarters and villages (*ancemaatin vergi*) was terminated and an individual taxation system introduced, though Şener stated that it occurred in 1859-60 with the introduction of the income tax (*temettü vergisi*). Abdüllatif Şener, *Tanzimat Dönemi Osmanlı Vergi Sistemi*, Istanbul, 1990, pp. 225-26. See also, Çadırcı, *Tanzimat Döneminde Anadolu Kentleri'nin Sosyal ve Ekonomik Yapıları*, pp. 340-48.

5 As for *kaza* chief, see Çadırcı, *op. cit.*, pp. 240-48. We do not have enough information about the kaza council, but it is regarded as the continuation of *muhassıllık* council. On *muhassıllık* council, see İlber Ortaylı, *Tanzimattan Sonra Mahalli İdareler (1840-1878)*, Ankara, 1974, pp. 15-18.

The Temettuat survey of 1845 was the first important mission the government imposed on local officials as their collaborative task. When they carried out the Temettuat survey as governmental officials, investigating the individual property and income of quarter members, this experience could bring a turning point in their role, because each of them gained a foothold in local society as a key person having direct connections with the government.

They were, however, not only government administrators, but also members of local communities. Though the development of the autonomous local administration system remained insufficient,[6] neither could the government control them completely, at its own convenience. They also tried to protect local interests. They sometimes bargained with the government in favor of local notables. In this connection, we can regard the failure of the Temettuat survey in many regions as, paradoxically, evidence that local officials could successfully protect local interests against the government.

After the failure of the Temettuat survey in 1845, the Ottoman government never attempted to perform a later survey on the same scale. In the second half of nineteenth century, however, the gradual transformation of administration systems could take place in the local societies. Although the Temettuat survey carried out by the Ottoman government in the middle of nineteenth century was a failure as a governmental enterprise, it left a legacy of native administrators in local societies, as well as a large amount of information recorded about local societies.

---

6 *Ibid.*, pp. 235-37.

Appendix I: Residents of a Quarter

In the Case of the Ortacami Quarter in Tatarpazarcığı[1]

No.1 İmam Kulan oğlu Ahmed Efendi, *imam*
—Tax paid in previous year: exempted
—Property: livestock (2 head)
—Estimated income: 400 *kuruş*

No.2 Halil oğlu Hüseyin, wool comber, the first *muhtar*
—Tax paid in previous year: exempted
—Property: a shop rented from Manavzade Hüseyin Ağa
—Estimated income: 180 *kuruş* from the occupation of wool comber

No.3 Ahmed oğlu Molla İbrahim, candle maker, the second *muhtar*
—Tax paid in previous year: 41 *kuruş*
—Property: a shop rented from the pious foundation of Hüsrev Kethüda and subleased to someone; a shop selling fur caps rented to someone; a broker's shop rented to someone; a hardware dealer's shop rented to someone; a shop rented from an orphan named Mumcu Acemi Mehmed; livestock (7 head)
—Estimated income: 500 *kuruş* from rent and animals, plus 400 *kuruş* from candle making

No.4 Mustafa oğlu Ali, saddler
—Tax paid in previous year: 28 *kuruş*
—Property: a shop rented from Hacı Hafiz Efendi
—Estimated income: 200 *kuruş* from saddlery
—Estimated income of his wife: 150 *kuruş* from a shop rented to someone and livestock (4 head)

No.5 Abdullah oğlu Receb, assistant master of tanner
—Tax paid in previous year: 20 *kuruş*
—Property: none
—Estimated income: 250 *kuruş* from occupation of assistant master

1 ML. VRD. TMT. no. 6340.

No.6 Mehmed oğlu Molla Mustafa, servant
—Tax paid in previous year: 32 *kuruş*
—Property: livestock (5 head)
—Estimated income: 65 *kuruş* from animals, plus 400 *kuruş* from the occupation of servant
—Estimated income of his brother: 200 *kuruş*

No.7 Nebi oğlu Arnavud Ali, coffee seller
—Tax paid in previous year: 30 *kuruş*
—Property: a shop rented from Tahtacı Hacı Ağuş Ağa
—Estimated income: 250 *kuruş* from coffee trade

No.8 Halil oğlu Kuşgözlü Osman, transporter
—Tax paid in previous year: none
—Property: livestock (3 head)
—Estimated income: 250 *kuruş* from transportation
—Note: Because of his eye illness, he did not get any income or pay any tax in previous year.

No.9 Hüseyin oğlu Seyyid Hüseyin, hair rope maker
—Tax paid in previous year: 35 *kuruş*
—Property: a shop rented from the pious foundation of Paşa Camii
—Estimated income: 350 *kuruş* from hair rope making

No.10 Ali oğlu Molla Mehmed, student of *ilim*
—Tax paid in previous year: exempted
—Property: a shoemaker shop rented from the pious foundation of Hüsrev Kethüda and subleased to someone; a storehouse rented to someone
—Estimated income: 40 *kuruş*

No.11 Ahmed oğlu Molla Mehmed, shoemaker
—Tax paid in previous year: 41 *kuruş*
—Property: a shop subleased from the wife of Hamamcı Hacı İbrahim, which was rented by her from the pious foundation of Hüsrev Kethüda
—Estimated income: 350 *kuruş* from shoemaking
—He has farmland and water mills outside of the city, which were recorded in the registers as belonging to the village concerned.
—Estimated income of his son: income from a coffeehouse and a wool comber's shop both rented to someone by him, 220 *kuruş*

No.12 Mehmed oğlu Mustafa Ağuş, transporter
—Tax paid in previous year: 41 *kuruş*
—Property: livestock (9 head)
—Estimated income: 35 *kuruş* from animal, plus occupation of transportation using animals

No.13 Abdullah oğlu Manav Ahmed, jobless
—Tax paid in previous year: none
—Property: none
—Estimated income: none

No.14 İsmail oğlu Hacı Tahir, wool merchant
—Tax paid in previous year: 136 *kuruş*
—Property: a shop owned and used by himself; a quarter share of a bakery rented to someone; a room in the inn called Han-ı Kebir which he rented from a pious foundation and subleased to someone; a furrier shop rented to someone; a hair rope maker's shop rented to someone; tailor's shop rented to someone; a silk shop rented to someone; a goldsmith shop rented to someone; a *boza* seller's shop rented to someone; livestock (2 head)
—Estimated income: 1020 *kuruş* from his properties, plus 600 *kuruş* from occupation of wool merchant

No.15 Abdullah oğlu Ali, having no property and jobless
—Tax paid in previous year: none
—Property: none
—Estimated income: none

No.16 Elhac Ahmed Efendi oğlu Hacı Ali Molla, hardware dealer, farmer
—Tax paid in previous year: 136 *kuruş*
—Property: a shop rented from the pious foundation of Güllük Camii; a shop rented from the pious foundation of Sadi Hoca Camii and subleased to someone; livestock (15 head)
—Estimated income: 105 *kuruş* from his properties, plus 1500 *kuruş* from hardware selling
—Estimated income of laborer (*hizmetkar*) working in his farmland: Yıkov *zimmi*, 610 *kuruş*; Minho *zimmi*, 610 *kuruş*

No.17 Adbi oğlu Hacı Alişah, shoemaker
—Tax paid in previous year: 66 *kuruş*
—Property: a shop rented to someone; a shop subleased from wife of Taktakzade Ahmed Ağa, which was rented by her from the pious foundation of Hüsrev Paşa
—Estimated income: 50 *kuruş* from his properties, plus 550 *kuruş* from shoemaking

No.18 Abdi oğlu Hacı Alişah, shoemaker
—Tax paid in previous year: 70 *kuruş*
—Property: a shop owned and used by himself; a shop rented to someone; livestock (13 head)
—Estimated income: 160 *kuruş* from his properties, plus 550 *kuruş* from shoe-making
—Estimated income of his wife: 70 *kuruş* from a hardware dealer's shop rented to someone
—Estimated income of laborer working in his farmland: Nikola *zimmi*, 620 *kuruş*;

Beled oğlu Petro *zimmi*, 650 *kuruş*; Şerif bin Hüseyin, 610 *kuruş*; Angel *zimmi*, 630 *kuruş*

No.19 Elhac Hüseyin Ağa oğlu Emin Ağa, grocer
—Tax paid in previous year: 250 *kuruş*
—Property: three grocery shops rented from the pious foundation of Hüsrev Kethüda and used by himself; a shop rented from the pious foundation of Hüsrev Kethüda and subleased to someone; a store house rented from the pious foundation of Hüsrev Kethüda and subleased to someone; a soap maker's shop rented to someone; three butcher's shops rented to someone; a soap factory rented from the pious foundation of Hacı Kılıç Camii and subleased to someone; livestock (29 head)
—Estimated income: 1855 *kuruş* from his properties, 1350 *kuruş* from the occupation of grocer, plus 250 *kuruş* from soap factory
—Estimated income of laborer working in his farmland: Metra *zimmi*, 740 *kuruş*; Nikola, a horse keeper, *zimmi*, 400 *kuruş*

No.20 Seyyid Mustafa, an orphan of Seyyid Mehmed
—Tax paid in previous year: 20 *kuruş*
—Property: a share of one-third of a tabacco shop rented to someone
—Estimated income: 395 *kuruş*

No.21 Seyyid İsmail, another orphan of Seyyid Mehmed
—Tax paid in previous year: 30 *kuruş*
—Property: a share of one-third of a tobacco shop rented to someone
—Estimated income: 335 *kuruş*

Appendix II: The Variety of Occupation found in the Five Cities

S: Samokov, T: Tatarpazarcığı, B: Balıkesir,
G: Güzelhisar-ı Aydın, E: Erzurum

1. Religious and Educational Occupations

cabi (collector of the revenue of a pious foundation)........G
cami-i kitabet hizmetkarı (mosque attendant)........E
daskal (teacher)........S
ders hocası, ders-i am (teacher)........B-E
derviş (dervish)........S-E
emin-i fetva (custodian of *fetwa*)........E
erbab-ı kitap (expert on books)........E
fakih (expert on the canon law of Islam)........E
hafiz (mosque attendant)........S-E
haham (Jewish rabbi)........S-G
hatib (preacher)........S-T-B-G
imam (prayer leader)........S-T-B-G-E
imaretçi (manager of soup kitchen attached to mosque)........B
kayyum (mosque keeper)........B-G
keşiş (Christian monk)........S-E
kilise hizmetkarı (verger of a church)........E
mahzarcı (scrivener)........T
mektep hocası (teacher of primary school)........T-E
metropolit (bishop)........S
mevali-i kiram (chief judges)........E
muallim-i sıbyan (teacher)........S-B-G-E
muallime-i sıbyan (female teacher of small children)........E
müderris (madrasah teacher)........S-T-B-G-E
müezzin (prayer caller)........S-B-G-E
müfti (scholar of Islamic law)........B-G-E
mütevelli (*vakıf* trustee)........S-B-G-E

nakşibendi tarikatı hülefası (dean of the Nakşibendi sect) .... E
papaz (priest) .... S
seyyid (descendant of Prophet) .... S
şeyh (sheikh) .... S-B-G
talebe (student) .... S-B-G-E
türbedar (keeper of a tomb) .... G
ulema .... T-B-G

2. Military and Administrative Occupations

asker (soldier) .... S-B
bağbekçisi (watchman) .... E
beglikçi hizmetkarı (chancery officer) .... S
bekçi (night watchman) .... T
beybaşı (soldier) .... E
binbaşı (major) .... E
bostancı (warden) .... E
bölge emini (custodian) .... E
cizye kolcusu (watchman for the *cizye* collection) .... E
çavuş (sergeant) .... S-E
dergah-ı ali kapıcıbaşısı (head of the palace doorkeeper) .... E
emir (commander) .... S
enderun ağası (eunuch of the Sultan's palace) .... E
gececi (watchman) .... E
gümrükçü (official in charge at the Customs) .... E
hacegan-ı divan-ı hümayun (the department chief of the Imperial chancery) .... E
ihtisapçı (supervisor of market) .... S-E
jurnal (census official) .... B
kabzmal-i mahalle (income collector of quarter) .... B
kapıcı (doorkeeper in the Sultan's court) .... B-E
kapıaltı askeri (soldier in a governmental building) .... G
karakullukçu (military officer) .... G
katib-i mahkeme (clerk of court) .... S
katip (clerk) .... S-T-B-G-E
kavvas (archer) .... S-E
kaymakam (head official of *kaymakamlık*) .... S
kaza müdürü (director of *kaza*) .... E
kolağası (adjutant major) .... E
korucu (warden) .... T-E
maden katibi (clerk of mine) .... S
maden müdürü (administrator of mine) .... S
maden yazıcısı (scribe of mine) .... S
mahalle ağası (notable of a quarter) .... G

mahalle kahyası (bailiff)....G
mahkeme başkatibi (head of the clerks in a court) .... E
menzilci (manager of a government post house) .... B-G
muameleci (money lender)....G
muhtar (headman of quarter) .... S-T-B-G
muhzır (officer of a court of justice)....S-B-G-E
mukayyid-i nüfus (census registrar) .... S-G
müdür (director).... E
müfettiş (inspector) .... E
mülazim (lieutenant) .... E
mültezim (tax contractor).... T
müşir (governor) ....G
mütesellim-i sabık (former magistrate of *sancak*)....B
naib (substitute judge) .... E
nüfus nazırı (census inspector).... S-E
onbaşı (corporal).... E
pasban (watchman) .... S-B-E
paşa hazinedarı (accountant of *paşa*).... S
paşa katibi (clerk of *paşa*).... S
pazvandbaşı (chief of watchmen)....G
rahtar (served at the Customs and important passages) .... E
sa'i (foot messenger) ....S-G
sancaktar (standard bearer).... E
sandık emiri (treasurer)....G-E
sekban (formerly, keeper of the imperial hounds; a soldier)....G
sipahi (cavalry soldier) ....G-E
su nazırı (superintendent of the distribution of water) .... E
süvari zaptiyesi (cavalry gendarmerie).... E
şehbender (consulate).... E
tabur katibi (battalion clerk) .... E
tahmis mültezimi (tax contractor for coffee and similar items).... E
tahsildar (tax collector) .... T
tatar (courier, especially a state courier, who worked as a messenger or postman) .... E
teğmen (lieutenant) .... E
tellal (town crier) .... E
teroğlanı (assistant of *cizye* collector) .... S
timar me'muru (*timar* officer).... S
timarlı (one who has a fief).... E
topçu (gunner).... E
topçu yüzbaşı (gunner captain) ....
tüfenkçi başı (head of the guard).... E
tüfenk-endaz (musketeer) .... E

tulumbacı (fire engine man)........ T
yazıcı (scribe)........ S-G-E
yevmiyeci (daybook registrar)........ S
yiğitbaşı (formerly, the man responsible for carrying out the regulations of a guild; or a foreman in the army)........ G
zabıtada neferi (policeman)........ B
zaptiye (gendarmerie)........ E

3. Occupations Pertaining to Agriculture

ashab-ı çiftlik (owner of farm)........ S
avcı (hunter)........ T
bahçevan (gardener)........ S-B-G
celeb çobanı (shepherd to the cattle)........ E
çeltik kahyası (head of the rice cultivation plant)........ T
çeltik yamağı (apprentice to the *çeltik kahyası*)........ T
çiftçi (farmer)........ G
çiftlik kahyası (steward)........ T
çiftlik kethüdası (manager of a farm)........ B
çoban (shepherd)........ S-T-B-G-E
erbâb-ı ziraat (agriculturist)........ G
ortakçı (sharecropper)........ G
rençber (farmer)........ B-G
seyis (horse keeper)........ S
sığırtmaç (herdsman)........ S-B-G

4. Craftsmen, Tradesmen and Master Constructers

abacı (maker of coarse woolen cloth)........ S-T-B-G-E
alaftar (merchant)........ E
alçıcı (plasterer)........ E
arpacı (barley seller)........ T-B-G
ashab-ı fabrika (owner of iron enterprise)........ S
asiyabcı (miller)........ E
aşçı (cook)........ S-T-G-E
attar (herbalist)........ S-T-B-G-E
aynacı (mirror maker)........ T
ayrancı (maker of a drink made from yogurt)........ E
bakırcı (coppersmith)........ B-G-E
bakkal (grocery)........ S-T-B-G-E
balcı (honey seller)........ B
balıkçı (fish seller)........ G
baltacı (ax maker)........ E

bardakçı (mug and glass maker)........G
barutçu (gunpowder maker)........B-E
basmacı (maker of printed material)........B
bezci (cloth seller)........T
bezir (dealer in linseed oil)........T
bezzaz (textile merchant)........S-T-B-G-E
bıçakçı (knife maker)........S-T-B-G-E
bileyci (knife grinder)........E
billurcu (cut-glass ware maker)........G
borucu (pipe maker)........B
boyacı (dyer)........S-T-B-G-E
bozacı (maker/seller of *boza*)........T
börekçi (*börek* maker)........B
buzcu (ice transporter)........E
bükücü (twister)........E
cambaz (horse dealer)........S-T-G-E
camcı (glazier)........T
celep (cattle dealer)........S-T-E
çakıcı (knife maker)........B-E
çakmakçı (flint maker)........B
çamurcu dülgeri (mortar worker)........S
çanakçı (seller of pottery)........T
çarhçı (knife-grinder)........B
çarıkçı (sandal maker)........S-T-E
çarkçı (wheel maker)........S
çenberci (hoop maker)........G
çengelci (hook maker)........G
çerçi (haberdasher; peddler)........S-T-B-G-E
çerezci (hors d'oeuvres seller)........G
çeşmeci (fountain founder)........S
çeyrekçi (seller of meat products)........E
çıkrıkçı (latheman)........B-E
çiçekçi (florist)........E
çilingir (locksmith)........B-G-E
çinici (tile maker)........E
çivici (nail maker)........B-E
çizmeci (boot maker)........B-E
çorbacı (soup maker)........G
çömlekçi (potter)........T-B-E
çubukçu (pipestem maker)........S-T-B-E
çuhacı (draper)........S-T-G
çulha (weaver)........G-E
dana boğazlayıcı (heifer slaughterer)........G
debbağ (tanner)........S-T-B-G-E

değirmenci (miller) .... S-B-G
dellal (broker) .... S-T-B-G
demirci (blacksmith) .... B-G-E
derici (leather dealer) .... T
destici (pitcher maker) .... B-G
dikçi (stitcher) .... S-T-B-E
dinkçi (*aba* finisher) .... T-B
doğramacı (carpenter) .... S-T-B
dondurmacı (ice-cream maker) .... G
dökmeci (founder) .... T-E
duhancı (tobacco seller) .... S-T-B-G-E
duvarcı (bricklayer) .... G-E
dülger (carpenter) .... S-T-B-G-E
ekmekçi (baker) .... T-B-G-E
elekçi (sieve maker) .... G
enfiyeci (snuff seller) .... E
eski yamacı (old-clothes mender) .... G
eskici (dealer in second hand wares) .... S-T-B-G-E
fahimci (coal dealer) .... S
fenerci (torch maker) .... G
fesci (fez making) .... G
fıçıcı (cooper) .... S-T-E
fırıncı (bakery) .... S-T-E
fişekçi (cartridge maker) .... S
gaytancı (maker of woolen braid lace) .... S-T-E
gömlekçi (shirt making) .... G
göncü (saddler, leather worker) .... E
gülcü (rose dealer) .... E
habz tablakarı (bread vendor) .... B
haffaf (shoemaker) .... S-T-B-G-E
hallaç (wool comber) .... S-T-B-G-E
hasırcı (mat maker) .... T-G-E
hatab kesici (wood chopper) .... S
hayyat (tailor) .... E
helvacı (sweet maker) .... S-B-G
hırdavatçı (hardware seller) .... E
hızarcı (pit sawyer) .... E
hoşabcu (stewed fruit seller) .... B
hurdacı (scrap dealer) .... E
ibrişim bükücü (silk thread spinner) .... G
ihramcı (seller of ihram, a seamless garment worn by pilgrims in Mecca) E
ipek bükücü (silk spinner) .... G
iplikçi (thread maker) .... G
kabakçı (squash seller) .... G

kadayıfçı (maker/seller of sweet called *kadayıf*)..B
kaftancı (wardrobe maker)..T
kahve döğücü (coffee pounder) ....E
kahveci (coffee seller)...S-T-B-G-E
kal (metal refiner of smelting)...B
kalaycı (tinsmith)..S-B-G
kalburcu (sifter)..G
kaldırımcı (paver)...B
kalpakçı (seller of fur caps)..T
kaltakçı (saddletree maker)..B-G-E
kantarcı (steelyard maker)..S-G-E
kapamacı (dealer of ready-made clothing)...S
kasacı (safe maker)..G
kasap (butcher)...S-T-B-G-E
katmerci (flaky pastry maker)...G
kavcı (punk seller)..E
kayışçı (belt maker)..E
kazancı (cauldron maker)..E
kazzaz (silk manufacturer)..T-G-E
kebabçı (*kebap* seller)..G-E
keçeci (felt maker)...B-G-E
kemaneci (violin maker)...S
kepçeci (hardware maker)..E
keresteci (timber dealer)...T-G-E
kerpiççi (seller of sun dried bricks)...T-E
kestaneci (chestnut seller)...G
kılıççı (sword maker)..E
kırbacı (water skin maker) ....E
kırmızcı (seller of *kırmız*, paint acquire from a tiny insect)..........................G
kısrakçı (mare dealer)...G
kıyıcı (mincer of tobacco)...B
kibritçi (dealer of flammable substances)...E
kilci (clay seller)..B
kireççi (lime seller)...E
kiremitçi (tile maker)..T-G
kirişçi (catgut maker)..B-G
koltukçu (armchair maker)..G-E
kovaç (blacksmith)..S-T
kovancı (hive seller)...G
koyuncu (sheep dealer)...E
köhneci (dealer in secondhand or antiquated wares)..E
kömürcü (coal dealer)..T-B-G-E
köşeci (who changed money or carried out small transactions with his drawer in the streets or at the corners of shops)..................................E

kundakçı (gunstock maker)....................G-E
kunduracı (shoemaker)....................S
kutucu (box maker)....................G
kuyumcu (goldsmith)....................S-T- B -G-E
küleci (?)....................S-E
kürkçü (furriery)....................S-T-G-E
leblebici (raosted chickpeas seller)....................B-G
limoncu (lemon seller)....................G-E
lokmacı (morsel maker)....................G
lüleci (pipe bowl maker)....................E
macun satar (pill maker)....................B
manav (greengrocer)....................G-E
manifaturacı (draper)....................G
mestçi (maker of light thin-soled boots worn indoors or inside shoes)......E
meşinci (roan seller)....................E
mıhçı (nailer)....................E
mısırcı (corn seller)....................S-G
mineci (enameller)....................G
mukavvacı (who produced paper)....................E
mumcu (candle maker)....................S-T-B-G-E
muvazene (who weighs or measures)....................B
muytab (goat woolen cloth maker)....................S-T-B-G-E
mücellit (book binder)....................S-T
nakkaş (decorator)....................S-E
nalband (farrier)....................S-T-B-G-E
nalbur (hardware dealer)....................T
nalçacı (iron heel making) ....S-G-E
nalinci (clog maker)....................E
neccar (carpenter)....................E
nohudcu (chickpea seller)....................B
oduncu (firewood dealer)....................B-G-E
oturakçı (ready-made goods dealer)....................G-E
pabuççu, pabuşçu (shoemaker)....................S-B-G-E
pabuş dikiçisi (shoe/slipper sewing)....................G
pabuş tamircisi (shoe/slipper mending)....................G
palancı (who produced harnessing equipment for the animals)....................E
panayırcı (fair business)....................G
pazarcı (marketer)....................G
penbe burucu (cotton twister)....................G
penbeci (cotton dealer)....................E
perakendeci (retailer)....................T
peştemalcı (seller of large bath towels)....................E
postalcı (long boots making)....................G
püskülçü (tassel making)....................G

rişmeci (who produced the bit of a bridle) .... E
saatçi (watch maker) .... S-B-G-E
sabuncu (soap maker) .... T-G-E
sağmalcı (dealer of milch-giving animals) .... E
salatacı (salad seller) .... G
samancı (fodder dealer) .... E
sandıkçı (chest maker) .... B-G-E
sandukacı (sarcophagus maker) .... B
sarraç (saddler) .... S-T-B-G-E
satıcı (seller) .... G
sebzevatçı (seller of vegetables) .... E
seleci (wicket basket maker) .... G
semerci (pack saddle maker) .... S-T-B-G
sepetçi (basket maker) .... S-G
sergici (keeper of a stall for the sale of goods) .... E
sermaye tüccarı (capital merchant) .... E
sırçacı (glass maker) .... S
sıvacı (plasterer) .... G
silahçı (gunsmith) .... T
simitçi (seller of *simit*, a kind of bread) .... S-T
simsar (broker) .... G
sirkeci (vinegar maker) .... B
soğancı (onion seller) .... G
sucu (water-carrier) .... E
süpürgeci (broom maker) .... T-B-G
şalcı (seller of shawls) .... E
şekerci (sugar seller) .... G
şerbetçi (sherbet master) .... T-G-E
şeridci (lace maker) .... G
şilteci (seller of thin mattresses) .... E
şişeci (bottle maker) .... S-E
tablakar (itinerant vendor) .... S-B
tahmis döğücü (grinder of coffee) .... G
tahmisci (roaster of coffee) .... S-T-G
tahtacı (sawer) .... T-E
takkeci (skull cap seller) .... S-T
tarakçı (comb maker) .... S-T
taşçı (stonemason) .... S-G
tavukçu (who dealt with buying and selling animals) .... E
taycı (colt dealer) .... E
tehril bükücü (spinner of *tehril*, silk thread spun thickly) .... G
tenekeci (tinsmith) .... S-T-G-E
teraş (shaver) .... S
terzi (tailor) .... S-T-B-G-E

tiftikçi (mohair dealer) .... E
tikeciler (patch maker) .... E
tohumcu (seed dealer) .... E
topaviçar (gunsmith) .... S
tömbekici (seller of water pipe tobacco) .... T-G
tuzcu (salt seller) .... S-G
tüccar (merchant) .... S-B-G
tüfenkçi (gunsmith) .... S-T-E
tülbentçi (muslin seller) .... G
tütüncü (tobacconist) .... B
uncu (flour dealer) .... T-B-G-E
urgancı (rope maker) .... B-G
usturacı (razor maker) .... G-E
ütücü (iron making) .... G
yağcı (oil seller) .... T-G
yağhaneci (oil mill manager) .... B
yapağıcı (wool merchant) .... T
yapıcı (builder) .... G
yemenici (seller of colored cotton handkerchief) .... E
yemişçi (greengrocer) .... S-T-E
yoğurtçu (yogurt seller) .... T
yorgancı (quilt maker) .... G-E
yüzükçü (ring maker) .... E
zahire-fürüş, zahireci (dealer of wheat and cereal grains) .... T-E
zenbilci (rush basket maker) .... E
zencirci (chain maker) .... G

5. Transporters

arabacı (transporter by horsecart) .... S-T-G
deveci (transporter by camel) .... B-G-E
eşekçi (transporter by donkey) .... G
herbendeci (muleteer) .... E
himarcı (donkey driver) .... E
hintocu (coachman) .... S
katırcı (transporter by mules) .... G-E
kervancı (who dealt with organization of the transportation) .... E
kiracı (transporter) .... S-T-G-E
koçucu (coachman) .... S
mekkareci (who hires out pack animals and looks after them) .... B
seyis (horse keeper) .... G
sürücü (drover) .... B

6. Physical Laborers

amele (worker) .... S-B
aylak (laborer) .... S
çırak (apprentice) .... S
çukadar (footman) .... G
dellak (*hamam*, public bath, worker) .... B
deşteban (watcher set over sown field) .... G
gündelikçi (daily worker) .... T
hademe (servant) .... S-T-G
hammal (porter) .... B-G
hizmetkar (servant) .... S-T-B-G-E
ırgad (workman, day-laborer) .... S-B-G
işçi (worker) .... S-G
kazıcı (engraver) .... E
kuyucu (well digger) .... B-G
maden amelesi (mine worker) .... S
mezarcı (gravedigger) .... S
saraydar (steward) .... S
tabi (servant) .... S

7. Occupations of Service Sector and Others

arzuhalci (writer of petitions) .... T-E
ayıcı (bear trainer) .... E
baytar (veterinarian) .... E
berber (barber) .... S-T-B-G
cerrah (surgeon) .... T-G
çalgıcı (musical instrument player) .... G-E
çamaşırcı (laundry) .... G
çarşıpasbanı (market sentry) .... T
çöpçü (garbage collectors) .... E
davulcu (drum player) .... E
dilenci (beggar) .... S-T-G-E
ferraş (cleaner of mosques) .... E
hamamcı (keeper of a public bath) .... S-T-B-G
han odabaşı (room manager of inn) .... B
hancı (inn-keeper) .... S-T-B-G
hattat (calligrapher) .... E
hekim (physician) .... S-B
meyhaneci (tavern keeper) .... S-T-G
mimar (architect) .... G
mimarbaşı (manager of architect) .... B

natır (attendant in a woman's bath) .... T-B-G
saka (water carrier) .... E
suyolcu (man responsible for the maintenance of water conduits) .... G-E
zurnacı (*zurna* player) .... G

Appendix III: İrade Masâil-i Mühimme no. 65, lef 4, Model Entries for Temettuat Surveyors

(p.2)
Filân eyâleti mülhâkâtından filân sancak kazâlarından filân kazâdan filân karyede mukîm ahâlînin emlâk ve arâzî ve temettü'âtlarını mübeyyin defterdir

erbâb-ı zirâ'atden idüğü
hâne
0

numara
0

sene-i sâbıkada vergü-yi muhassasadan
bir senede vermiş olduğu
guruş
000

a'şâr ve sâ'iresi dahi
bu siyâk üzere yazılması
a'şâr ve rüsûmât olarak sene-i sâbıkada bir senede vermiş olduğu

hınta		*şa'îr*		*burçak*	
keyl	*fî-i*	*keyl*	*fî-i*	*keyl*	*fî-i*
000	*beher keyl*	*000*	*beher keyl*	*000*	*beher keyl*
guruş	*guruş*	*guruş*	*guruş*	*guruş*	*guruş*
000	*0*	*000*	*0*	*000*	*0*

cem'an yekûn
guruş
0000
0000 maktû' sûretiyle meblağan verdigi

----	*guruş*	
0000	*000*	*bedel-i 'öşr-i bostân*
	000	*mukâta'a-i zemîn-i âsiyâb*

	0000	

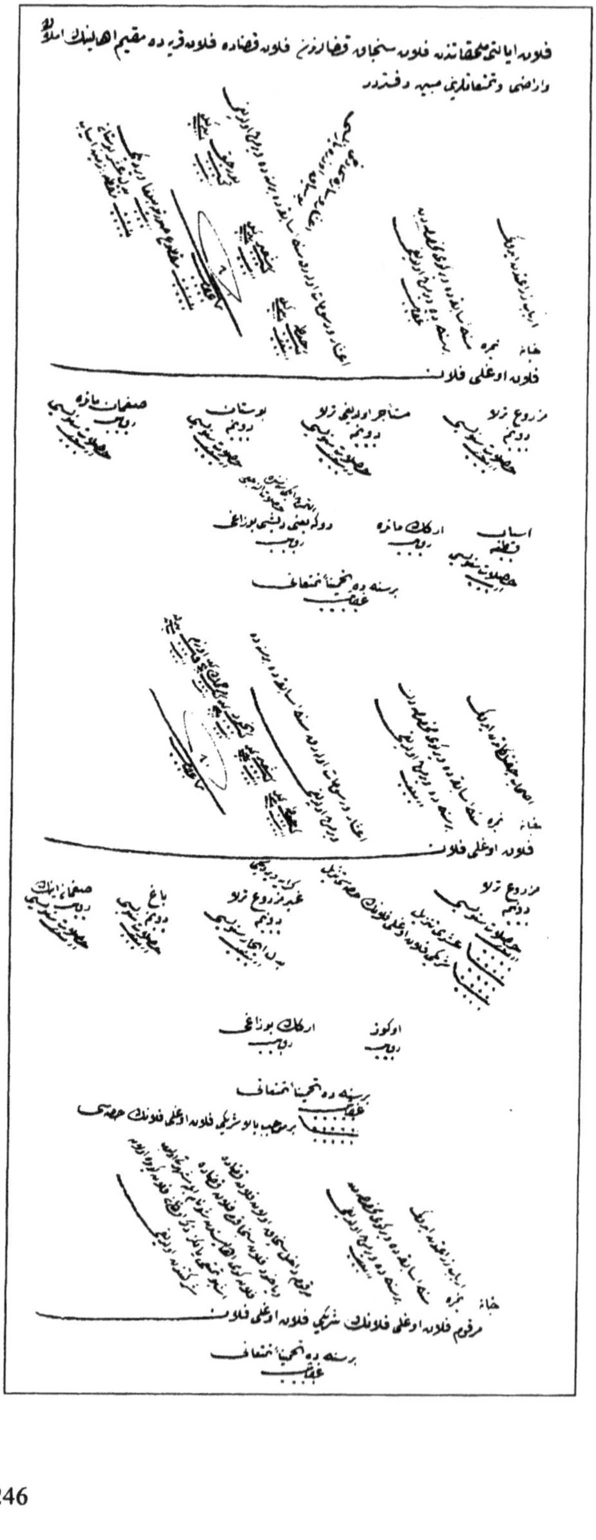
فلان ایالتنده ملحقاتنده فلان سنجاغی قضالرندن فلان قضاده فلان قریه‌ده مقیم اهالینک املاک
واراضی وتمتعاتلرینی مبین دفتردر

Filân oğlu filân

mezrû' tarla	müste'cir olduğu tarla	bostân	sağman manda
dönüm	dönüm	dönüm	re's
000	000	000	000
hâsılât-ı senevîsi	*hâsılât-ı senevîsi*	*hâsılât-ı senevîsi*	*hâsılât-ı senevîsi*
guruş	*guruş*	*guruş*	*guruş*
000	*000*	*000*	*000*

âsiyâb	erkek manda	*altmış iki senesinde hâsılât alınacağı* düğe ya'nî dişi buzağı
kıt'a	re's	re's
00	000	000

hâsılât-ı senevîsi
guruş
000

bir senede tahmînen temettü'âtı
guruş
0000

ashâb-ı çiftlikâtdan idüğü
hâne
0

numara
0

sene-i sâbıkada vergü-yi muhassasadan
bir senede vermiş olduğu
guruş
000

a'şâr ve rüsûmât olarak sene-i sâbıkada bir senede vermiş olduğu

hınta		*şa'îr*		*nohud*		*mercimek*		*üzüm*	
keyl	*fî-i*	*keyl*	*fî-i*	*keyl*	*fî-i*	*keyl*	*fî-i*	*kıyye*	*fî-i*
000	*beher keyl*	*000*	*beher keyl*	*000*	*beher keyl*	*000*	*beher keyl*	*000*	*beher kıyye*
guruş	*guruş*	*guruş*	*guruş*	*guruş*	*guruş*	*guruş*	*guruş*	*guruş*	*para*
000	*0*	*000*	*0*	*000*	*0*	*000*	*0*	*000*	*0*

cem'an yekûn
guruş
0000

Filân oğlu filân

mezrû' tarla	*kîrâya verdiği* gayr-i mezû' tarla	bâğ	sağman inek
dönüm	dönüm	dönüm	re's
000	000	000	00
hâsılât-ı senevîsi	*bedel-i îcâr-ı senevîsi*	*hâsılât-ı senevîsi*	*hâsılât-ı senevîsi*
guruş	*guruş*	*guruş*	*guruş*
0000	*000*	*000*	*000*

0000 'öşrü tenzîl

0000
0000 şerîki filân oğlu filânın hissesi tenzîl

0000

öküz	erkek buzağı
re's	re's
000	000

bir senede tahmînen temettü'âtı
guruş
00000
00000 ber-mûceb-i bâlâ şerîki filân oğlu filânın hissesi

00000

erbâb-ı zirâ'atden idüğü
hâne
0

numara
0

sene-i sâbıkada vergü-yi muhassasadan
bir senede vermiş olduğu
guruş
000

merkûm dâhil-i sancak olan filân kazâda
veyâhûd filân sancakda filân kazâda
filân köy ahâlîsinden şu nâm ile şöhreti olup
işbu temettü'ü yalnız zikr olunan filân köyde olan
şerîkinden olduğu

merkûm filân oğlu filânın şerîki filân oğlu filân

bir senede tahmînen temettü'ü
guruş
0000

Appendix IV: Pages of the Erzurum Temattuat Register

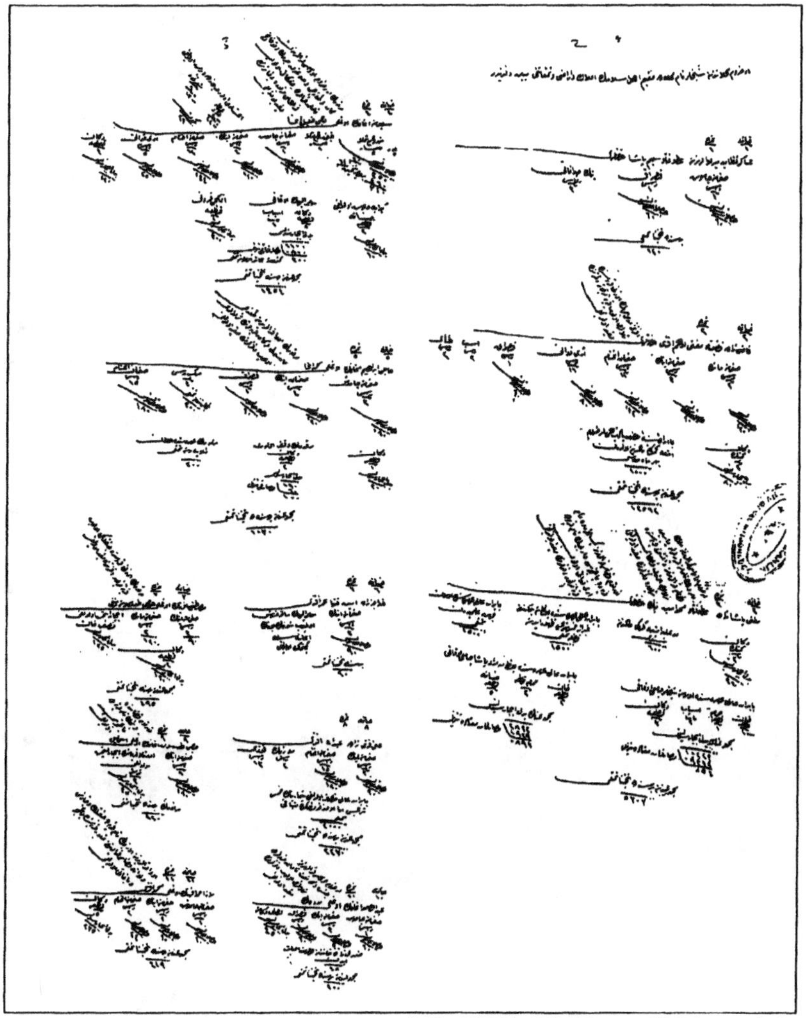

ML. VRD. TMT. no. 6856, pp. 2-3

1. Şeyhler Mahellesi, hane 1 (ML. VRD. TMT. no. 6856, p.2)

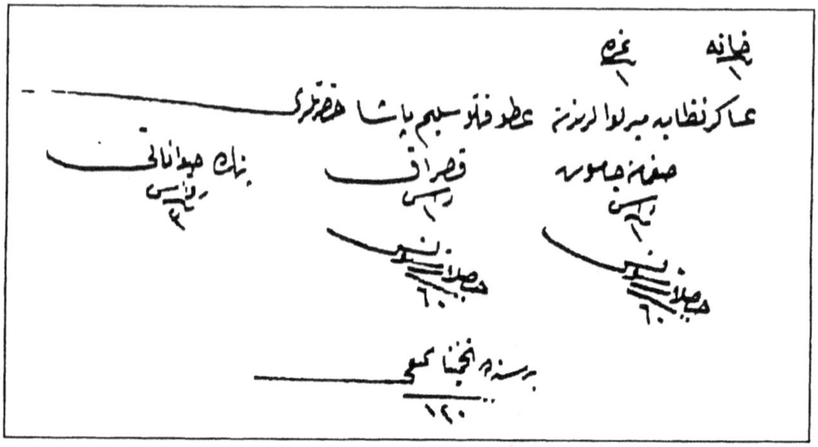

خانه	نمره
عدد	عدد
١	١

عساكر نظاميه مير لوالرندن عطوفتلو سليم پاشا حضرتلری

صغمان جاموش	قصراق	بنك حيواناتی
رأس	رأس	رأس
عدد		عدد
١	١	٣

حاصلات سنويسی	حاصلات سنويسی
غروش	غروش
٦٠	٦٠

بر سنه ده تخمينا تمتعی
غروش
١٢٠

2. Şeyhler Mahellesi, hane 2 (ML. VRD. TMT. no. 6856, p.2)

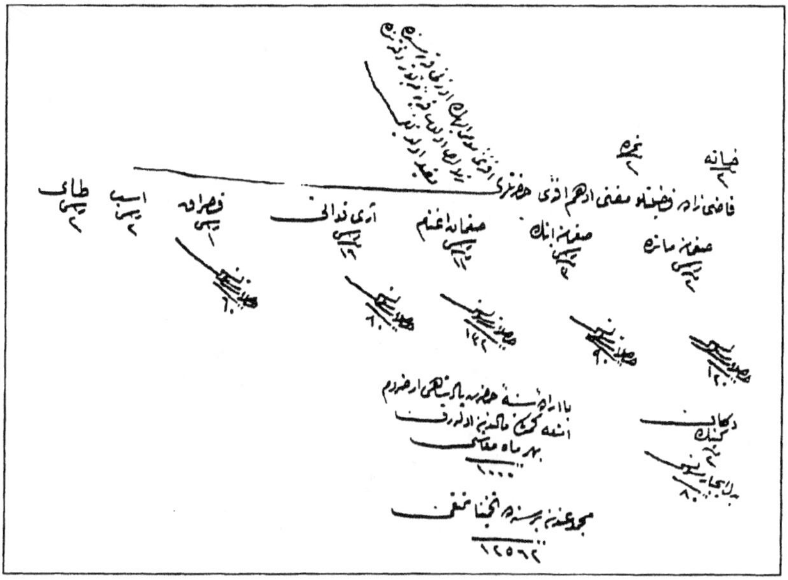

خانه	نمره	
عدد	عدد	افندئ مومی الیهك اوزنی قریه سنده
٢	٢	ترلالری اولوب قریهٔ مزبور دفترنده
		مقید اولدیغی

قاضی زاده فضیلتلو مفتی ادهم افندی حضرتلری

صغمان مانده	صغمان اینك	صغمان اغنام	آری قوانی	قصراق	اسب	طای
رأس	رأس	رأس	رأس	رأس	رأس	رأس
عدد	عدد	عدد	عدد	١	٢	٢
٢	٣	١١	١٦			
حاصلات سنویسی	حاصلات سنویسی	حاصلات سنویسی	حاصلات سنویسی	حاصلات سنویسی		
غروش	غروش	غروش	غروش	غروش		
١٢٠	٩٠	١٣٢	٨٠	٦٠		

دكان	با ارادهٔ سنیهٔ حضرت پادشاهی ارضروم
كپنك	امتعه كمركی مالندن اوله رق
عدد	بهر ماه معاشی
٢	غروش
بدل ایجار سنویسی	١٠٠٠
غروش	
٨٠	مجموعندن بر سنه ده تخمیناً تمتعی
	غروش
	١٢٥٦٢

3. Şeyhler Mahallesi, hane 8 (ML. VRD. TMT. no. 6856, p.3)

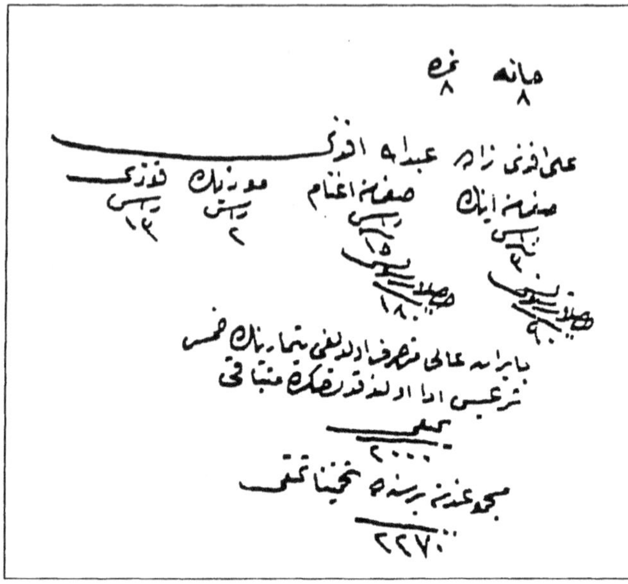

خانه نمره
عدد عدد
٨ ٨

علی افندی زاده عبد الله افندی

صغمان اینك	صغمان اغنام	موزیك	قوزی
رأس	رأس	رأس	رأس
عدد	عدد	٢	١٣
٣	١٥		
حاصلات سنویسی	حاصلات سنویسی		
غروش	غروش		
٩٠	١٨٠		

با برات عالی متصرف اولدیغی تیمارنك خمس
شرعی ادا اولندقدنصكره متباقی
تمتعی
غروش
٢٠٠٠

مجموعندن بر سنه ده تخمیناً تمتعی
غروش
٢٢٧٠

Bobliography

1. Archival Sources

The Prime Ministry Ottoman Archives of Turkey (Başbakanlık Osmanlı Arşivi)

Registers

•Maliye Nezareti Defterleri

Temettuât Defterleri (ML.VRD.TMT.)

no. 11197, 11199-11201, 11206, 11207, 11213, 11214, 11216, 11217, 11227, 11233, 11236, 11238, 11239, 11244, 11249, 11250, 11252, 11258 (Samokov)

no. 6295, 6312, 6314, 6318, 6319, 6321, 6324, 6336, 6340-6342, 6346, 6347, 6349, 6352, 6350, 6354, 6356, 6364 (Tatarpazarcığı)

no. 7225-7228 (Balıkesir)

no. 1977, 1981, 1985, 1989, 1996, 2006-2008, 2011-2013, 2015, 2019, 2020, 2023, 2025, 2030, 2031, 2037, 2039, 2042, 2043 (Güzelhisar-ı Aydın)

no. 6850-6897 (Erzurum)

no. 17534 (Example for the 1840 survey)

Cerîde Odası Defterleri (ML.CRD.) no. 1146.

Cizye Defterleri (ML.VRD.CMH.) no. 136.

•Kâmil Kepeci Tasnifi Defterleri no. 60/7, 2791, 3860, 3900, 3904, 5938, 6479.

•Mühimme Defterleri no. 259.

•Tapu Tahrir Defterleri no. 166, 205, 387.

Individual Documents

•Bâb-ı Âlî Belgeleri

Sadaret Âmedî Kalemi Belgeleri (A.AMD.) dos. 95/19.

Sadaret Divân Kalemi Belgeleri (A.DVN.) dos. 13/44.

Sadaret Mektubî Kalemi Belgeleri (A.MKT.) dos. 24/19, 24/36, 24/60, 25/4, 25/9, 25/15, 25/16, 25/17, 25/18, 25/20, 25/27, 25/30, 25/32, 25/36, 25/46, 25/48, 25/52, 25/54, 25/55, 25/58, 25/63, 25/64, 25/68, 25/72, 25/75, 25/77, 25/79, 25/80, 25/83, 25/90, 25/94, 25/95, 25/96, 25/99, 26/4, 26/6, 26/7, 26/8, 26/9, 26/10, 26/11, 26/19, 26/20, 26/23, 26/32, 26/34, 26/36, 26/37, 26/41, 26/47, 26/48, 26/54, 26/67, 26/68, 26/70, 26/87, 26/89, 27/23, 27/35, 27/42, 25/56, 27/63, 27/68, 27/70, 27/74, 27/75, 28/5, 28/14, 28/64, 28/65, 29/41, 29/42, 29/63, 29/91, 30/1, 30/6, 30/8, 30/42, 30/83, 31/34, 32/34, 32/55, 35/16, 35/29, 35/61, 35/86, 35/94, 37/56, 37/91, 38/30, 38/40, 39/14, 40/9, 40/24, 40/29, 40/45, 40/81, 40/83, 43/57, 43/78, 43/87.

Sadaret Mektubî Kalemi Meclis-i Vâlâ Yazışmalarına Ait Belgeler (A.MKT.MVL.) dos. 1/73.

Sadaret Mektubî Kalemi Umum Vilayet Yazışmalarına Ait Belgeler (A.MKT.UM.) dos. 86/38, 99/42.

•Cevdet Tasnifi Belgeleri

Dahiliye: no. 7217, 9031, 9122, 12901, 14948.

İktisat: no. 499.

Maliye: no. 8570, 22496, 23670.

•İrâdeler Tasnifi

Dahiliye: no. 567, 5220.

Meclis-i Vâlâ: no. 1290.

Mesâil-i Mühimme: no. 9, 58, 65, 70, 72, 73, 74, 102, 147, 176.

•Yıldız Sarayı Arşivi Belgeleri

Sadaret Resmî Maruzat Evrakı(Y.A.RES.) dos. 62/11.

The Oriental Department of the National Library (Narodna Biblioteka Sv. Sv. Kiril i Metodii, Orientaliskiya otdel) in Sofia

•NBKM OO, D506, D 598, D687.

2. Manuscripts

Ahmed Arif Hikmet Beyefendi, *Rumeli Teftiş Defteri*, İstanbul Üniversitesi Kütüphanesi, T.Y., no. 2475.

Katip Çelebi, *Cihannüma*, Wien, Österreichische Nationalbibliothek, Mxt 389.

Said Muhib Efendi, *Memalik-i Şahanede 1247 Senesinde Mevcud Olan Nüfus Defteri*, İstanbul Üniversitesi Kütüphanesi, T.Y., no. 8867.

3. Books and Articles

Abdurrahman Vefik, *Tekâlif Kavâ'idi*, 2 parts, Istanbul, 1328-1330.

Adıyeke, Nuri, "Temettuat Sayımları ve Bu Sayımları Düzenleyen Nizamname Örnekleri," *Ankara Üniversitesi Osmanlı Tarihi Atarştırma ve Uygulama Merkezi Dergisi*, no. 11, 2000.

Ahmed Lûtfi Efendi, *Târîh-i Lûtfî*, 8 vols, Istanbul, 1290-1328.

Akgündüz, Ahmed and Said Öztürk (eds.), *Yozgat Temettuat Defterleri*, n.p., 2000.

—— *Darende Temettuat Defterleri*, 3 vols., Istanbul, 2002.

Akın , Himmet, *Aydın Oğulları Tarihi Hakkında Bir Araştırma*, Ankara, 1968.

Aktüre, Sevgi, "Osmanlı Devleti'nde Taşra Kentlerindeki Değişimler," *Tanzimat'tan Cumhuriyet'e Türkiye Ansiklopedisi*, Vol. 4, Istanbul, 1985.

Akyıldız, Ali, *Tanzimat Dönemi Osmanlı Merkez Teşkilâtında Reform (1836-1856)*, Istanbul, 1993.

Andreev, St. & E. Grozdanova, *Iz istoriyata na rudarstvoto i metalurgiyata v balgarskite zemi prez XV-XIX vek.*, Sofia, 1993.

Aydın, Dündar, "Erzurum Şehri'nin Osmanlı Fethini Müteakip Yeniden İmârı, İskânı ve İlk Sâkinleri," *Atatürk Üniversitesi Edebiyat Fakültesi Araştırma Dergisi*, no. 1, 1970.

Aydın, Mahir, "Sultan II. Mahmud Döneminde Yapılan Nufûs Tahrirleri," *Sultan II. Mahmud ve Reformları Semineri 28-30 Haziran 1989 Bildiriler*, Istanbul, 1998.

Ayhan, Aydın and Mücteba İlgürel, *Tarih, Balıkesir Bir Kentin Kimliği*, Ankara, 1997.

Ayhan, Aydın, "Balıkesir'e Ait Eski Bazı İsimler ve Bilgiler," *Balıkesir Ekspres*, 1998, issued on February 5.

Ayverdi, Ekrem Hakkı, *Avrupa'da Osmanlı Mimari Eserleri*, Istanbul, 1982.

Bağış, Ali İhsan, *Osmanlı Ticareti'nde Gayri Müslimler, Kapitülasyonlar, Beratlı Tüccarlar, Avrupa ve Hayriyye Tüccarları, 1750-1839*, Ankara, 1983.

Barkan, Ömer Lütfi, "Tarihî Demografi Araştırmaları ve Osmanlı Tarihi," Türkiyat Mecmuası, Vol. 10, 1951.

Baykara, Tuncer, *XIX. Yüzyılda Aydın Eyaleti*, Graduation thesis of Department of History, Istanbul University (unpublished), 1966.

Bayraktar, Kaya, *Maliye Nezareti Temettuat Defterlerine Göre 1844 Yılında Çorlu, Silivri ve Ereğli Kazalarının Sosyo-Ekonomik Durumu*, Master thesis of Istanbul University (unpublished), 1996.

Behar, Cem, "The Ottoman Empire and the Population of Turkey 1500-1927," *Devlet İstatistik Enstitüsü Tarihi İstatistikler Serisi*, Vol. 2, Ankara, 1996.

Berki, Ali Himmet, "İslâmda Vakıf, Zağanos Paşa ve Zevcesi Nefise Hâtun Vakfiyesi," *Vakıflar Dergisi*, no. 4, 1958.

Beydilli, Kemal, *Recognition of the Armenian Catholic Community and the Church in the Reign of Mahmut II (1830)*, Harvard University, 1995.

Cezar, Yavuz, *Osmanlı Maliyesinde Bunalım ve Değişim Dönemi (XVIII. yy dan Tanzimat'a Mali Tarih)*, n.p., 1986.

Cuinet, Vital, *La Turquie d'Asie: Géographie administrative statistique descriptive et raisonnée de chaque province de l'Asie-mineure*, Paris, 4 vols., 1891-94.

Cumhuriyetin 50. Yılında Aydın: 1973 İl Yıllığı, Izmir, 1973.

Çadırcı, Musa, "Türkiye'de Muhtarlık Teşkilâtının Kurulması üzerine," Belleten, no. 135, 1970.

—— *Tanzimat Döneminde Anadolu Kentleri'nin Sosyal ve Ekonomik Yapıları*, Ankara, 1991.

Çoruh, Haydar, *Temettüat Defterlerine göre Erzurum Şehri*, Master thesis of Istanbul University (unpublished), 1997.

Danova, N., *Konstantin Georgiev Fotinov v kulturnoto i ideino-politicheskoto razvitie na Balkanite prez XIX vek.*, Sofia, 1994.

Darkot, Besim and Mükrimin Halil Yınanç, "Aydın, " *İslam Ansiklopedisi*, Vol. 2, Istanbul, 1943.

Demir, İsmail (ed.), *Kayseri Temettuât Defteri (H. 1250/M.1834 Tarihli)*, 3 vols., Kayseri, 1998-99.

Dimitrova, D., "Statistitcheski danni ot 1840 godina za madandzhiiskite sela Banya Kostenets i Mahalata, Samokovsko," *Izvestiya na natsionalniya istoritcheski muzei*, no. 2, 1978.

Egawa Hikari, "The Tanzimat Reforms and Provincial Society: Analysis of the Temettü'ât Defteri in Balıkesir District (1840) from the Viewpoint of Land Possessions," *The Toyo Gakuho (The Journal of the Research Department of the Toyo Bunko)*, no. 79/2, 1997 (in Japanese).

—— "The Urban Society and Commerce-Industry of Balıkesir in the Middle of the Nineteenth Century: Especially from the Point of Aba Industry," *Ochanomizu Shigaku*, no. 42, 1998 (in Japanese).

—— "The Use of GIS to Locate Abandoned Villages Listed in the Temettuat Registers of Balıkesir County, Anatolia," Atsuyuki Okabe ed., *Islamic Area Studies with Geographic Information System*, 2004, London & New York.

Emecen, Feridun, "Aydın," İslam Ansiklopedisi, Vol.4, Türkiye Diyanet Vakfı: Istanbul, 1989.

Engelhardt, Ed., *La Turquie et le Tanzimat*, 2 vols., Paris, 1882.

Eren, Muharrem, *Zağnos Paşa*, Balıkesir, 1994.

Ergenç, Özer, "Osmanlı Şehrindeki 'Mahalle'nin İşlev ve Nitelikleri üzerine," *Osmanlı Araştırmaları*, no. 4 , 1984.

Erim, Neşe, "Trade, Traders and the State in Eighteenth-Century Erzurum," *New Perspectives on Turkey*, no. 5-6, 1991.

Evliya Çelebi, *Seyahatname*, 10 vols, Istanbul, 1314-1938.

Genç, Mehmet, "Osmanlı Esnafı ve Devletle İlişkileri," *Ahilik ve Esnaf 1*, Esnaf ve Sanatkarlar Dernekleri Yayınları: Istanbul, 1986.

Gerber, Haim, *Economy and Society in an Ottoman City: Bursa, 1600-1700*, Jerusalem, 1988.

Gökbel, Asaf & Himmet Şölen, *Aydın İli Tarihi*, Vol. 1, Aydın, 1936.

Güran, Tevfik, *Structure économique et sociale d'une région de compagne dans l'Empire Ottoman vers le milieu du XIXe s., étude comparée de neuf villages de la nahiye de Koyuntepe, sandjak de Filibe*, Sofia, 1980.

—— "XIX. Yüzyıl Ortalarında Ödemiş Kasabası'nın Sosyo Ekonomik Özellikleri," *İstanbul Üniversitesi İktisat Fakültesi Mecmuası*, Vol.41, no. 1-4 (*Ord. Prof. Ömer Lütfi Barkan'a Armağan Özel Sayısı*), 1985

—— "Osmanlı Tarım Ekonomisi 1840 -1910," *Türk İktisat Tarihi Yıllığı 1987*, Istanbul, 1987.

—— *19. Yüzyıl Osmanlı Tarımı Üzerine Araştırmalar*, Istanbul, 1998.

—— "19. Yüzyıl Temettüat Tahrirleri," Halil İnalcık and Şevket Pamuk (eds.), *Osmanlı Devleti'nde Bilgi ve İstastik*, T. C. Başbakanlık Devlet İstastik Enstitüsü: Ankara, 2000.

Ivanova, Sv., "Danachnoto oblagane na naselenieto v balgarskite gradove i formiraneto na negovite instituzii (XVII - XVIII vek)," *Izvestiya na darzhavnite arhivi*, no. 65, 1993.

İlgürel, Mücteba, "Balıkesir," *İslam Ansiklopedisi*, Vol. 5, Türkiye Diyanet Vakfı: Istanbul, 1992.

İnalcık, Halil, "Köy, Köylü ve İmparatorluk," *V. Milletlerarası Türkiye Sosyal ve İktisat Tarihi Kongresi Tebliğleri*, Ankara, 1990.

Kaynar, Reşat, *Mustafa Reşit Paşa ve Tanzimat*, Ankara, 1954.

Kazıcı, Ziya, "Osmanlılar'da Mahalle İmamlarının Bazı Görevleri," *İslam Medeniyeti Mecmuası*, Vol. 5, no. 3, Istanbul, 1982.

Kenderova, St., "The Town of Samokov: A Centre of Creative Activities, XVIII.—Beginning of the XIX Centuries." Paper presented at the International Symposium on Islamic Civilisation in the Balkans, Sofia.

Khoury, Dine Rizk, "The Introduction of Commercial Agriculture in the Province of Mosul and its Effects on the Peasantry 1750-1850," Çağlar Keyder & Faruk Tabak (eds.), *Lndholding and Commercial Agriculture in the Middle East*, Albany, 1991.

Kırzıoğlu, M. Fahrettin, "1753 ve 1846 Yıllarında Erzurum Çarşıları ile Esnafını tanıtan Kağızmanlızadelerin İki Vakfiyesi," *Atatürk Üniversitesi Edebiyat Fakültesi Araştırmaları Dergisi*, no. 7, 1976.

Küçük, Cevdet, "Erzurum," İslam Ansiklopedisi, Vol.11, Türkiye Diyanet Vakfı: Istanbul, 1995.

—— "Osmanlılarda Millet Sistemi ve Tanzimat," *Tanzimat'tan Cumhuriyet'e Türkiye Ansiklopedisi*, Vol. 4, Istanbul, 1985.

Kütükoğlu, S. Mühabat, "Asakir-i Mansure-i Muhammediyye Kıyafeti ve Malzemesinin Temini Meselesi," *Doğumunun 100.Yılında Atatürk'e Armağan*, Istanbul, 1981.

—— (ed.), *Osmanlılarda Narh Müessesesi ve 1640 Tarihli Narh Defteri*, Istanbul, 1983.

—— "Osmanlı Sosyal ve İktisâdî Tarihi Kaynaklarından Temettü Defterleri," *Belleten*, no. 225, 1995.

Lewis, Bernard, *The Emergence of Modern Turkey*, second edition, Oxford University Press: London, 1968.

Mahiroğulları, Adnan, "Fransız Seyyahı Vital Cuinet'nin Notlarıyla 100 Yıl Önce Erzurum," *Tarih ve Medeniyet*, no. 25, 1996.

Martal, Abdullah, "Osmanlı İmparatorluğu'nda Su Yolculuk," *Belleten*, no. 161, 1977.

Masters, Bruce, "The Treaties of Erzurum (1823 and 1848) and the Changing Status of Iranians in the Ottoman Empire," *Iranian Studies*, no. 24/1-4, 1991.

Mecmû'a-i Kānûnnâme-i Cezâ ve Ta'lîmâtnâme, Süleymaniye Ktp. Es'ad Efendi, no. 1877.

Mehmed Arif, "Rusya ile 1244 ve 1245 Senelerinde Vuku Bulan Harbe Dair Bir Vesika," *Tarih-i Osmani Encümeni Mecmuası*, no. 14, 1328-1330.

Nagata Yuzo, *Tarihte Ayanlar: Karaosmanoğulları Üzerinde Bir İnceleme*, Ankara, 1997.

—— "Turkish Rural Society in the sixteenth century", *The Toyo Gakuho (The Journal of the Research Department of the Toyo Bunko)*, no. 58/3-4, 1977 (in Japanese).

Ortaylı, İlber, *Tanzimattan Sonra Mahalli İdareler (1840-1878)*, Ankara, 1974.

Özer, İlbeyi, *Darende, Tanzimat Döneminde Bir Anadolu Şehri (1844): 19. Yüzyıl Ortalarında Şehrin Sosyal, Ekonomik ve Demografik Yapısı*, Istanbul, 2000.

Özey, Ramazan, "Fırat-Karasu Kaynakları Çevresindeki Kırsal Yerleşmelerin Başlıca Sosyo Ekonomik Sorunları ve Çözüm Yolları: Erzurum Merkez İlçesi ve Çevresi," *Atatürk Üniversitesi Fen-Edebiyat Fakültesi Edebiyat Bilimleri Araştırmaları Dergisi*, no. 18, 1990.

Öztürk, Said, "Temettuat Tahrirleri," *Akademik Araştımalar Dergisi*, no. 4-5, 2000.

Pakalın, M. Zeki, *Osmanlı Tarih Deyimleri ve Terimleri Sözlüğü*, 3 vols., Istanbul, 1993.

Pamuk, Şevket, *Osmanlı Ekonomisinde Bağımlılık ve Büyüme (1820-1913)*, Istanbul, 1994.

Quataert, Donald, "The Age of Reforms, 1812-1914," H. Inalcık & D. Quataert (eds.), *An Economic and Social History of the Ottoman Empire 1300-1914*, Cambridge, 1994.

Salname-i Vilayet-i Erzurum, Year 1288.

Salname-i Vilayet-i Erzurum, Year 1299.

Scheben, Thomas, *Verwaltungsreformen der frühen Tanzimatzeit: Gesetze, Maßnahmen, Auswirkungen; von der Verkündigung des Ediktes von Gülhane 1839 bis zum Ausbruch des Krimkrieges 1853*, Peter Lang: Frankfurt am Main, 1991.

Semerdzhiev, Hr., *Samokov i okolnost'ta mu: prinos minaloto im ot turskoto zavoevanie do osvobojdenieto*, Sofia, 1913 (rep. 1986).

Sertoğlu, Midhat, *Osmanlı Tarih Lügatı*, Istanbul, 1985.

Shaw, Stanford, "The Nineteenth Century Ottoman Tax Reforms and Revenue System," *International Journal of Middle East Studies*, no. 6, 1975.

Su, Kamil, *XVII ve XVIIIinci Yüzyıllarda Balıkesir Şehir Hayatı*, Istanbul, 1937.

—— "Balıkesirde Eski Tarihlerde Abacılık," *Kaynak*, no. 50, 1937.

—— *Balıkesir ve Civarında Yürük ve Türkmenler*, Istanbul, 1938.

Süleyman Sudi, *Defter-i Muktesid*, 3 vols., Istanbul, 1307.

Şener, Abdüllatif, *Tanzimat Dönemi Osmanlı Vergi Sistemi*, Istanbul, 1990.

Texier, Ch. *Küçük Asya*, 2 vols, trans. Ali Suad, Istanbul, 1339.

Tsvetkova, B. (ed), *Frenski patepisi za Balkanite XV-XVIII v.*, Sofia, 1975.

—— *Frenski patepisi za Balkanite XIX v.*, Sofia, 1981.

Uzunçarşılı, İsmail Hakkı, *Karasi Vilâyeti Tarihçesi*, Istanbul, 1925.

—— *Osmanlı Devleti'nin Saray Teşkilâtı*, Ankara, 1988.

—— *Karasi Meşâhiri*, new ed., 3 vols, Balıkesir, 1991-92.

Ünlüyol, Aynur, *Şeriyye Sicillerine göre XVIII. Asrın İlk Yarısında Balıkesir (1700-1730)*, dissertation to Uludağ University (unpublished), 1995.

Wittek, Paul, *Menteşe Beyliği*, trans. Orhan Şaik Gökyay, Ankara, 1944.

Yazıcı, Nesimi, "Tanzimat Döneminde Osmanlı Haberleşme Kurumu," *150. Yılında Tanzimat*, Ankara, 1992.

Yılmaz, Ahmet, *19.yy. İlk Yarısında Yabanâbâd Kazası Sosyal İktisadi Durumu*, Ankara, n.d.

Index

Not all of the occupations are cited in this index. A comprehensive list of occupations is in Appendix II.

For Product Safety Concerns and Information please contact our EU representative GPSR@taylorandfrancis.com
Taylor & Francis Verlag GmbH, Kaufingerstraße 24, 80331 München, Germany

www.ingramcontent.com/pod-product-compliance
Lightning Source LLC
LaVergne TN
LVHW021038011026
849160LV00008BA/451

9781138010765